Mr. Ruehle, You Are a Free Man

My Fight for Justice

William J. Ruehle

The person who lived it

To Julie – My wife and my inspiration

Contents

PROLOGUE

"Unless executives possess an extraordinary ability to forecast the future marketwide movements that drive these predicted returns, the results suggest that at least some of the awards are timed retroactively." With those words, an obscure professor from the University of Iowa set off a firestorm that would eventually consume the energies of hundreds of companies, destroy (or threaten to destroy) the lives of some of corporate America's most productive citizens, and burn through hundreds of millions of shareholders' and taxpayers' dollars—all of this with the ostensible purpose of "protecting" shareholders' interests.

In today's media-driven society, words like these can never be allowed to just sit there. The 24/7 news cycle jumped on this report like a pack of wolves devouring raw meat. A relatively little-known shareholder watchdog organization called the Center for Financial Research and Analysis (CFRA) analyzed a hundred companies that actively granted stock options to employees and concluded that at least seventeen of them showed a pattern suggesting that some of the dates when they did so were likely selected with the benefit of hindsight. One of the identified companies was Broadcom Corporation, a very successful Irvine, California-based semiconductor company and an embodiment of the American Dream.

Before we get caught up in the frenzy, a little background information is important. First, we'll define stock options and the alleged crimes that were supposedly committed. Then we'll go into some detail on the great American success story that is Broadcom. Following that, we'll go back to the frenzy and the story of how a handful of entrepreneurs and executives at Broadcom were caught up in it and how it played out through the federal criminal court system. As one of those entrepreneurs and executives, I will tell this story from my own very personal point of view.

What Is a Stock Option, Anyway?

A stock option gives a person the right to purchase a share of stock at a specified price at some date in the future. Stock options are most frequently granted to employees of corporations. They are also often granted to members of a corporation's board of directors and sometimes to individuals who provide consulting services.

The price at which the option is granted is referred to as the *grant price* or the *strike price*. If the market value of the company's stock increases above the grant price, the option can be exercised: the underlying shares are sold and the holder of the option realizes a profit. There is an important catch here, however: the option cannot be exercised until it is vested. If the market value of the stock does not rise above the grant price, the option is said to be "underwater," and it is worthless as long as it remains underwater. So, to be of any value, a stock option must be both vested and "in the money" (i.e., have a strike price that is less than market value on the date of proposed exercise).

Almost all stock options are granted with a vesting period, which means that an employee has to stay employed for the options to acquire any value. This is referred to as the *retentive value* of the options, or sometimes more colloquially as "golden handcuffs." Vesting periods vary, but Broadcom's was typical. No employees had vesting in their first year. On the first anniversary of the option grant, they were deemed 25 percent vested, and an additional 1/48th of the grant would vest in each succeeding month. At the end of four years, the grant would be fully vested. The options would expire ten years after the grant date. Options granted in succeeding years generally started vesting monthly from the date of grant.

The reports that suggested that grant dates may have been selected with hindsight slapped the media-friendly term "backdating" on them. Backdating works like this: say that on June 1, a company's stock was trading in the open market for $15.00 per share. Then on June 30, it is at $20.00 a share. On June 30 the company wants to grant options to many employees, but it uses the June 1 price of $15.00.

This is perfectly legal to do, but under the accounting guidelines in place prior to 2005, the company would be required to recognize a noncash accounting charge of $5.00 per share times however many shares were included in the grant. Let's say it was a company-wide grant and that five million shares were granted. The company would then be required to take a $25 million charge and amortize it over the vesting period of the options. Did the company have to make a payment of $25 million to anyone? No. That's why the charge is referred to as a "noncash" charge. Does it guarantee that the employees will collectively realize a $25 million gain from the grant? No. If the stock went to $100 a share, they would earn far more. If the stock fell to $10 a share and stayed there, the options would be underwater and would never be exercised. So what is the point of the $25 million charge? Good question!

So, How and Why Did Backdating Become a Crime?

If backdating is a perfectly legal process, how and why was it criminalized? The answer to that is in how the accounting is done. If the noncash expenses are "properly" recorded on the company's books, no problem. If they are not, it's a big problem. The criminal charge of securities fraud is for "lying" to shareholders by not recording the noncash charges. (It turns out that no one really cared about those charges anyway, as we'll show later.)

But a simple securities fraud charge would be much too...well, simple. So the prosecutors pile on charges of lying to accountants, maintaining false books and records, mail fraud, wire fraud, and anything else that can be added to make an innocent misinterpretation of an accounting principle sound like the basis of a criminal enterprise. They also used a prosecutor's favorite charge of "honest services." It would be too much of a diversion to go into that issue here. Suffice it to say that this principle, originally designed to punish government officials who took bribes and then was grossly overbroadened to mean anything a prosecutor wanted it to, was overthrown in a 2010 Supreme Court case (involving Jeffrey Skilling of Enron fame).

That's how backdating was criminalized. But what was the reason? Unfortunately, there has been a trend of overzealous prosecutors motivated by the desire for political gain (some very famous politicians were once prosecutors), for financial gain (landing a high-paying position with a prominent defense firm), or just plain ego (let's get our names in the paper).

Some of these prosecutions were later undone when the full truth emerged, but often too late. When the US Supreme Court, in 2005, reversed the Enron-driven 2002 conviction of Arthur Andersen, it was too late. The company had liquidated, throwing about twenty-six thousand people out of work. When the Attorney General demanded the reversal of Senator Ted Stevens' 2008 conviction, it was too late to allow him to try to regain the Senate seat he had held for forty years.

Then there is the underlying accounting guidance. It all starts with a twelve-page publication entitled Accounting Principles Board Opinion 25 (APB 25), which was first issued in 1972 and then subject to numerous complaints and updates. It was ultimately discarded in 2005. Failing to interpret this literature in the 1990s and early 2000s with the same politically correct hindsight subjected certain companies and executives, including yours truly, to criminal prosecution after 2006.

To put the story in context, I will begin with a brief history of Broadcom Corporation, the company at the center of this case.

Chapter 1

The Broadcom Story—An American Dream

Every company has to start somewhere. Broadcom started in a condo in Redondo Beach, California. Every company needs to raise start-up capital. Many raise millions, tens of millions, or even hundreds of millions of dollars from venture capitalists who then take control and cause the business to be run in a way that will maximize their investment. Broadcom started with the two cofounders writing checks for $5,000 each. Therefore, the founders could run the business their way. And they did. From the beginning, Broadcom was an unconventional company.

By retaining most of the initial ownership within the company rather than in the hands of outside investors, the founders could provide attractive stock option packages to potential and current employees, thereby maximizing their incentive to have the company succeed.

Who were the two founders? They can be succinctly described as a quiet electronics engineering professor from UCLA (Henry Samueli) and his not-so-quiet student (Henry Nicholas). Having two Henrys could be confusing, so everyone (including me) always knew Henry Samueli as "Henry," while Henry Nicholas was always "Nick."

Before There Was a Broadcom

Henry Samueli rose from very humble beginnings. His parents had grown up in Poland and escaped from the Holocaust to try to build a life in America. They settled in Buffalo, New York, then moved to Los Angeles in search of opportunity when Henry was ten years old.

Ultimately, they opened a liquor store. It would provide Henry his first after-school job.

Henry knew he was destined to be an engineer as soon as he built his first Heathkit radio in junior high school. At UCLA, he pursued electrical engineering, taking his bachelor's, master's, and PhD degrees straight through without a break.

His first post-PhD job was at the large defense contractor, TRW. There, in addition to working on advanced technology projects designing state-of-the-art semiconductor chips for military applications, he fortuitously met a young engineer and fellow UCLA graduate, Henry Nicholas.

Nick also grew up in a family of modest means. They lived in Cincinnati, Ohio and then moved to Los Angeles when he was still young. He aspired early to be an Air Force fighter pilot; as a good student, he secured an appointment to the Air Force Academy in Colorado. However, his body refused to cooperate with his aspirations. When he reached a full six feet, six inches in height, he was deemed too tall to fly a fighter jet. Flying a large, lumbering tanker just didn't appeal to him, so he left the Academy and enrolled in the engineering program at UCLA.

Following his graduation from UCLA, Nick also went to work at TRW. He too aspired to earn a PhD but that was not to happen for another thirteen years —literally on the eve of Broadcom's Initial Public Offering (IPO).

By 1985, Henry Samueli was offered a faculty position at UCLA, realizing a lifelong dream. In spite of the relative financial hardships this imposed on his family, he never wavered in his decision to enter the academic world. One of the position's appeals was the University's policy to allow its faculty members to consult in private industry one day a week. This time in the real world complemented their ivory-tower existence.

Henry eventually became one of the founders of a fledgling telecommunications company called PairGain. When they needed a

2

brilliant and driven engineer to head their semiconductor development, Henry knew just the candidate: his old TRW colleague, Henry Nicholas.

American industry is replete with stories of would-be entrepreneurs working inside a corporate entity, trying to persuade their bosses to invest in some promising new technology. PairGain was no exception. It was doing well and had had a successful IPO. Sometime after that, Henry and Nick tried to persuade its board of directors that there was a lot of promise in the developing market for broadband digital communications. Specifically, Henry and Nick had the vision that cable television would be converting subscribers' set-top boxes from analog to digital, which offered far more channels and a higher quality of video. In parallel, digital cable modems would receive and transmit content orders of magnitude faster than the dial-up modems then in use.

The board's response was all too predictable: No. Not to be deterred, Henry and Nick decided they would start their own company to address these markets. Eventually, they settled on a name for it that they believed best described its target *broad*band *com*munications markets: Broadcom Corporation.

Broadcom: The Early Years

From 1991 through 1993, Broadcom rented modest office and lab space near the UCLA campus in Westwood. A small, dedicated team of engineers developed groundbreaking products for digital set-top boxes and high speed networking products.

When the company recorded its first revenue in 1994—a whopping $3.6 million—no one could have guessed that just twelve years later in 2006, revenue would be $3.7 billion. That's right: a thousandfold increase in just twelve years. From 1994 through 1996 and into 1997, Broadcom continued to grow and to fund its operations almost entirely through internally generated cash flow. A mere $4 million of outside capital was raised through a combination of individual private investors and two corporate investors. By 1996, revenue had grown to $24 million.

My Introduction to Broadcom

In 1987, I joined a small private company in Silicon Valley called SynOptics Communications, Inc., as chief financial officer (CFO). SynOptics had developed systems products that helped provide the infrastructure on which modern, large-scale computer networks are built. That year, they had annualized revenue of $2 million and about thirty employees. The next year, we grew to $40 million and had a very successful IPO. By 1994, we had grown to $700 million in revenue and merged with a firm with complementary products: Wellfleet Communications. The combined company was renamed Bay Networks, Inc. By early 1997 Bay had grown to over $2 billion in annual revenue and employed over six thousand people world-wide.

Retirement at that time was certainly something I considered. At age fifty-five and with sufficient financial resources, I could have. But I wasn't done yet. I wanted to see if I could help guide another company from early stage to industry leader. In my search for such an opportunity, I was thrust into immediate contact with the newly forming Internet culture. I had very smart people explain to me why such-and-such company was going to be a great success because of the number of "eyeballs" it was attracting. (I learned that this referred to the number of people who were visiting a company's website and therefore could be a proxy for the advertising revenue they could earn if they could figure out how to charge for it.)

Having been a CFO for many years in private and public companies, I had a keen appreciation for the concept of earnings per share. What I could not understand was eyeballs per share. I was beginning to feel that I just didn't get it, because these very smart people all seemed to be enthralled with this new technology. Clearly, some of these new-age companies have thrived (Amazon, Yahoo, eBay and others), though most just did not have a viable business plan

(Pets.com, WebVan, and others). In another three years, most of the "eyeballs" companies had crashed and burned, leaving a lot of damage in their wake.

Finally, I was introduced to the dynamic young company down in Orange County named Broadcom. By this time, I had lived for over twenty-five years in the San Francisco Bay Area (specifically in what came to be called Silicon Valley shortly after I arrived there in 1970). Broadcom's location was a challenge, but I solved it by commuting for nine-plus years.

First Impressions of an Outsider

My first interview was scheduled in Irvine with Nick and Henry on a warm Friday. By this time, the casual dress code was ubiquitous in Silicon Valley and I assumed it would also apply in Orange County, particularly on a Friday. Just to be sure, though, the day before my interview I phoned Nick's administrative assistant to confirm. She informed me that suit and tie were expected every day of the week. Okay, that was different...I was glad I called.

I had read up on the company and seen profiles of the rather colorful founders. My first interview was with Nick, who kept me waiting maybe a half an hour. I soon learned it was one of the shortest waits on record for an interview with him. He was as intense as I had been led to believe. He also was clearly a brilliant business strategist who had a vision of the markets that Broadcom could enter and lead. Most of them barely even existed yet, but they did grow quite large, and Broadcom did indeed become the leader in almost all of them.

If Nick was the yang, Henry was the yin. He was intense in his own way; it was just sort of a low-key intensity, if that's not an oxymoron. He was the technologist, and I soon learned that he was sort of an "Uncle Henry" to the engineers. At this time, about two-thirds of the hundred-fifty employees were engineers, not an unusual ratio for an early-stage company—but I privately predicted that the ratio would gradually decline over time. I was wrong: by the time I left the company in 2006, engineers accounted for over 70 percent of its then five thousand employees.

For many years, I had used a simple set of four criteria to evaluate companies, either as a potential investment or as a place I wanted to work. First, is the company in a series of dynamic growth markets? Second, do the company's products or its technology address the mainstream of those markets? Third, does the team have a proven ability to execute? Fourth, does the company have a financial model that will be attractive to the investing public? Of all the companies I evaluated after leaving Bay Networks, Broadcom was the only one to earn strong affirmatives from me on all four criteria.

Without getting into the details of negotiations, I will say that I agreed to a base salary that was a small fraction of what I had been earning, but also to a generous option grant that would ultimately be worth much more than I had ever imagined.

People on a Mission

The culture at Broadcom could best be described as "people on a mission." These were not just employees working for a paycheck. For one thing, their actual paychecks were relatively small. The only way they could earn a decent living was if they performed extraordinarily and helped the company to succeed. That's the whole point of employee stock options.

In addition to the strong financial motivation, people were hired for their dedication to their craft. The pride of developing and bringing to market a new technology was a powerful motivator. How could the company ensure that it was hiring the right people?

Interviewing for a position at Broadcom was an excruciating process for the interviewee. It was often a multiday affair, with interviews going late into the night. Nick used to say, only partially in jest, that it was his goal to send potential recruits "screaming into the night." There was no sugarcoating the job, saying how cushy it would be.

We needed to make sure our hires had the fire in the belly necessary to join the mission. The compensation structure, so heavily biased toward equity, assured us that no one would want to join the company just so they could sit back and draw a large salary whether the company succeeded or not. We were all on the same page. Delivering value to ourselves required delivering value to our shareholders.

Let's Step Back and Look at the Environment

It's long been common knowledge that, particularly in the technology industry, the company's principal assets get in their cars and drive home every night. This was even truer during Broadcom's formative years. The technology industry's business environment in the late 1990s was unprecedented. The Internet boom spawned hundreds of aggressive, young companies that were out to change the world and grab as much market share as possible in the process. Most of them failed—some spectacularly and some quietly, but they failed. Broadcom was a notable exception.

In my experience, the scarcest resource for any start-up in the 1970s and 1980s was money. In the 90s, money was readily available, though often at a very steep cost: the higher the percentage of the company owned by investors, the more control they had. Venture capitalists (VCs) raised huge war chests and competed vigorously with each other to fund as many deals as they could.

In the 90s, the scarcest start-up resource was people. Young companies with very limited cash resources could not pay the salaries and cash bonuses that large companies offered. Nor could a guaranteed stream of cash payments provide enough incentive to get large groups of very talented people (with young families they only infrequently saw) to work virtually (and even literally) around the clock. The most compelling incentive a start-up could offer was equity, provided through employee stock options.

The future of any technology company depends directly on a reliable flow of new products with enhanced performance and at reduced cost. It must work very closely with its major customers and assist them in their own development efforts. Engineers and others routinely work extraordinary hours to complete designs on time and get products to customers before competitors can. To excel, a company has to focus unremittingly on being first to market with the highest-performance products, and then be able to repeat that for the next generation of product and the next, and so on. This all requires extreme dedication from a very highly talented cadre of engineers.

Now Back to the Story...

I had been with early-stage companies before, so I was accustomed to not having a large staff to delegate to. I had arrived at SynOptics when it was an early-stage company. It began an explosive growth path shortly after I arrived, but it still took seven more years to reach a billion-dollar revenue level—and that was assisted by a merger in the seventh year. Broadcom was to reach the billion-dollar level only three years after I joined it—from a $20 million annual run rate to $1 billion, representing a fiftyfold increase in that very short time. None of the early Broadcom growth was generated by acquisitions.

A company doesn't grow at Broadcom's rate by accident. It takes a lot of very dedicated people performing at a very high level, working to implement a brilliantly conceived strategy. Nick and Henry conceived the strategy and drove its implementation through the culture they had instilled from day one. Was everything perfect? Not by a long shot. One of the casualties of the hyper growth rate was administrative process. A lack of process was at the core of the employee stock option accounting issues that no one realized *were* issues until the hindsight of 2006 was applied.

When I joined Broadcom, I inherited a finance organization consisting of two professionals, neither of whom had more than five years of business experience, and two or three overworked clerical staff. One of my first actions was to hire the people I needed to upgrade our financial and accounting capabilities. I hired a controller (Glenn Josephson), a head of shareholder services to record and track stock option grants and exercises (Carol Prado, who testified as a government witness at my trial), a highly qualified financial reporting specialist (Gail Patton, who always appeared on the government's witness lists but was never called at my trial) and a senior financial planning and analysis person (Kourosh Kohanteb). I also hired an experienced human resources executive with whom I worked very closely (Nancy Tullos). To my dismay, Nancy ultimately became the government's primary witness in the options-related charges that were filed against me in 2008.

Still, it was always a struggle to keep up. The primary focus of the company was always on developing new products and getting them to market ahead of the competition. The growth rates I have cited testify to the success of that focus.

Staff Meetings: A New Level of Agony

It would be tedious to recount the many anecdotes that could give the flavor of working at Broadcom during those early days, so I will focus on just one: staff meetings. These represented the best and the worst of what the internal operations were like.

Nick called all executive staff meetings, and he dominated them. Nick had many very positive attributes, as I've noted, but Nick and the clock were archenemies. Staff meetings were generally scheduled to start at 6:00 or 7:00 p.m., but often didn't really get started until 8:00 or 9:00. They often ran into the early morning hours.

Then there was the matter of agendas. I have been in many staff meetings with crisp agendas. I ran my own finance staff meetings that way: bring up the principal issues confronting the company, let each person describe his or her own perspective regarding their own area of responsibility, designate some action items, and adjourn. Good theory, but not even close to the practice in Nick's meetings.

His would often start with what came to be known as the "crisis du jour." These were never twice the same, so that's actually a good thing. For any executive in whose area the crisis arose, it was not to be a pleasant evening. Particularly in the early days, Nick was likely to be fully informed on every detail of every development project and every customer interaction. Any executive who was confident of countering Nick's attacks with superior knowledge of the issue was soon proven embarrassingly wrong.

Once we finally dispensed with the crisis du jour—it could take an hour, or several—we moved on to lesser crises or potential crises. Having seen one of their peers thoroughly skewered already, the next people in the hot seat would be quick to acknowledge their shortcomings and to propose solutions. If their solutions weren't robust enough or could not be implemented soon enough, Nick was not shy about pointing that out in his own inimitable way.

Most of Nick's attacks were well founded, such as when someone failed to make a timely response to a customer request. Others were a little misdirected. I recall one late-night staff meeting when Nick verbally attacked Vahid Manian, the head of manufacturing, and accused him of doing nothing to solve a technical problem with a new silicon chip. Knowing that he and his limited staff had been working around the clock on the issue, Vahid sarcastically agreed he had been doing nothing but enjoying the Club Med environment at Broadcom. That was a great tension-breaker, and it helped Nick to realize he'd gone a little overboard.

As crazy and dysfunctional as all this seemed, it actually worked. Again, the evidence is in the company's growth and its creation of shareholder value.

Getting Ready for the IPO

Put quite simply, an IPO is a big deal. An initial public offering is the first time a company offers its shares to the public. Unlike a privately owned corporation, a public company is required to make fulsome disclosures of all its financial operations, risk factors, and any other events or circumstances that could be important to investors.

Only a small fraction of the thousands of companies that are started every year in this country ever do an IPO. The vast majority of start-ups are small-scale companies (often referred to as Mom & Pop operations) with no aspirations of ever going public. And whether they start with Mom & Pop or even Masters-of-the-Universe aspirations, a significant number ultimately fail and liquidate. Some companies that start with great aspirations never get beyond the stage of being marginal private enterprises. Many are acquired by larger companies and cease to exist. So, just to get to the point of launching an IPO meant that Broadcom was in rare company.

Broadcom's aspirations were always clear: to be a successful public company with the capability and financial resources to bring great products to market. By 1997, Nick and Henry and their team had done all the right things. They had developed cutting-edge products that were in great demand in their growing markets. They were operating profitably and were generating positive cash flow. They had three solid product lines and the vision to see how they could diversify into additional areas. They had assembled a very solid team. It was a young team; most of the members were under age forty, including the CEO. What they lacked in experience, they more than made up for in intelligence and drive.

To complete the team, they needed an experienced CFO who could handle the Wall Street interface and guide the internal growth. I was fortunate enough to be in the right place at the right time and was chosen for the role. The next major item on our agenda was to tell our story to the Street.

All of us believed we had a tiger by the tail, but the only thing that would really matter was to convince the potential investors with the big checkbooks that we were worthy of them. Marketing an IPO requires some very detailed financial and operational filings with the Securities and Exchange Commission (SEC). It also includes a so-called "road show," where the principal executives and the lead investment bankers spend about two weeks traveling in Europe and the United States to meet with potential investors in group presentations and one-on-one meetings.

One way to measure the success of an IPO is the conversion rate on the one-on-ones: the percentage of investors visited who actually buy shares. In Broadcom's case, of the 72 investors we visited all 72 purchased shares in our offering. Can't do much better than 100 percent. Demand exceeded supply dramatically. Our issue price was $24.00 per share. At the end of the first day of trading, April 16, 1998, the stock closed at just over $53.00. Prior to our IPO, the largest percentage increase on the first day of trading had been Netscape's, and we eclipsed it. We didn't realize that this was really the beginning of the Internet bubble. Within the next year, many IPOs would surpass our first-day record.

(Broadcom has had several stock splits since the IPO. If the $24 IPO price is adjusted to allow for all the splits as of early 2012, the equivalent price would now be $2.67 per share. I cite this fact in case any readers want to compare the IPO price with current market price.)

Living through the Bubble

You might think that as the bubble was inflating and stock prices seemed to be on a one-way trajectory upward that everyone would be happy. That would not be correct. The inflation of the bubble presented its own set of challenges. Hiring new people was one of them. Two individuals could start a week apart and each have their options priced at their respective start date. Because the stock was so volatile, the strike prices could differ by $25 to $30 or more—in either direction. The stock could rise $50 one week, plunge $25 the next, and then rise another $50 the week after.

It was very hard to plan with any discipline. As soon as a production plan was put in place, it had to be scrapped and replaced with a more aggressive one. The normal discipline of conserving resources was replaced by a culture that said that if a company did not take advantage of every possible opportunity, it would be left in the dust.

Before the IPO, Broadcom's top management had architected a plan to diversify the company's technology base through a combination of aggressive hiring and aggressive acquisition of early-stage companies. We consummated our first acquisition in 1999. Less than two years later, we completed our twenty-first acquisition. With only one exception, these were all early-stage companies with little or no revenue, but they had solid technology and a cadre of thirty to fifty highly talented engineers.

As always, the primary motivation for all of these new Broadcom employees was the opportunity to share ownership interest in the corporation. As the stock value continued to grow, the employees felt rewarded for their hard work and continued to work even harder. The higher stock price also provided a valuable currency for making acquisitions. In those early days, all acquisitions were made by issuing new stock instead of spending cash. This initially diluted the current shareholders' interests, but almost all of them understood the value of diversification and approved of Broadcom's acquisition strategy. As soon as acquisitions were publicly announced, the stock price almost always rose by an amount greater than the dilution created by issuing new shares.

We never decided specifically how many acquisitions would be enough. Because these were small entities, they were relatively easy to absorb. The market told us when it was time to stop acquiring and focus on rationalizing our acquisitions.

The Bubble Deflates. Now What?

By late 2000 and early 2001, the market spoke loudly and clearly: the bubble had burst. The NASDAQ market index plunged from a historic high of 5,048 in March 2000 to 2,470 by the end of 2000. It eventually dropped to a low of 1,114 in October 2002. In mid-2012, the index was hovering around the 2,700 mark.

Broadcom's stock drop paralleled the NASDAQ drop. From a split-adjusted high of $182.51 in August 2000, BRCM fell to $56.03 by the end of the year and eventually to an all-time low of $6.47 in October 2002. For a group of dedicated employees who depended on the value of their options to sustain their lifestyle, this was a devastating time. For a current perspective, in mid-2012, Broadcom stock was trading around the $30-to-$35 level.

As employees' options were rendered valueless by the market meltdown, we scrambled to find alternative approaches to retaining our people and being able to hire new talent. In 2001, we instituted a so-called "tender offer" that allowed eligible employees to exchange their underwater options for new ones that would be priced six months and a day after the offer commenced. People were able to exchange options with strike prices as high as $200 or more (on a presplit basis) for new ones priced at $39.75 (also presplit).

That looked good for a while, but within a few months, the $39.75s were underwater also. Finally, in mid-2002 when the stock was approaching its all-time low, we made a major stock option grant to about 2,000 employees for the 2002 year. At the same time, we accelerated the company-wide focal grant that had originally been planned for 2003. Priced at $15.74, this grant finally reestablished the proper level of equity incentive.

As the stock market deflated, so also did the markets for technology products. Many of the companies Broadcom competed against saw their revenues plummet by as much as 80 percent from 2000 to 2001. Broadcom was much better positioned and suffered only a 15 percent revenue drop. But compared to annual revenue increases that had exceeded 100 percent in each of the previous three years, a 15 percent decline was very serious.

Many competitors went into hunker-down mode, laying off significant portions of their workforces and seriously limiting research and development expenditures, all in an effort to conserve cash and to minimize the financial losses they would have to report. Broadcom took a more measured approach. Doing a relatively modest layoff of about 5 percent of the workforce in 2001, Broadcom continued to invest in its diversification program. We put a freeze on new acquisitions of companies and focused on absorbing what we had already acquired.

Our commitment to continued investment in new product development at this time was a defining moment in Broadcom history. Among other products developed during this period were chips for Bluetooth and wireless LAN (also known as Wi-Fi). These two forms of wireless technology were to provide the technology base that propelled Broadcom into a position of market leadership for the next decade.

In late 2002, we had completed most of the development for a series of new products, but our market had not yet fully recovered and our expense base was too high. In a very painful process, we had a major reduction in force by five hundred people—about 15 percent of our workforce.

Our Charismatic Leader Leaves and We Never Miss a Beat: Nick Had Built a Solid Base

The net result of all this was that we entered 2003, which turned out to be a recovery year, with a broad product line and a streamlined expense structure. We were well positioned. It has often been said that we can't control our circumstances, but we can control how we react to them. Instead of panicking or going into "woe is me" mode, we calmly and rationally determined where we could eliminate excess without damaging our future prospects, and we executed on our plan. One saving element was that we had consistently generated good cash flows, so we were in no danger of running out of money. In fact, 2002 was the only year of my tenure when our cash flow from operations was negative—but only by $69 million (a very small number compared with over $1 billion of revenue). Cash flow was slightly positive in 2003; it then surged to a positive $502 million by 2004, as we were able to reap the benefits of the well-targeted investments we had made in the down years of 2001 and 2002.

In early 2003, Nick left the company he had founded and was replaced in the interim by Lanny Ross, a member of the board. Lanny had had substantial big-company experience in the technology area. He brought solid organizational skills and an orientation toward supporting process improvements. I and my staff wholeheartedly endorsed implementing rigorous controls. We had become a large company and we needed to act like one, while still retaining an entrepreneurial edge.

When the strategies implemented under Nick were combined with a more rational organization structure, Broadcom revenue increased by more than 120 percent over the next two years. The company generated over half a billion dollars in cash flow from operations. In 2005, Scott McGregor replaced Lanny as CEO, and revenue over the next two years increased by over 50 percent. Clearly, Broadcom was doing some things right in those early days to provide a product and technology base that supported such a dynamic rate of growth.

During this time, our internal processes improved substantially, including in the handling of employee stock options. Based on the 2006 reassessment of the accounting guidelines, Broadcom recorded a restatement in early 2007 that added an additional $2.2 billion of noncash stock option expenses spread from1998 to 2005. All of the restated grants related to grants made prior to mid-2003, when the process improvements were implemented.

Although the company reported large noncash expenses during my tenure from 1997 through 2006—over $7 billion related to acquisitions and stock option expenses, before the additional $2 billion of restated expenses—the company continued to be very successful as measured by revenue growth, employee growth, and cash flow generation. Revenue increased a hundredfold: from $37 million in 1997 to $3.7 billion in 2006. Employee headcount grew from 150 to 5,000. And the company generated positive cash flow from operations of more than $2.1 billion.

I have remarked that Broadcom was an unconventional company. Certainly, the financial metrics it has been able to achieve—and still achieves to this day—are outside the norm. As a key member of the management team for almost ten years, I can say that the experience took me through the full gamut of emotions. It was exhilarating to grow at such a rate. It was very satisfying to enable the creation of products that people use to improve their everyday lives. It was challenging to be moving so quickly in what sometimes seemed to be a random manner. It was frustrating to be making rapid-fire decisions with such incomplete information. What I love most in my professional life is building companies. There were a lot of very high points at Broadcom and a number of not-so-high points. On balance, I feel very fortunate to have been part of a team that built a company to be proud of.

Chapter 2

The Search for the Guilty—Whether They're Guilty or Not

Once the media had created the frenzy about purported stock option backdating in mid-2006, the Wall Street firms were quick to jump on the bandwagon. Any hint of a scandal drives a flurry of trading activity. Since trading volume per se is a great profit generator for the Street, it's not surprising that there is competition to see which firms can convert a purported scandal into a trading opportunity.

Once the media and Wall Street create froth, the regulators can't be far behind. Having missed most of the real misbehavior (Enron, WorldCom, and more recently, Madoff), the SEC pounces on opportunities to show how tough their enforcement operations can be. If this means they have to create the appearance of wrongdoing where none existed, so be it. The United States Attorney's Office (USAO) needed a high-profile case in 2006, and this one sure looked like it would fill the bill.

Our Initial Response to the Frenzy

As soon as the CFRA report was issued and Broadcom's stock option practices were attacked, I took the first internal action. I immediately called the member of my staff, Gregg Morrison, who oversaw our stock options reporting function, and asked him to conduct a thorough analysis of our granting practices. My instinctive reaction was to gather all the facts in response to the allegations. I wasn't about to engage in a war of words in the media or make unfounded statements to the public markets.

However, because allegations were being made about possibly erroneous accounting on my watch, I was in a delicate situation. While I was not, by any means, the internal accounting expert, I was responsible for the function. I made sure that an internal analysis was launched immediately, empowered my people to dig in without restriction, and stepped back to avoid even any appearance of bias in the analysis. Again, this was my instinct. Let's find all the facts and let them speak for themselves.

In May 2006, I had no reason to believe I would eventually become the designated bad guy. I sat in on most of the analysis reviews with my finance staff, the company's independent public accountants, Ernst & Young (E&Y); the company's attorneys, the Los Angeles-based law firm of Irell & Manella; and the audit committee. My interactions with the Irell law firm, who initially represented both the company and certain executives (including me) took an unexpected twist that I will describe in more detail later in this chapter.

My first indication that things were taking an inappropriate turn was in August 2006, as we were preparing a memorandum for the SEC that we planned to deliver personally in Washington, DC. I still remember the meeting with a number of senior Broadcom executives where we reviewed it. At some point, something was said about the forthcoming SEC visit, but I hadn't realized it had been scheduled. When I asked the CEO, Scott McGregor, why I hadn't been informed, he advised me that I would not be attending.

Following that, I was generally excluded from further meetings as the analysis progressed. By this time, the Broadcom Audit Committee had retained the services of the Kaye Scholer law firm to act as independent counsel. I soon learned that this is standard procedure in these cases. The company's own attorneys are arguably too closely affiliated with the company to be fully objective.

Soon thereafter, the independent counsel asked to interview me in an alleged fact-finding meeting. By this time, I had also been advised to retain personal legal representation. On the advice of Broadcom's corporate attorneys, I initially retained the services of the well-known Silicon Valley law firm of Wilson, Sonsini. They wisely recommended that I not grant the interview, since it was clear that I was at least "a person of interest" and was possibly at risk of being used as a scapegoat.

Later in the process, when I finally was able to see the notes the independent counsel had prepared for the proposed interview, it was clear that it was never meant to be anything like an impartial search for the truth. It was more of a setup. Their notes read like an indictment: it appeared to me that they had already made up their minds that I was guilty of some evil crime.

This was a real turning point for me. I had a series of conversations with Scott McGregor about the consequences of whether I should take the interview or not. He understood my dilemma and counseled me to do whatever I believed was best for myself. When I asked about specific consequences to my position at Broadcom should I decline to be interviewed, he gave me a very direct answer. He told me that as an officer of the corporation, if I declined to "cooperate fully" in the process, I had three choices: I could retire, I could resign, or I could be fired. That's pretty clear.

I had already decided on retirement, but this was not my chosen timeframe, and these were certainly not my chosen circumstances. I thought long and hard about the decision and consulted in depth with my attorneys. Finally, I opted to take my attorneys' advice and declined to be interviewed. Simultaneously, I presented Scott with a brief letter announcing my retirement.

In my trial, the government tried to liken my refusal to take the interview with a bank robber leaving the scene of a crime. Shame on them. They knew full well that no responsible attorney would ever advise a client to jeopardize Fifth Amendment rights in such a situation. But if they could make my decision sound to a jury like an admission of guilt, they were going to do so.

The result was that, as of September 19, 2006, my forty-year business career officially ended. The last nine-plus years of my career had been spent helping Broadcom to evolve from a small, aspiring private company to an industry powerhouse. Now that company was throwing me under the bus.

Why Would a Company Turn On Its Own?

The motivation for a company to look for potential suspects within its own ranks was codified in the Holder Memorandum of 1999. Eric Holder wrote it when he was Deputy Attorney General in the Clinton administration. To be fair, the Holder Memorandum provided suggestions. The 2003 Thompson Memorandum (see Appendix A), authored in the aftermath of the Enron and WorldCom scandals, hardened these suggestions into demands. The Thompson Memorandum was ultimately deemed so overreaching that it was toned down by the McNulty Memorandum, but not until 2008—after the indictments in the Broadcom case had been issued and Department of Justice (DOJ) intimidation tactics had been implemented.

The Thompson Memo laid out criteria enabling a corporation to earn "points" of cooperation to prevent it from being indicted. As I noted earlier, any indictment of a corporation could well be a death sentence for that corporation (viz., Arthur Andersen).

One of the most significant criteria in the Memo was whether a corporation would waive its attorney-client privilege. This violates a basic tenet of our justice system, namely that any information exchanged between attorney and client cannot be divulged to any outside party—particularly not to a party with an interest in prosecuting the client. This principle is necessary so that clients can offer full disclosure to their attorneys without fear that their comments will be twisted and used against them. Thompson to corporate attorneys: forget your privilege.

In an even more blatant misuse of government power, Thompson promised corporations cooperation points if they took action "to discipline or terminate wrongdoers." In other words, give us some sacrificial lambs and maybe we won't prosecute you as a corporation. And, by the way, offering up sacrificial lambs draws attention away from yourself (whether you be other corporate executives or board members).

To be fair, many of the tools DOJ directives design to elicit cooperation from corporations are appropriate and necessary. There have been cases of genuine fraudulent behavior by corporate officers; these need to be uncovered and punished. The problem arises when sanctions designed to expose crimes are used instead to create the appearance of criminal activity.

Being Fast Is More Important Than Being Accurate

There are a lot of good reasons for a corporation to conclude an investigation of this nature as soon as possible. First, there is the distraction of having senior executives and the board focusing on a witch-hunt rather than on normal business issues. Second, until the corporation can complete its restatement, it cannot be in compliance with SEC requirements for financial reporting. If not in compliance, no employee options may be sold. If not in compliance for an extended period, the corporation can be delisted from the securities exchanges. All of these factors place extreme pressure on the corporation to reach some conclusions, even if they are the wrong ones.

Accounting is not an exact science. A company's financial statements are compiled using a combination of facts, assumptions, and estimates. This is certainly true when assigning a value to noncash charges. Since no one ever writes a check, how can anyone be sure what the exact amount is? In doing a large restatement for stock-based compensation charges, assumptions are piled on top of assumptions. Many different dates can be used as "measurement dates" (i.e., the date when an option grant is priced). The amount of the restatement is critically dependent on which measurement dates are used. Since there is no fixed rule declaring exactly which date should be used, assumptions must be made.

Whichever dates are chosen, there will always be Monday-morning quarterbacks who will say they were incorrect. If some of those quarterbacks happen to work for regulatory agencies like the SEC, their opinion is very important. If the regulators deem the amount of the restatement to be understated, they can and will require that the company restate again. That would be a very bad thing. Broadcom assigned measurement dates that created the highest possible restatement amount so they would not be required to do it again.

The Broadcom restatement was large: just over $2.2 billion of expenses were deducted from Broadcom's reported earnings for the years 1998 through 2005. The government did their best to try to dramatize the size of the restatement, implying that greedy Broadcom executives had realized billions of dollars of illegitimate gains from the alleged backdating. What they never mentioned was that the $2.2 billion was a hypothetical number based on abstract accounting theory and did not represent any actual payments to anyone. Furthermore, most of the options that had to be restated wound up underwater after the NASDAQ meltdown and were never exercised.

So far, we have just been talking about accounting. Accounting is important, but not nearly as important as the lives of individuals. It appeared to me that as part of the effort to complete the restatement expeditiously and to redirect the government's attention (both DOJ and SEC) away from the company, Broadcom offered up some sacrificial lambs. There was no time to do a thorough investigation of who, if anyone, was to blame for the purported accounting errors that led to the restatement.

The "Independent" Investigation Begins

As soon as Broadcom was named in media and Wall Street analyst articles as a company at risk for having improperly accounted for its employee stock options, the inevitable plaintiff strike suits were launched. Recognizing the inevitability of this even before the first suits ever appeared, Broadcom retained the services of its principal law firm, Irell & Manella, to represent it as a corporation and some of its executives as individuals. I was one of the executives

Irell represented, in this case and in another we had concluded a few months earlier.

Within a week or so, two Irell partners interviewed me about the case. At the time, I had never heard of something called an "Upjohn warning"—it's sort of a corporate Miranda warning advising individual executives that any privilege in the interview belongs to the corporation and not the individual. I was never given one. A year and a half later, I learned that everything I told them had been passed on by Broadcom to the prosecuting attorneys from the DOJ. For the record, I had not given them anything incriminating; I merely recited the facts as I knew them. I later learned that some of my comments to them appeared to have been twisted to make them sound incriminating. The presiding judge in my case, Judge Carney, ruled that their disclosure violated both my privilege and their duty of loyalty to me as a client. (Judge Carney's ruling about my privilege was later reversed by the Ninth Circuit. More on that later.)

As I noted earlier, Irell had advised that the Broadcom Audit Committee retain the services of an independent law firm to investigate the conduct of certain Broadcom officials. Irell had determined, somewhat belatedly, that it would be a conflict for them to advise the company and investigate individuals who had been their clients: people like me.

This independent law firm was retained to ferret out the guilty. It was Kaye Scholer of Los Angeles, a firm well known to Irell. Within the first week of their investigation, it appeared to me that they had concluded that certain individuals, including me, were to blame. Clearly, their conclusions were not based on an exhaustive investigation, but seemed to me to have been handed to them on a silver platter by the attorneys at Irell. It was as though the independent law firm were brought in as a hired gun, that the Irell attorneys provided the bullets, and then showed them where to aim. (This metaphor actually originated with the judge in my case. See Chapter 6.)

And aim they did—squarely at Nick, Nancy Tullos, and me. The first two had left the company in 2003, so they were convenient targets.

I was still there, but I had signed the SEC filings and the lawyers found a few twistable e-mails, so I was thrown under the bus, too.

E-mail—God's Gift to Prosecutors

I'm not sure how prosecutors developed fraud and conspiracy cases before there was e-mail. Maybe they had to have actual evidence. Anyway, e-mails are a prosecutor's best friend. Who has never written an e-mail using colorful language that could be taken out of context and made to sound like something insidious?

In this case, lawyers for both sides estimated that they reviewed in excess of six million pages of documents, many of them e-mails. For the heart of their case, the prosecutors in trial used and reused about a dozen. They showed some others, but they kept coming back and hammering on those. In our cross-examinations, the defense would show dozens of messages on either side of the allegedly incriminating e-mails to put them in context. The jurors later told us that they were not fooled by the government's attempt to create something out of nothing, and that they were grateful for the defense's ability to "teach" them.

But long before the case came to trial, or even before indictments were handed down, the independent counsel formed a biased case against me using some of the same e-mails the prosecutors would ultimately use. We saw tangible evidence of this in the trial when a former senior member of the Broadcom board, Werner Wolfen, testified. Although Werner and I had worked very closely together for over nine years and shared a great mutual respect, after a couple of hours of being shown out-of-context e-mails, this former director did a one-eighty and decided that I was not trustworthy.

The same tactics were applied repeatedly with other potential witnesses who were cowed into believing that the only way they could save their own skins was to buy into the government's twisted interpretation of the e-mail traffic.

The Search for the Truth (As We See It)

The most fundamental principle of the American criminal justice system is that the accused is presumed innocent unless and until the government proves the accused guilty beyond a reasonable doubt. That's a very high bar, and one the government was never able to achieve in this case. But it's a different story for the special investigators. There are no real standards. A convenient presumption of guilt can be all it takes to move the investigation along to its next stage.

In this case, the investigators somehow reached conclusions in a few weeks. From the revelations of Broadcom's internal investigation until my acquittal, it was three and a half years! This proves once again that the quick answer is not always the correct one. And when a person's liberty is at stake, it is vital to find the correct answer.

The first quick answers appeared to me to have been served up by Irell and then "verified" by the independent counsel. Both law firms then aggressively provided incriminating data to the government, which used them to conduct a deeply flawed grand jury process.

The grand jury process is primarily controlled by the prosecuting attorneys. Any witnesses they call are not permitted to have their own attorneys in the jury room. Witnesses are supposed to be able to break and talk with their attorneys outside the jury room at any time, but this is also at the whim of the prosecutors.

In addition to offering all the out-of-context e-mails, the prosecutors in our case also regaled the grand jury with lurid tales attributed to Nick. Nick was a colorful, larger-than-life character. Many stories circulated alleging drug use and other aberrant personal behavior. To my knowledge, none of these allegations has ever been proven, but the stories were just too juicy to die.

You might ask, what does this have to do with accounting for stock options? Good question. It has absolutely nothing to do with it. But apparently, the government's theory was that if you throw enough mud around, someone is going to get dirty. In the end, the grand jury returned three criminal indictments. Nick and I were indicted on fraud charges relating to stock options accounting and Nick was indicted on charges of distributing narcotics.

The salacious charges against Nick were widely publicized. After all, that makes much more interesting reading than something as arcane as accounting for stock options. We will never know how much influence the bogus narcotics charges (the government ultimately dropped them) had on the grand jury's willingness to return indictments for the stock options accounting. What is painfully obvious is that what should have been a search for the truth was instead perverted into a search for convictions.

It Doesn't Really Matter Who We Prosecute, but We Have to Go after Someone

Once they decided that something evil had happened at Broadcom, the USAO needed to find someone to prosecute. Prosecutors knew they could get their best cooperation from the companies they targeted at that time if they armed themselves with the Thompson Memorandum. Charging decisions could be seen as sort of an unholy joint venture between a corporation and the USAO. The USAO needed defendants and corporations needed cooperation points. Voila! Here are your defendants.

In the case of Broadcom, Nick was an obvious target. With his well-documented personal quirks, he provided frequent fodder for the local media. Certainly, any case that involved Nick would generate a lot of publicity. And if you're going to create a case where there is really no evidence, you're going to need a lot of publicity. If someone is incredibly wealthy, that also makes for an attractive target. Never mind that Nick obtained his wealth by creating a fantastic company that has provided thousands of jobs and hundreds of innovative products. In the current populist environment, wealth equals greed, and greed can only be satisfied by cheating. Okay, let's go after Nick.

What about Nick's partner and cofounder, Henry? He meets the wealth criterion, so he must be greedy and therefore a cheater. Henry and Nick were the stock options committee and were responsible for granting options to employees. There was a problem, though: Henry's public persona was largely that of an epic philanthropist. Inside the company, Henry was the antithesis of Nick, whose style was vociferous and led to a sometimes rather harsh treatment of employees. The bottom line was that Henry is universally well liked and is not the kind of person jurors would be likely to convict. What to do about Henry? We'll address that in the next chapter.

Let's see: who else signs the SEC documents? That would be Bill Ruehle, the CFO: always a convenient target. The prosecutors would really like to get the top guys, but maybe if they can get the CFO, they can flip him and get to the top. I was a pretty frequent e-mail communicator, so the prosecutors would inevitably find something they could twist into looking nefarious.

One of the lessons of this case is that we should always be extra careful when writing e-mails. Many years later, some zealous prosecutor may try to use your own words against you. However, being careful is easier said than done; the average e-mail is probably composed and sent in a few seconds. That's hardly enough time to do a thorough scrubbing of all the language.

One person at Broadcom could have given a course on how not to write e-mails. Nancy Tullos, Vice President of Human Resources, created e-mails that were just too juicy for the prosecutors to resist. She let her very frequent frustrations flow into flaming e-mails that often sounded conspiratorial, even in the absence of any conceivable conspiracy. Whether she did anything wrong or not, her e-mails sounded so conspiratorial that they could be good tools for the prosecutors to use to intimidate her into cooperating.

Other potential targets included David Dull, the general counsel, but apparently he was not attractive enough, so he was just left to twist slowly in the wind for a few years. But as we shall see, dealing with him proved to be the prosecution's undoing.

We don't have an accurate count of how many people in Broadcom's accounting and shareholder services functions the USAO and their close colleagues at the SEC interviewed. Clearly, there were dozens they thought they could potentially target or intimidate. Some had only the remotest connection with Broadcom and its stock options program. Many of the interviews were solely about trying to add substance to the flimsy narcotics case against Nick. (That alone is patently unfair. Why should a grand jury impaneled to hear evidence about the alleged illegal backdating of stock options be inundated with salacious charges about drugs and other personal behavior?)

The Path to the Charging Decisions

If a real crime has been committed, one would think that decisions about whom to charge with it would not be very complicated. There might be some difficult calls about whether certain individuals were involved or not, but at least it would be clear that there *was* criminal activity. When accounting for stock options that may or may not have been backdated, it gets a lot fuzzier.

As I've mentioned, backdating stock options is not illegal per se as long as they are accounted for properly. Many regulators, public accounting practitioners, and media pundits would opine that the "rules" for doing it were simple, and that anyone who failed to follow them correctly could only have done so intentionally. Therefore, if any improper accounting was done—as measured by post-2006 hindsight—it was with intent to defraud. In the course of my case, it came out very clearly that the so-called "rules" for the proper accounting of employee stock options were anything but clear themselves. It turned out that hundreds of companies had misinterpreted accounting guidelines whose interpretation only became crystal-clear in hindsight after the events of 2006.

Second, the evidence at this trial showed that sophisticated investors did not consider noncash charges related to stock options when they evaluated whether or not to invest in a stock. The only witness the government produced at trial to comment on stock-based compensation charges was unable to even identify where they might appear on a company's financial statements.

So, if it's not clear whether the accounting was correct or not and it's not clear that investors even care, where is the crime? Since the decision of whom to charge with what crimes was such a torturous path in this case, it is further evidence that the government was grossly overreaching when it tried to criminalize behavior that was in no way criminal.

Chapter 3

Let's Make a Deal

The prosecutors' dilemma: if there is no crime, how do we make it look like there was one? The prosecutors' weapon: intimidation. There are a lot of seats in a courtroom. The judge has one. The court reporter has one. The clerk has one. The jury has fourteen (or sometimes, as in this case, sixteen), including the alternates. There are ample seats for spectators, including media and lawyers just curious to learn. There are seats for the prosecutors and seats for the defense attorneys. But there is one seat that no one wants to occupy: the defendant's seat. I know. I sat in it for eight interminable weeks.

How does one avoid sitting in that seat? The simple answer is: just don't do anything wrong. Well, I didn't think I had done anything wrong, and in the end it was determined by judge and jury that I hadn't. But it didn't keep me out of that seat. When the powers that be decide that someone is going to sit in the defendant's seat, then you better believe that someone will, whether he or she should or not.

Given this background, the best way for anyone to assure that they won't be in the defendant's seat is to deflect responsibility from themselves and, ideally, onto some convenient target. If the government and the "independent" attorneys have already determined who the most likely occupants will be, the rest is fairly simple. Tell the investigators what they want to hear, and they'll go pursue the designated bad guys.

I was deeply saddened that so many people with whom I had worked closely over the years, and with whom I had thought I shared a mutual respect, turned on me when they thought it would save their own skin. One of the few advantages of being a defendant is that you get to see the recorded memoranda of all the government's and the independent investigators' interviews of potential witnesses. These are confidential documents, so I can't expose their contents here, except to the extent those individuals testified in the trial. Suffice it to say that there were many people who suddenly took a revisionist view of history when the government led them to believe that they could be in the defendant's seat if they were not sufficiently "helpful." It's amazing how "helpful" a person's recollections can be when their situation is explained that way.

I Just Want You to Tell the Truth (As I See It)

Reading the summaries of the USAO interviews with potential witnesses presents a very clear picture of the government trying to develop the "truth" as they see it. This really came through in the testimony of the government witnesses during the trial.

As a primary example, take the concept of backdating. In my years at Broadcom I don't recall ever even hearing the word until the media frenzy that kicked off in 2006. Suddenly, it became the buzzword to imply nefarious acts by greedy executives. It was a very convenient term for the media to lock onto because it required no thought or understanding of nuance. It was therefore important for the government to make sure the term was used extensively by its witnesses.

The award for compliance with this requirement should go to Carol Prado. Carol was hired at Broadcom shortly before its IPO to set up and maintain the shareholder services function, which managed the employee stock options program. Carol input option grants into the database, produced documentation for employees, and assisted them in the exercise of their options. She did this with care and dedication throughout her tenure.

In the course of the trial, we presented evidence of at least a dozen interviews she had had with the government. As with others who had multiple government interviews, there was considerable drift in her testimony. By the time she got on the stand, the word "backdating" had been firmly inculcated into her vocabulary. In her direct testimony, Carol dutifully used the word many times. During the years I worked with Carol, I never heard her use it once.

The ultimate example of testimony seemingly molded to the government version of the truth was that of Nancy Tullos. At trial, her testimony came off as thoroughly scripted and lacking in credibility. We learned during trial that Nancy had been subjected to twenty-six government interviews.

With this distorted view of the truth held by the government entity with the power to prosecute, it is easy to see how some individuals could be pressured into making whatever plea deal they could.

The Strong Arm of the Law

From my perspective, I believe the government process went something like this: (1) with the help of the corporation and their "independent" investigators, identify the primary prosecution targets; (2) interview anyone who could potentially have any knowledge of the alleged crime; (3) try to convert some to cooperating witnesses; (4) try to gain informal cooperation from others through intimidation; (5) find some way to neutralize the ones who could otherwise be really helpful for the defense.

I've already indicated the unholy alliance of corporation and government that pointed the finger at Nick, Nancy Tullos, and me. It was very much in the government's interest to make it appear that there could be, and very likely would be, additional targets. This satisfied #1 above.

Next, the government cast a very broad net to include anyone who could possibly have been involved or who could possibly provide incriminating evidence against any real or potential targets. The obvious interviewees were any executives or finance or human resources personnel who were at Broadcom any time from 1998 through 2003. They also interviewed the whole board of directors from that period. They interviewed all Ernst & Young people who had been involved in Broadcom's audits. They interviewed attorneys from outside law firms who had advised Broadcom.

Just to make sure they were getting everyone they could, they also interviewed people who provided personal security for any of the executives, or who provided transportation services (including pilots of the founders' private aircraft). They interviewed family members and ex-family members. Very early one morning, the FBI banged on the door of the home where I was living with my wife-to-be, Julie. They presented her with a subpoena to appear before the grand jury. No stone was left unturned in the government's effort to dig up dirt. This all satisfied #2 above.

In the course of the trial, we heard various witnesses describe the experience of being interviewed by the Feds. The interviewee was there with one or two of their attorneys. There would typically be two or three attorneys from the USAO (i.e., prosecutors). There would always be two FBI agents taking notes and flashing their badges. There would almost always also be at least two attorneys from the SEC. During the interview, many of the government representatives would furiously take notes. I have actually been very kind in referring to the experience as an interview. "Inquisition" would probably be a better descriptor.

From the many interview notes I have seen, it was very clear that such an event was nothing like an objective search for the truth. It was dedicated to intimidating witnesses and extracting any comments that could be used in support of the government's preconceived notions of what had happened and who was responsible for it. Even in the face of all this power play, the government was only able to persuade one witness to plead guilty and to cooperate with them, which is a testimony to the flimsiness of their case. This satisfied #3 above, though their inability to convert any more than one witness scores the effort as unsuccessful.

They were more successful with #4: gaining informal cooperation through intimidation. When she was responding very nervously on the stand, Carol Prado acknowledged that she was fearful that the

USAO would seek an indictment against her. Her profuse use of the word "backdating," not to mention the middle-of-the-night epiphany we will discuss later, clearly showed the extent of her intimidation. The befuddled ramblings of former Broadcom board member Werner Wolfen and his effort to place blame on me appeared to me to be trying desperately to divert prosecutorial attention away from himself. These people didn't plead to any offense, but they appeared to have a clear idea of the direction their testimony should take.

Finally, there is #5: neutralizing anyone who could be of most help to the defense. It became obvious from the government interview notes that there had been several instances of this. The intimidation factor was working overtime. The two most extreme examples of "frozen" potential witnesses were Henry Samueli and David Dull. Each was placed in a totally untenable position. If they testified to what they knew to be the truth of the matter, they knew that the government could (and most likely would) seek indictments against them and twist any testimony on my behalf into something that appeared to incriminate them. The USAO was very successful with #5 until the fateful day when Judge Carney stepped up, did the right thing, and granted them defense immunity.

Here's an Offer You Can't Refuse

I have no way of knowing how many or what kind of plea deals may have been offered. I do know about the two that were entered into and I know about the government's unsuccessful attempts to get me to plead.

The Nancy Tullos Plea

Nancy Tullos was the only person to enter into a plea agreement with the government that included her cooperating with the prosecution. It didn't come easily. It was not as though Nancy one day walked into the government offices and said that she knew crimes had been committed at Broadcom and that she was there to see that justice was done.

What came out at trial was that, during late 2006 and most of 2007, the government attempted to get her to talk with them. Since it was clear that she was a target, she resisted as best she could. Obviously frustrated by their inability to elicit her cooperation, the USAO implemented a new ploy. Since leaving Broadcom in 2003, Nancy had found a job that, by her own testimony, she loved. She was Vice President of Human Resources at another highly respected high tech company in Orange County.

One day, the lead prosecutor on the case picked up the phone and called the general counsel (GC) at that company. The prosecutor asked the GC what the company's policy was if a corporate officer refused to cooperate with a government investigation. He went on to offer the gratuitous advice that such a circumstance would create a reporting obligation for the corporation. Some internal conversations ensued at Nancy's company, and the next day she "voluntarily" resigned: another tangible example of the long, strong arm of the law.

Now the government had Nancy's attention. They had proved they could mess with her life. In the ensuing weeks, the USAO presented Nancy with a stack of her own conspiratorial-sounding e-mails from her Broadcom days. They had come back to bite her.

I don't know what alternative plea agreements Nancy may have had to choose from, but the one she accepted is a matter of public record. She pleaded guilty to one count of obstruction of justice. What did she obstruct? Good question. In a 1999 e-mail to one of her HR subordinates (and on which she copied another), she wrote, "Please delete this e-mail." Now, had there been a current investigation, asking someone to delete what could be a piece of evidence would indeed be a crime.

The first problem with her plea was that it involved a 1999 request to delete an e-mail that eventually may have had some peripheral relevance to an investigation that would start in 2006—seven years later. That's even two years beyond the statute of limitations. The e-mail in question was never even deleted by Nancy. Nor did she request the other subordinate on the e-mail to delete it. If she was trying to obstruct an investigation, she didn't do a very good job of it.

Significantly, the charge Nancy pleaded to had nothing to do with the alleged backdating conspiracy. It was a felony charge, though, and carried a maximum potential penalty of five years in prison. We learned at trial that the government had told her attorney that her plea had to be to a felony, because that would make the jury believe she had done something seriously wrong.

She had been told the government would recommend a sentence of probation if she cooperated fully. We also learned that at some of the government's twenty-six coaching sessions, her responses did not please them and that she was told that if she testified in that manner, she could not be guaranteed that her sentence would be limited to probation. A standard government response when her testimony drifted from what they wanted to hear was to express displeasure, but using the words "we just want you to tell the truth." I've pointed out that, in my opinion, those words were really code for "we just want you to tell our version of the truth."

The Henry Samueli Plea

Henry was a prime target for the government, but as I've said, they would have some serious problems. Henry is very well liked and projects a sincerity and innocence that would be bound to impress even the most jaded juror. On top of that, he was one-half of the options committee that the government tried to convince everyone never met. If Henry were to testify, as he did to the SEC (and why wouldn't he?), it would destroy the government's theory that the options committee was a sham and that all options dates were actually selected after the fact by me.

If Henry were to say that on the stand, the jury would have to decide between his credibility and that of Nancy Tullos. No contest! Okay, if you're the government, how are you going to keep Henry off the stand? Aha! Let's get him to plead to a non-existent crime also. The one they selected for Henry was a statement he made in his SEC testimony that he was not involved in pricing options for Section

16 officers (i.e., the top officers of the company). They found one answer to one of over thirteen hundred questions he was asked in the course of some four days of SEC testimony that could be interpreted as false. They conveniently overlooked the fact that about seventeen lines later in his testimony, he corrected his earlier statement. In fact, in presenting his proposed plea agreement to the judge, the government prosecutors had redacted the part of the testimony that included Henry's correction. (In Chapter 11, the Defense Case, details of Henry's trial testimony regarding his plea will be presented).

So the government presented to Henry's attorneys an opportunity for him to assure he would not sit in the defendant's chair. Remember, the defendant's chair came with a potential prison sentence of over three hundred years. So even if the charge made no sense, it could solve a problem for both sides. For Henry, it could keep him out of the defendant's chair; for the government, it could keep a popular and charismatic person out of the courtroom.

Unlike Nancy, Henry was not willing to hope that his ultimate penalty would not include jail time. Nancy said at trial that she was hoping she would receive probation, but she had no assurances. And, she had to agree to cooperate with the government to even get that. Henry was a different story. The government really, really didn't want him in the courtroom. And he refused to cooperate with the government because he didn't think he or his colleagues at Broadcom had done anything wrong, and he wasn't about to make something up.

The government had a dilemma. How could they guarantee Henry probation when he wasn't even a cooperating witness? Let's see: Henry is a man of substantial means, so let's let him pay a fine so large that it appears he has been punished. After much negotiation, the parties agreed on a fine of $12 million plus probation in addition to a guilty plea on one felony count of lying to the SEC.

Now, the government can recommend a penalty, but only the Court (i.e., the judge) has the authority to impose one. When the government and Henry appeared before the court for approval of his plea deal, the judge rejected it. He cited the fact that Henry was not cooperating and was paying a very large monetary penalty. In rejecting the plea deal, Judge Carney commented that he did not want any appearance that "justice was for sale" in his court. As could be expected, there was considerable media comment about the outrageous $12 million fine. What never made it to the media was the government's original demand for a fine. Their initial offer was that if Henry wanted to be assured of a sentence of probation, he needed to pay a fine of several times the amount ultimately agreed to! That demand was rejected out of hand by Henry and his attorneys. One can only imagine what Judge Carney's reaction would have been to that sum.

Who Else Could Cause the Government Trouble?

Another person who was problematic for the government was David Dull, Broadcom's general counsel (a corporation's top in-house lawyer). Anyone would know that such a person has a very sophisticated understanding of the law. David was not an easy mark.

Having such a large number of defendants can be a serious burden for the prosecution. Each has to be tried based on a different, specific set of facts. Multiple defendants can be tried together—as the government attempted and failed to do in this case—but it is still very cumbersome to have to try more than one or two.

For reasons known only to them, the government apparently decided that David Dull was too difficult to convict and too dangerous to be called as a witness, so they needed to freeze him. The government can tell each potential defendant, "We will charge you," or "We will not charge you," or "We may or may not charge you." It generally best suits their purposes to go with the "maybe we will, maybe we won't" approach. That's what they did with David.

David testified before the SEC twice in 2007. The government said that they did not believe his testimony had been entirely truthful and were considering indicting him in the criminal case. By the time my criminal trial began, their tactic had kept David on the sidelines for two years. They made sure he was well aware that if he were to testify for the defense at trial, anything he said could and would be used against him and that they might very well seek the threatened indictment.

That tactic worked very well until the day it blew up in their faces.

Could a Prime Target Be Flipped?

Very early on, it was clear that I was a prime target (although certainly, I wasn't as dramatic a target as Nick or Henry). I often felt that one of the main reasons was the government's hope that if they put enough pressure on me, they would be able to flip me against Nick and Henry—to get me to agree to cooperate with them against the high-profile cofounders.

By the time I left the company in September 2006, I was working with the law firm of Wilson, Sonsini. Toward the end of the year, they discussed my possible plea agreement with the USAO. The government originally offered that if I pleaded guilty to two felony counts (each of which carried a maximum prison term of five years) and that if my cooperation was strong enough, they would recommend what is euphemistically called a "downward departure" from the maximum sentence.

Later, they hinted that maybe confessing to "only" one felony count would be sufficient. That would carry a five-year max and they would recommend downward departure from that—depending, of course, on how "helpful" I was in my cooperation. I interpreted that to mean that if I could help them convict Nick or Henry (or both), I would get a lighter sentence than if either went free. One of the fatal flaws in the government's rationale was their assumption that I was aware of evidence that, if exposed, would convict Nick or Henry.

The other fatal flaw in their reasoning was that they could induce me to make my testimony sound like Henry and Nick had done something criminal just for the chance at a lighter sentence. Nancy Tullos tried that approach, giving a strained portrayal of a witness claiming to have evidence that she really didn't have. The prosecutor would lob a loaded question at her and she would dutifully bounce back the answer he wanted, with the spontaneity and sincerity of a trained seal.

So far, that's two reasons for me not to take a government deal: (1) I had no incriminating evidence against Nick or Henry and (2) I wouldn't have allowed the evidence to be twisted to make it appear as if I did. As a defendant in a criminal trial, I cannot be forced to testify or even to submit to an interview by hostile government investigators because of my constitutional protection under the Fifth Amendment.

If those reasons weren't enough, the government wanted me to confess to a crime I didn't commit. The charges in my indictment carried a maximum prison sentence of 380 years if I were convicted on all twenty-one counts. That is not something to take lightly. Even five years in prison would be a horrible experience, particularly when you know you have not committed a crime, but there could still be life at the end of five years. Still, I refused to take the bait, which was first offered in December 2006 to January 2007, and my attorneys from Wilson, Sonsini carefully walked me through the implications of pleading versus fighting. They painted a very vivid picture of how overwhelming it could be to fight the federal government.

I listened carefully and weighed the alternatives. I could even understand how a person could be pressured into pleading guilty to a nonexistent crime rather than face the specter of spending the rest of his or her life in prison.

The statistics are overwhelmingly against fighting the government. The US Government presents an annual report on the disposition of federal court cases, sorted by type of charge. For the year 2009, the year my case went to trial, criminal fraud cases were decided for 11,679 defendants. In 88 percent of those cases, the defendant pleaded guilty. About 8 percent of the cases were dismissed before going to trial. Therefore, only 4 percent went to trial. In 2009, that amounted to 470 cases. Of those 470 cases, 81 percent resulted in conviction (so, only 19 percent in acquittal). Looking at the bigger picture, once an indictment has been handed down, the probability in 2009 that a defendant would be acquitted at trial was only 7/10 of 1 percent. Hardly encouraging odds.

I was never seriously tempted to plead, but I was concerned at how my attorneys seemed to be encouraging it as the low-risk approach. When I decided to fight, I also decided to change attorneys. In February 2007, I made the seminal decision to retain the services of Skadden, Arps. Specifically, I had been referred to Skadden's lead white-collar defense attorney, Richard Marmaro, by Frank Quattrone. Frank was a long-time business colleague who knew what it was like to be on the receiving end of a government prosecution. This was a turning point in my case. Rich, his partner Jack DiCanio, and a team of incredibly skilled and diligent attorneys constituted the team that ultimately set me free.

This was not the last government attempt to gain my cooperation. In January 2009, Nick's trial and mine were separated, much to the government's consternation. My defense counsel believed that the government would prefer that I be tried first so that if I were convicted, they could get me to flip on Nick in exchange for a lighter sentence. They never got the opportunity to test their theory, since I was acquitted and the judge ordered the charges against Nick dismissed. Even if I had been convicted, I would never have flipped on Nick.

The government made yet another attempt a few weeks before my trial. Through my attorneys, they invited Julie and me to discuss a potential plea deal. By this time, Judge Carney had gone on record several times with comments that if the defendants in this case were found guilty, they could spend the rest of their natural lives in prison.

That is not a comment anyone ever wants to hear about oneself. In fact, the harshest sentence ever imposed in a backdating case has been two years. I have to believe that Judge Carney was aware of this, but he continued to reference a virtual life sentence. With that threat hanging over, if the government is going to offer something much less onerous, it is tempting to at least listen.

We wound up proposing that the prosecutors meet with my attorneys at the Skadden offices just to feel them out. At first, that seemed acceptable to the government, but the next day, the prosecutors said they would only have a meeting if Julie and I attended, and only in their own offices. The intent could not have been clearer: to parade a few gun-toting FBI agents in and do their best to intimidate Julie and me into believing that the way to salvage anything out of our lives would be to cop a plea and serve some jail time. Hearing that, my response was immediate and unequivocal: I will not plead guilty to a crime I did not commit. End of discussion.

Chapter 4

The Day of Indictment

Never in my life did I imagine that one day I would be the subject of a federal indictment. That is, never until the politically motivated, media-driven backdating frenzy of mid-2006. By August 2006, it became clear to me that I was a logical scapegoat in a dynamic that demanded that someone be scapegoated. It wasn't until twenty-two months later that I was actually indicted.

To say that those months constituted a strange and surreal time would be a vast understatement. It was certainly a time of great personal change. I was forced to retire early from a job I had held for over nine years. I retired from a career that had spanned just over forty years and had more than its share of ups and downs (though fortunately, the last twenty years had had far more ups than downs). Yet through all this, I maintained an abiding faith that ultimately the truth would prevail and that I would be exonerated.

I recall with anguish the day in early 2007 when, returning from a trip, I did my customary cell phone voicemail check as soon as the plane landed. The first message was from my personal banker empathizing with how terrible I must have felt when I saw that morning's *Wall Street Journal* (see Appendix B for a copy of the article as well as my comments and trial testimony providing context rebutting the opening drama created by the article's authors, with some obvious help from the government). Since I hadn't yet seen the *Journal* that day due to my travels, of course I headed for a newsstand as soon as I got inside the terminal at SFO. There, on the front page, was my picture at center column, appended to a story about alleged options backdating at Broadcom.

There are times and circumstances when any business executive would be proud to have his or her picture adorn the front page of the *Wall Street Journal*. This would not be one of them. Nick's picture also appeared with the article, though on a continuation page. Both of our attorneys vigorously protested this inexcusable breach of propriety on the part of the government. We didn't get anywhere with our protests just then, but later on, it proved to be only one piece in the mosaic of government misconduct.

The First Look at the "Evidence"

Late 2006 and early 2007 was probably the low point. My attorneys (Wilson Sonsini) were very skilled at pointing out to me all the evidence the government was amassing through collecting e-mails and their intimidating grilling of potential witnesses. That, combined with company directors who seemed to me to be more concerned with aiding and abetting the government in a search for scapegoats than they were in a rigorous search for the truth, created a very trying environment (no pun intended).

With my new legal team from Skadden on board and coming up to speed, the truth began to emerge, slowly and painfully. The government could easily pick off the low-hanging fruit in the form of a small number of incendiary e-mails. Only dozens of other e-mails and documents could recreate the context that showed the true meaning of each negative sounding e-mail.

A Time of Major Changes

Throughout 2007, my defense case slowly built. It was not an intense experience; it was more like a dull, throbbing headache. It was always there in the background, and I was determined not to let it dominate my life. This was when my personal life went through a dramatic transformation.

After my retirement, I had begun a warm friendship with Julie. I had hired her in 2005 to set up the internal audit function at Broadcom. She did so with great skill, and I had the highest professional regard for her. As any of my former Broadcom colleagues (or Bay Networks colleagues, or colleagues from anywhere else I ever worked) could tell you, I've always been a very private person. I never formed strong friendship bonds at work and always stayed outside company social activities.

My relationship with Julie at Broadcom was no exception. It was purely professional and characterized by a great deal of mutual respect. After I left the firm, we had a chance meeting in a most unlikely location, and our true friendship began. Well, as they say, one thing led to another, and by the following summer we had made a lifelong commitment to each other. As I write this nearly five years later, I see that no decision I ever made was more prescient.

As I've said, I refused to allow the government's intrusion into my life take away my life. Julie knew full well what she was getting into when she decided to build a life with me—a life that could have been rudely interrupted by a prison sentence and by financial penalties that could have expropriated my entire net worth. To her enduring credit, she shared in my commitment to treat the case against me very seriously, but not to let it dominate our lives.

Waiting for the Shoe to Drop

As 2007 progressed, the question increasingly became not if, but when (and how), I would be indicted. We have all been entertained by high-profile arrests for white-collar crimes. Often, a posturing US attorney or other law enforcement official solemnly decries the crimes against humanity committed by some formerly high-flying executive. If the individual was wealthy, that made for even better copy.

Almost without exception, the person being arrested presents no more physical risk than a puppy dog. Notwithstanding the total lack of physical risk, it makes a much better media event if a couple of burly, uniformed officers clasp the cuffs on the target and conduct a finely orchestrated "perp walk." Would I be subjected to a perp walk? Would law enforcement bang on my door early one morning and cuff me in front of my eight-year-old twin stepdaughters? Would I be arrested at an airport? Would I be pulled over on the highway?

My attorneys had ongoing dialog with the USAO about my inevitable indictment and, assuming it was to happen, how it would be handled. My attorneys made it very clear that I would surrender voluntarily and that the government didn't need to create any media sideshow.

One of the important elements in filing charges in any kind of lawsuit, whether criminal or civil, is the statute of limitations (SOL). In my case, the limit for the issues on which I was being accused was five years. That means that any act that occurred more than five years earlier could not be included in the charges. As the government began building their case, they took the normal step of requesting a tolling agreement. That means that both sides would agree to, in effect, extend the SOL while the case was being built. Why would a defense team want to agree to that? In the absence of a tolling agreement, the government would most likely have filed their charges immediately, thereby giving the defense less opportunity to build their own case. The government would also have less time, but low-hanging fruit generally favors the prosecution. Therefore, it was in our interest to delay the indictment as long as possible.

Tolling agreements always have an end date. The defense would not allow the prosecution to take as long as it wanted. The typical allowance is six months. One of our agreements was scheduled to expire in December 2007. While I was at breakfast one day with Julie in San Francisco shortly before the holidays, one of my attorneys called to advise me that the government might be on the verge of filing charges. This certainly did not add much to the festiveness of the holidays for us.

Only a few days earlier, before we had left San Diego, two FBI agents pounded loudly on our front door at 6:45 a.m. and handed Julie a grand jury subpoena. With that experience still fresh in our minds, we speculated that when we returned from San Francisco, the FBI might be waiting at our home. Or they might have an arrest warrant for me at the airport. Needless to say, this was very stressful.

The episode ended benignly: the defense agreed to extend the tolling agreement and the government did not file charges at that time.

How Criminal Charges Are Filed

The United States Attorney's Office does not file criminal charges itself, although the effect is the same. The power to file criminal charges rests with a grand jury. A federal grand jury, of between sixteen and twenty-three citizens, is impaneled for up to twelve months. The USAO presents evidence and calls witnesses for them to hear. The witnesses can only consult their own attorneys outside the grand jury room, and then only with permission of the USAO. The USAO is not obligated to present a balanced case. They present the evidence they choose to present.

I haven't seen any statistics, but I would guess that it is very rare that a grand jury does not hand down an indictment the USAO seeks. No defense attorney is allowed to have any contact with a grand jury. The jury proceedings are secret as a matter of law.

Once the grand jury determines that an indictment should be issued, their decision is relayed to a magistrate to be officially logged into the court's records. From that moment forward the court could issue an arrest warrant for the target of the indictment. That target is now referred to in the system as the "defendant."

Still Waiting for the Shoe to Drop

As I've mentioned, my attorneys had tried to determine how I would be treated when I was indicted. The USAO was assured that I would surrender promptly and peacefully and that they wouldn't need to send out the Feds for a humiliating arrest at an airport, my home, or any other inappropriate place. The USAO refused to commit.

By the time indictment paperwork was completed after one of the grand jury's Wednesday meetings, I expected to be indicted on a Thursday. Rather than risk a perp walk, we considered the possibility of me spending all my Thursdays in the Santa Ana courthouse so that the Feds wouldn't have very far to go, but we rejected the plan as too disruptive.

Eventually, my attorneys got signals from the USAO that I would be allowed to surrender voluntarily. Still, it's a feeling that as Americans we never expect to have: the power of our own government's representatives to arbitrarily inflict profound embarrassment on us. And this is really just the tip of the iceberg, because a prosecution like the one I was forced to endure could deprive us of liberty for literally the rest of our lives.

Meanwhile, the waiting game went on. My attorneys and I planned my defense, and Julie and I planned our wedding. Life went on, albeit with a giant, dark cloud hanging overhead, the months dragging as the government worked on building their case.

From the interview notes we saw later, it was clear that the government's cajoling of witnesses was a major reason for the delay. A truly objective search for the truth probably would have taken a lot less time, but it would never have resulted in the USAO's desired indictments. They wanted a high-profile criminal case, and they were willing and able to do what it took to get one.

No indictments were handed down in January, February, or March. Nothing in April. On May 14, 2008, the SEC formally filed charges against Nick, Henry Samueli, David Dull, and me. Since the SEC and DOJ had been joined at the hip throughout this process, it was clear that the criminal indictments were on their way.

What do I mean by "joined at the hip?" The USAO interviews of potential witnesses are memorialized in a document called a *302*, prepared by attendant FBI agents. In one section, a 302 describes all parties at the meeting. All of the 302s that were made available to the defense team showed at least one, generally two, and sometimes three SEC attorneys present.

By this time, neither Henry nor David Dull had been indicted. The signs were that the USAO would effectively freeze both of them by simply threatening to indict them without actually doing so.

In June, the shoe was about to drop. A few days before the indictment we received assurance from the USAO that I would be allowed to voluntarily surrender. Finally, on Wednesday, June 4, 2008 the grand jury reached the decision the USAO had prompted it into. They handed down indictments against Nick and me related to alleged backdating of stock options and a second indictment against Nick for alleged drug trafficking.

At Last, the Day of Indictment is Here

I was required to be at the Santa Ana Federal Courthouse by 2:30 pm on Thursday, June 5—the day before my sixty-sixth birthday. You can be sure that I and my attorneys were there with plenty of time to spare. Julie was by my side, as always.

It had been nearly five years since I had seen Nick. After he left Broadcom in January 2003, I had only seen him a couple of times. He always prided himself on being a rather formal dresser. No business casual for Nick. He showed up for work every day in a three-piece suit, French-cuffed shirt, a nice silk tie: always well turned out.

In this particular courtroom, the defense table is on the left, set back near the spectator area. The jury box is on the right, near the front. I first caught sight of Nick diagonally across the courtroom from me. He was seated in the jury box for a reason I did not immediately understand.

Looking far from his normal natty appearance, he was wearing a suit, but no tie; he looked rather disheveled. Soon I learned that Nick had attempted to surrender voluntarily on arrival at the courthouse first thing in the morning as instructed. The prosecutors had deemed him a danger to society and had him booked into a cell. Standard operating procedure for anyone booked into a cell is to take away their belt and necktie, lest they attempt to hang themselves.

When he was escorted into the courtroom, before any of the rest of us had arrived, Nick was in handcuffs. That would certainly be enough to make a person appear disoriented.

Is the Defendant a Danger to the Public or a Flight Risk?

If the defendant in a criminal case is neither a danger to the public nor a flight risk, posting a bail bond is standard procedure. In extreme cases, the defendant is immediately incarcerated for one or both reasons. The terms of my bond had been previously agreed to and were confirmed at the original indictment hearing before a magistrate.

The prosecutors had declared Nick both a flight risk and a danger to society in their constant search for headlines. The latter was because of some death threats he had allegedly made, but which the prosecutors were never able to even partially substantiate, much less prove. The magistrate presiding over the bail hearing put the absurdity of the government's allegations in proper perspective when he commented, "as far as threats of death, I haven't seen any dead bodies, so if there are any dead bodies, I'd like the government to produce them."

Knowing the arduousness of preparing for a trial of this nature, with so many documents to be reviewed, I can't even imagine how a person could adequately prepare if he were incarcerated. Under those conditions, the government might just as well impose a guilty verdict and save all the time, trouble, and expense of a trial.

To his credit, the magistrate had the air of a person who has heard it all and was not about to be swayed by some specious emotional argument. At the end of the hearing, both Nick and I posted our respective bail bonds and walked out of the courtroom, though we carried with us the stigma of being under federal indictment for having allegedly committed securities fraud and, in Nick's case, an alleged involvement in the illegal distribution of narcotics.

Time for the Mug Shot

At some time during the proceeding, I was instructed to report to an office on a lower floor of the courthouse building to be formally booked. Among the highlights of that process was the opportunity to be fingerprinted and to have my mug shots taken. I was now a statistic in the criminal justice system.

I also had to sign up for pretrial services. I was assigned an officer to call in to every Tuesday; I also had to visit in person within the first half of each month. The officer had to visit my home, paying special attention to the clothes in my closet as evidence that I was indeed living there. They also made me hand over my passport to make sure I didn't try to flee the country. I was free to travel within the country, but if I left the state of California, I was required to submit my itinerary.

It was very clear that the whole system was geared to handle individuals with unstable and unpredictable lifestyles. I will say that throughout the year and a half that I had to report into pretrial services, the officers I dealt with were always courteous and respectful. Even so, having been accustomed to traveling freely all over the world and never worrying that some inadvertent mistake could cause me to be immediately incarcerated, it was not a pleasant experience.

The Indictment Document

The indictment itself can be described as a sixty-five-page tirade posing as fact. My lead Skadden attorney, Rich Marmaro, had observed that when he was a federal prosecutor in the 1980s, an indictment was a fairly brief and factual description of the charges being brought. In more recent years, indictments have morphed into lengthy narratives that are virtually opening statements.

One of the uses the government always hopes to make of the indictment is to have it present in the jury room during deliberation. Of course, it is an extremely one-sided document. No attempt is made to put any of the allegations in context. To the contrary: the goal is to make the alleged crimes, and therefore the alleged criminals, appear as nasty and guilty as possible.

How much of my indictment would be included in the jury room was subject to many arguments from both sides. In the end, the question was never resolved, and since I was acquitted by the judge before the case went to the jury, the point was moot.

The indictment's twenty-one charges included securities fraud, lying to auditors, falsifying books and records, and, a then-current favorite of prosecutors (that was recently successfully challenged in the Supreme Court), depriving my employer of "honest services." Each charge carried a maximum potential sentence of five to twenty years.

In the indictment document, the prosecutors made generous use of inflammatory language. For example, once they had given a few pages of background on Broadcom and its option practices, the next section heading, in bold, was **Overview of Fraudulent Scheme**. This was not an "alleged" fraudulent scheme, a "charged" fraudulent scheme, or any other such subtlety. The words "fraudulent" and "scheme" are used for maximum pejorative impact. The paragraph then states the government's position, as though it were incontrovertible fact, that defendants Nicholas and Ruehle "engaged in a fraudulent scheme and conspiracy to disguise, conceal, understate, and mischaracterize compensation expenses Broadcom was required to recognize in connection with its stock options."

So much for presumption of innocence! A few pages later, the indictment goes on to describe the **OBJECTS OF THE CONSPIRACY**:

Nick and myself, together with "others known and unknown to the Grand Jury, knowingly combined, conspired, and agreed to commit the following offenses:" securities fraud; filing false reports with the SEC; accounting fraud; lying to Broadcom's outside auditor; and the ever-popular "honest services," mail, and wire fraud.

The government had basically laid out their entire case in a document of public record; it became a critical piece of information for my defense team. It defined the specific charges and the specific option grants (virtually all that were made from 1998 through 2002). At least we had a roadmap.

The Pleading

All that was established at the initial court appearance on June 5 were the terms of bail and that the magistrate felt the government had made a shameful attempt to categorize Nick as a danger to society who must be immediately incarcerated. The next appearance was set for June 16.

The June 16 hearing was the opportunity to plead Guilty or Not Guilty. My plea would be obvious, as is that of virtually every other defendant in a criminal case. One portion of our criminal justice system that really does work is the presumption of innocence. This very important part is also very mundane and takes all of a few seconds: "How does your client plead?"

"Not guilty, Your Honor."

To illustrate how perfunctory a process this was for Nick and me, the court transcript showed that our session was called to order at 10:19 a.m. and was adjourned at 10:25—a whole six minutes!

Chapter 5

How Could This Be Happening?

Some events in life are harder to process than others. Being indicted in a criminal case that could result in a prison sentence of decades, or even life, certainly falls into that category. By the time the actual indictment came down, it had been just over two years since the "backdating" scandal first broke. I had known I was a target for some time, but it was still shocking.

It's a little like the death of a family member who is very ill for a long time. I had experienced that with my mother in 2002. She had been in poor health for her last twenty years and very seriously ill for her last two. Still, when she finally did succumb, it was a shock. To be sure, an indictment is not the same as a death, but it also has some dire possible consequences.

Between my indictment and the eve of the trial, I would sometimes write about what I was feeling. I made my first such entry the day Henry appeared in court to formalize his plea agreement. I was appalled by the process that required a good and decent man like Henry to stand up in a public forum and talk about the shame of committing the sin of lying to the SEC. I reread the entry recently and was a little surprised at how much outrage I expressed.

That outrage came through again in an entry from late January 2009, the day that Judge Carney rejected Henry's plea deal.

In my emotional state, I saw only the harsh part of the judge's ruling at the time. In my notes I even referred to him as "Hanging Judge Carney." But now, I see that he did it for exactly the right reasons. He did not want it to appear that "justice was for sale" in his courtroom.

He said that if Nick and I were convicted, then Henry would have to do time also.

This was also when a blizzard of motions was being filed by both sides. I commented that the outcome is always predictable: government motion—GRANTED; defense motion—DENIED. It really did seem pretty one-sided in favor of the government at that point. We had a major status conference scheduled for the following week, on January 26. There were two critical motions to be ruled on: whether Nick's trial and mine would be severed and whether trial would start in April, as originally scheduled, or moved to a later date.

A Time to Philosophize

When I'm severely stressed, sometimes I find it helpful to write out abstract notions of what's going on. That day, I wrote the following allegory:

> There is a mountain whose top is a large plateau. All of the action in the trial takes place on this plateau. In fact, basically all of life takes place on the plateau.
>
> The mountain descends fairly gently at first, and then drops off steeply to a brackish marsh far below. Just below the plateau on the gentle slopes of the mountain are a series of caves. When things get cold and stormy on the mountaintop the caves appear to offer sanctuary. Upon closer examination, however, any appearance of sanctuary is illusory. If you look very closely, you can discern a theme for each cave: fear, sadness, self-pity, outrage, complacency, surrender and so on. In my allegory, if a person were to enter any of these caves there would be a real possibility they would never get out. They would be lost forever in sadness or self-pity or outrage or any of the other destructive emotions.
>
> The lesson: stay on top of the mountain and fight, no matter how dark and stormy and foreboding it might seem. To borrow a con-

cept from General Patton, if you are about to be vanquished, it's better to be vanquished while advancing than while retreating.

A Time to Fight

The fighting philosophy served us well. We were rewarded just a few days later when Judge Carney ruled our way on the two critical motions. Nick and I would be tried separately; I would go first. And the trial date was moved from April 7 to October 20 in recognition of the good-faith work of both sides and the need for additional time to make sure the trial would be what Judge Carney characterized as a "fair fight."

Another affirmation that we were right to fight came at the end of February in a hearing on my claim that the Irell law firm had violated my attorney-client privilege. I believe it was an important turning point in the case. The judge called for an evidentiary hearing, which spanned three days and resulted in a clear win for my side. This was the first time I had really seen Rich and the Skadden team in action, arguing in court. I was impressed and very thankful that they were on my side. More on this later in the next chapter.

A Time to Reflect

I made a note on March 17, St. Patrick's Day, saying that what we needed is a modern-day St. Patrick to chase all the snakes out of the US Government.

Being a few months away from the impending trial was agonizing. It was close, yet not close enough. In frustration, Julie began writing letters to anyone she thought could possibly introduce a little sanity to a process gone mad. She wrote to members of Congress who were on the Judiciary Committee. Those outside our district responded that they could only help people in their own districts. Those who were in our district replied with unhelpful form letters.

She wrote to the Attorney General Eric Holder and to President Obama himself. Needless to say, we received no response to those.

One day, I wrote a list of who would win and who would lose if I were convicted. First among the "winners" would be the US Attorney's Office for the Central District of California. Its members would acquire bragging rights and maybe even some lucrative job offers from private law firms. Next would be the SEC, who could proclaim how tough they were on white-collar crime (maybe diverting a little attention from the Madoff mess).

The plaintiff's attorneys would gain more opportunity to extract settlements (and therefore large contingency fees) from any deep pockets they could tap into. A few self-righteous pundits could crow about how those wealthy evildoers finally got their comeuppance.

As for the losers, let's start with innocent victims like me, who were arbitrarily prosecuted and then had our pockets picked by "our" government and plaintiff's attorneys in civil suits. Also losing would be our friends and family and anyone who cares about us.

The US taxpayers, who funded this overblown witch-hunt, would be victims, as would the shareholders of Broadcom and other victimized companies who have seen their investments diminished by these horribly burdensome expenses and distractions. Finally, the American people would be losers. They would see that no one can be safe from the overreaching powers of "our" government.

I reflected that someday, a hundred or so years from now, historians would look back on all the energy and misdirected resources that went into this process, scratch their heads, and ask, "What were they thinking?"

On a more positive note, I kept reminding myself that were it not for the circumstances surrounding this whole options fiasco, including my premature departure from Broadcom, I would not be with Julie today. If putting up with all this evil is the price for being with Julie, I gladly pay it—no matter the outcome.

I also felt major support from my twin stepdaughters, Sara and Delara. We tried to explain my case to them in a way eight-year-olds could understand. We said that the government was accusing me of making serious mistakes in reporting Broadcom's financial statements. Their response was priceless: "Bill wouldn't have made a mistake; he's smart. He went to Harvard."

Chapter 6

Going through the Motions

The indictments called for Nick and me to be tried together on the stock options matter and for Nick to be tried separately on the drug allegations. By law, defendants in a criminal case have the right to a speedy jury trial. "Speedy" is defined as within seventy days of indictment. In a case as complicated as this one, there is no way either the prosecution or the defense could be ready for trial in seventy days, so I and my defense team waived the right to one.

I was told to expect an avalanche of motions. I was not disappointed. Beginning almost immediately after indictment and continuing right up through the end of trial, a seemingly endless stream of them was filed on both sides.

Early motions concerned setting a trial date. As a general principle, a shorter time before trial favors the government and a longer time favors the defense. The government had had a small army of lawyers and FBI investigators working full time on the case for two years prior to the indictment. They had interviewed dozens of witnesses, including participating in secret grand jury sessions with many of the same witnesses and a few new ones.

The case was complicated, and my defense team knew it would take a very long time to comb through the six million documents and to talk with the very limited number of potential witnesses who were willing to talk with us—that is, those who had not been so thoroughly intimidated by the government that they were afraid to.

Our Introduction to Judge Carney

Our first opportunity to meet The Honorable Cormac J. Carney was on July 1, about three weeks after the indictment. If ever a person deserved to be called "The Honorable...," it was he (though I've admitted that, ironically, my first impressions of Judge Carney were negative). The man had a passion for the truth and the deepest respect for the Constitution and the Founding Fathers who crafted it.

No one on our team had had any prior experience with Judge Carney, so we were not quite sure what to expect. Although the judge in any case is required to be an impartial observer, one does not have to look very far to see many examples of judges with agendas who are anything but impartial.

Throughout the course of the trial preparation and the trial, we got to know him quite well. After the trial I looked him up on the Internet and the found the following Wikipedia entry (accurate as of April 29, 2010):

> **Cormac J. Carney** (born 1959) is a United States federal judge.
>
> Carney was born in Detroit, Michigan and grew up in Long Beach, California. He received a B.A. from the University of California, Los Angeles in 1983 and a J.D. from Harvard Law School in 1987. He attended the U.S. Air Force Academy for one year before transferring to UCLA. Prior to his appointment to the bench, Carney was in private practice for two firms in Los Angeles, California for 15 years. From 2001 to 2003, he was a judge on the California Superior Court in Orange County, appointed to the post by then Gov. Gray Davis.
>
> Judge Carney was a wide receiver on the UCLA Bruins football team and played for one year on the Memphis Showboats USFL team. During his three years with the Bruins, he was the team leader in receiving each year and had a 3.51 grade point average in psychology.
>
> For his outstanding performances on the football field, he was named to the GTE/CoSIDA Academic All-America football team

and to the All-Pacific 10 Conference teams in 1981 and 1982. He was the Bruins' all-time leading receiver with over 100 receptions for nearly 2,000 yards when UCLA was 26-7-2. The Bruins were rated as high as #5 in the national polls. Carney's highlight at UCLA was when the team beat Michigan in the 1983 Rose Bowl.

Carney is a federal judge on the United States District Court for the Central District of California. Carney was nominated by President George W. Bush on January 7, 2003, to a seat vacated by Carlos R. Moreno. He was confirmed by the United States Senate on April 7, 2003, and received his commission on April 9, 2003. At the district court, Carney has been handling complex civil and criminal matters, including patents, copyrights, trademarks, securities, business finance, civil rights, drug conspiracies and white-collar crime.

In 2005, Carney was inducted into the College Sports Information Director's of America Academic All-America Hall of Fame.

These are the facts, and they clearly describe a life of achievement. My defense team first suspected that he strongly favored the government's positions in general, but I learned that such a position is not unusual. After all, judges are government servants also, and they interact with the government's prosecutors almost every day. It was not until later that the true character of Judge Carney came into view.

Early Evidence of Prosecutorial Misconduct

Beginning very early in the case, the defense team was compiling evidence of misbehavior by the prosecutors. On October 20, 2008, the defense filed a motion to dismiss based on prosecutorial misconduct. The principal grounds included repeated instances of witness intimidation, including inappropriate leaks of confidential information to the media, such as those which led to the *Wall Street Journal* article in which I featured so prominently. The motion was denied; we were not even granted a hearing.

Nevertheless, we continued to build our file in the hope we would be able to use it later. We believed the misbehavior was so extensive that it could form the basis for an appeal if we were to get a negative verdict at trial.

Shameful Use of a Personal E-mail

The government reached a new low: attempting to enter into evidence a very personal e-mail that Nick had written in 2002 to his then wife. Besides its intensely personal comments, it included some rambling comments about drug use and gratuitous, though tangential, remarks about the business. Nick had filed a motion to have the e-mail excluded as privileged communication between him and his wife.

The court initially ruled that because the e-mail had already been widely publicized by some self-serving individuals inside Broadcom, it was in the public domain and therefore no longer privileged. Nick appealed the decision, and the Ninth Circuit sided with him. The government's criminal prosecutors were deeply dismayed, because the e-mail contained just the sort of sensationalism they wanted to use to influence the jury.

Out of desperation, the government protested the ruling to Judge Carney. They said that the e-mail had to be admitted because it contained potentially exculpatory evidence for me (i.e., it could be helpful in proving my innocence). After considering the appeal carefully, Judge Carney ruled that since the e-mail was not allowable against Nick but must be made available for my use if I wanted, our trials had to be severed.

This was the position that Nick and I both wanted, for many reasons. Now the government was really in a panic. They even went so far as to recommend that two juries be impaneled and the Nicholas jury be excused when the Ruehle jury was exposed to the controversial e-mail. Judge Carney wisely said that he had enough of a challenge managing one jury and that there was no way he was going to try to manage two. The trials were severed.

I have now become much more knowledgeable than I ever wanted to be about preparing and implementing a defense case. It's a huge undertaking. With two defendants instead of one, managing the defense is much more than twice as difficult. For example, two different executives at the same company may very legitimately have different reactions to any given event. Prosecutors could characterize those natural differences as "inconsistencies," making it seem that at least one of the executives must be lying. That would make the prosecutors' job much easier.

Because they overreached with this e-mail, the prosecutors in my case not only did not get it admitted against Nick, they now had to face the tougher challenge of two separate trials. I refer to this mistake as Government Foot Shot #1.

Privilege? What Privilege?

Attorney-client privilege is one of the cornerstones of the American legal system. In its absence, prosecutors could demand that defense attorneys turn over all notes from all conversations with their clients, including informal assessments of the relative value of alternative strategies and even the disclosure of irrelevant information that prosecutors could twist against the defendant. For the best possible defense, a client must be able to fully disclose information to the attorney without fear that anything might be taken out of context and used against the client.

Unfortunately, we live in a highly litigious society, so corporate executives tend to get a lot more experience with litigation than they might prefer. Whenever a corporation is notified of an actual or pending lawsuit, its outside counsel is generally the first line of defense for itself and for the senior officers.

Broadcom's principal outside counsel, Irell & Manella, had represented the company and its officers in other legal matters. In May 2006 they let the corporation know that the expected opportunistic lawsuits were being filed. Broadcom's internal general counsel, David Dull, advised the senior officers that Irell would immediately defend us.

Shortly after that, partners from Irell asked me to help them set up a series of fact-finding meetings with various Broadcom employees, including myself. I did so, and talked with the Irell attorneys in early June. By sometime in September, I was being represented by an independent outside law firm, but until then I had privilege with Irell. Even when I ceased being their direct client, they had a "duty of loyalty" to me. That means they were obligated never to do or say anything that would be adverse to my interests.

In late 2008, an issue arose in the civil case that involved disclosure of the content of my June 2006 conversations with Irell. My defense team protested, and the special master appointed to assist in the civil cases deemed that the material was privileged. The civil judge agreed, so my Irell conversations were not allowed to be used in the civil cases.

In the criminal case, the government was figuratively sweeping the floors to gather every piece of potential evidence they could to bolster their case. They believed that comments I had made to Irell, though basically innocuous, could be spun against me. In February 2009, they argued to Judge Carney that the privilege should not hold because I had agreed to allow my conversations with Irell to be turned over to the authorities, and that because I never had a formal signed representation agreement with Irell, they did not actually represent me. My defense team argued that because I was never given an Upjohn warning, the special master's recommendation (in the civil court action) was correct and that the privilege should hold.

Judge Carney listened to both sides and then proclaimed that the issue was of sufficient importance that he would to a *de novo* review of the facts (i.e., a fresh review, not relying on anyone else's conclusion) and make the determination himself. This set up a very important event for my defense. The Judge set an evidentiary hearing for late February.

Before the formal hearing began the defense and government attorneys were wrangling over what facts should be brought into evidence. Judge Carney was obviously very troubled by the notion that my own attorneys (i.e., Irell & Manella) were taking a position adverse to my interest. In one memorable comment during the February hearing, Judge Carney said on the record:

> But if Irell is Mr. Ruehle's lawyer, isn't that a more serious ethical concern that they are now making recommendations that are very adverse to him, and it's your own lawyer who's loading the gun with the bullets?

At this hearing, two Irell partners were put on the witness stand to be questioned by the Judge, the defense, and the government. One of the partners had said under oath in a deposition for the civil case that he could understand how I might have believed that Irell was representing me because they had represented me as an officer of the corporation in other cases in the past. Incredibly, on the stand in the evidentiary hearing before Judge Carney, he recanted that sworn statement. That's never a good sign for a witness.

One of the best parts of the hearing was that I was asked to take the stand, which gave me a chance to interact directly with Judge Carney. The first part of my testimony was actually held *in camera* (a confidential hearing with the Judge, myself, and my defense counsel). Because some of the material on which I was to be questioned was clearly privileged, the government could not be present. This was an opportunity for me and Judge Carney to have a conversation, looking each other directly in the eye from a distance of maybe ten feet.

Defendants tend to get either a very friendly questioner (their own defense counsel) or a very hostile one (the prosecutor), but mine was very neutral. His only goal was to understand the facts. He asked intelligent, probing questions and I provided candid and credible answers.

Later on, the lead prosecutor, Andrew Stolper, tried to use this very limited-scope evidentiary hearing as a forum to get me to make on-the-record statements about factual elements of the criminal case. Mr. Stolper attempted several times to elicit comments about evidence completely irrelevant to the Irell issue, but I refused to be lured in. Judge Carney grew weary of Mr. Stolper's tactics and finally advised him:

> I have got to make a determination how much is fair game and I am about ready to shut you down because I don't think this is productive. And I have got to say I don't want any part of it. I am feeling very uncomfortable that this is very unfair to this man. He has certain due process rights.

The result was a solid victory for my side. Judge Carney ruled that my responses were very credible and that I did have a legitimate expectation of privilege. He further ruled that Irell was out of line in violating my privilege (which they had already done by turning over notes of their conversations with me, and, even adding their own spin on how cooperative they felt I was or was not). He found their behavior so offensive that he referred them to the California Bar Association for sanctions.

Judge Carney said, "All clients are equal under the Rules of Professional Conduct, and no lawyer can sacrifice the interest of one client for those of another." A little later in the same discussion, he added, "By sacrificing the interests of Mr. Ruehle in favor of those of Broadcom, Irell breached its duty of loyalty to him."

At the conclusion of the three-day hearing, the issue was so clear in Judge Carney's mind that he issued a ruling on the spot, saying that my conversations with Irell were indeed privileged and could not be used in his courtroom. His own words say it best: "Mr. Ruehle has had his privileged information disclosed and there is nothing I can do to get that back." He then looked directly at me as I sat in the defendant's chair and said, "And I regret that, sir. And as an officer of the court, I apologize that that happened to you." He added, "So I don't think it's a good day for justice."

As described earlier, the Ninth Circuit later reversed Judge Carney's ruling regarding my privilege, but by that time the damage had already been done to the government and to Irell. I had been given a golden opportunity to make a favorable firsthand impression on the Judge. He was also exposed to some of the interactions that were going on between the government and the company's lead counsel that I found troubling. I count this entire Irell privilege issue as Government Foot Shot #2.

Furthermore, Judge Carney continued to state his belief that the Irell attorneys had misbehaved. In a pretrial hearing in September 2009 the judge again expressed his concern when he said:

> And I vividly recall one email [from an Irell partner] where it was addressed to you, Mr. Stolper, it says "Dear Andy, here is another document that would be the nail in the coffin, smiley face". That, to me, is totally inappropriate, and especially inappropriate from a law firm that represents, on an individual basis, a client.

Following the hearing, I began to feel for the first time that maybe this was going to be a fair fight after all. I had a renewed faith that the system could work to produce a fair result.

In addition to our rational analyses, Julie and I were also open to less tangible signs. On a day just prior to the Irell hearings, Julie had dropped the kids off at school and was feeling down. Crying as she drove along, she was surprised at a stop sign when a hummingbird hovered just outside her car window. She had always considered a hummingbird sighting to be a good omen. In this case, it was.

Fast Forward to October 2009

My final personal journal entry was on October 18, 2009, the day before jury selection was to begin. By this time, I had been in the government's sights for just over three years. Julie and I were glad to finally be starting trial. As she said at the time, we could finally take the duct tape off our mouths and begin to speak our truth.

My concluding journal entries captured what I was feeling:

> It is a marathon we're starting. The trial is estimated to last about two months. Of course I have apprehension. But I can't really say I'm scared. That could change, but right now I feel at peace. I know the truth is on our side. We are out to win.

> Please, dear God, give us and our defense team the strength, the courage and the wisdom to prevail. Amen.

Chapter 7

A Jury of My Peers

Fundamental to our legal system is the right to be tried by a jury of one's peers. That right can be waived; the defendant can elect to be tried only by a judge, but it is unusual in a criminal case. This is partly because of probability: in a criminal case, a verdict must be unanimous. If a jury is used, that means twelve people have to agree whether the defendant is guilty or not guilty on each charge. When was the last time you tried to get twelve people to agree on anything? If unanimity is not reached, the trial ends in a hung jury and a mistrial is declared. At that point, the government must decide whether or not to retry the case.

Sometimes a retrial is based on a narrower scope of charges, but in many hung jury cases, the charges are subsequently dismissed. Either side wants unanimous victory. The statistical odds favor a conviction (as noted earlier, in 2009, 81% of federal white-collar crime trials resulted in one), but a hung jury is often considered a victory for the defense, so the defense usually insists on a jury trial as the best chance to avoid conviction.

You Have a Right to Be Tried By a Jury of Your Peers

What does a "jury of peers" really mean? Taken literally, it could mean that an indicted murderer has a right to be tried by a jury of murderers. Obviously, that's absurd. Equally absurd would be to insist that I have a right to be tried by a jury of high-tech CFOs. It really means that a defendant has a right to be tried by a jury representing a cross-section of the community where the trial is being held.

Having said that, neither side in a trial wants to trust some random selection of citizens to make such an important decision. Both sides want to root out obvious nutcases, people who lack the mental capacity to absorb the facts of the case, or those who lack the physical stamina to pay attention—particularly for an extended trial such as this one. Each side especially wants to weed out any potential jurors who they believe are strongly biased toward the other side.

It is a sad fact that many people look upon jury service with the same enthusiasm as they do going to the dentist. Most of us who have actually served on juries can say that the experience was valuable and fulfilling. I still recall a jury on which I served back in the 1970s as a memorable experience.

This Is Not a Random Process

Typically, both sides in a trial will have a formalized decision-making process for choosing and excluding jurors, particularly when the facts are as complex as in this one. Both sides commonly employ jury consultants. They may conduct focus groups with local members of the jury pool, though anyone used in a focus group is disqualified to serve on that case's jury. Some cases may even conduct mock trials to assess potential jurors' reactions to arguments presented by either side.

Jury consultants and good trial lawyers for both government and defense will have their own formal or informal databases of which characteristics make a juror more or less likely to side with the government or the defense. Both sides take account of these factors, and any additional research, such as focus groups and the like, in their decisions.

The Jury Pool

Sitting for this eight- or nine-week case could be a legitimate hardship for many potential jurors, but whether it would be boring, or just something they would rather not do, didn't qualify.

The process of choosing a jury begins when the judge has the Jury Commissioner send out hundreds of summonses to registered jurors. For this case, twenty-five hundred were sent. About a hundred jurors were led into the courtroom on the day of selection, with Judge Carney presiding. The prosecution and defense teams were in their places, and I, as the defendant, had to be present as well.

Before the jurors are led in, both sides examine jurors' questionnaires, and the jury consultants create demographic matrices from them. These include factors such as age, gender, ethnicity, education level, career, political affiliation, marital and family status, hobbies, and any other factors perceived as relevant.

Both sides strive to disqualify jurors who could be biased toward the other side. Although the jury questionnaires help, the *voir dire* process brings more detailed insight. (This French expression comes from a Latin one meaning an oath to tell the truth.) Each side is allotted a number of peremptory challenges, where a prospective juror can be dismissed without any reason being given. Typically, the defense is allowed more peremptory challenges than the government. In my trial, the defense was allowed fourteen challenges and the government ten. If a juror appears blatantly biased or otherwise incapable of understanding a case, either side can appeal to the judge to dismiss the person for cause, which doesn't count against the peremptory challenge limit.

For the final selection, sixteen jurors are called at random to the jury box. Judge Carney had already decided to add four alternates to the twelve regular jurors, who could substitute in case of illness, accident, or any other bona fide reason. (We only ended up needing one.)

Each juror was questioned in turn by Judge Carney, the defense, and the government. Queries included the names of their favorite book and movie. Interestingly, of the jurors selected, the most popular book was the Bible and the most popular movie was *Gone with the Wind*. (Showing his human side, Judge Carney said his favorite movie was *My Cousin Vinny*.)

It is surreal to observe the selection of twelve people empowered to make a decision that could send your life into one of two diametrically opposed directions. In this regard, the jurors are actually playing God. Rich asked the jurors if each would want someone like themselves on the jury if they or a loved one were on trial. Of course, no one responded in the negative, but I believe the question planted a seed of empathy in their minds and drove home the need for them to be impartial and diligent.

As much science is applied to the selection process as possible, but in the end, it comes down to a lot of intuitive decisions. I found myself making judgments as the prospective jurors were interviewed. I would hope that a certain one wouldn't be selected because he or she seemed much too self-assured. Or, those who worked in professions that required very black-or-white judgments, such as health care, were not favored because we were concerned they would not be able to deal with the uncertainties and nuances of my case.

I remember one man who looked like a free spirit. From his responses to questions, I knew he was clearly one I wanted on my jury, but I knew he would never survive the government's peremptory challenge. And he didn't. Another person I intuited would be favorable to me did survive. She ran a small business with her husband and seemed sharp and articulate. I remember one young man who always wore sunglasses in the courtroom; he was selected. I think neither side could figure him out, so he survived. He did nod off a few times during trial, and he caused a forty-five-minute delay one day by oversleeping. Judge Carney was not amused.

My jury wound up with seven men and five women; seven jurors were over fifty and only two were under thirty. Most had at least some college and several had degrees. In general, it was a slightly older and better-educated group than one might have expected. Their backgrounds were varied. They included a retired airline pilot, a retired teacher, a woman who provided job coaching for disabled adults, a young Mormon waiting for his mission assignment, a government accounting clerk, a stay-at-home mom, an avid gold miner (really!), a teachers' aide, a self-employed sales representative, a retired commercial banker, a small business entrepreneur, and a Los Angeles Water plant employee.

Every time the jurors entered the courtroom, at the start of the day or after breaks, they filed in in order of their seats. As they did, I silently repeated each of their names to myself. I didn't plan this reaction; it just happened. I think that, subconsciously, I was trying to establish a personal connection with each of them.

By the end of the trial, I felt I did know each of them personally. I even came to believe that I could intuit what at least some of the jurors' positions would be. When I spoke with them after the case, I learned that I was mostly correct.

I observed that with very few exceptions, they performed their civic duty with diligence. They listened to the evidence. I was gratified to see them taking notes appropriately when important points were being made. They did not seem to be swayed by the vitriol being spewed by the prosecutors.

After my vindication, Julie and I were permitted to talk with the jurors in the courtroom, but we followed up with many of them outside it as well. In late 2010, we even hosted a dinner for the regulars and alternates. Almost all attended with their spouses, and we had a very interesting evening learning about their views of the case as it had unfolded. From these discussions, it was clear that if the case had gone to the jury I would not have been convicted on any of the sixteen counts. (The government had reduced them from the original twenty-one shortly before trial, but the potential maximum sentence was still more than three hundred years.)

Jury selection in long, complicated cases can take several days, but to Judge Carney's credit, he kept the process moving. He gave both sides adequate time to ask important questions while making it clear he would not tolerate any diversions. As a result, the selection process only took one long, ten-hour day.

Chapter 8

Let the Games Begin

One of the many things I had never really wanted to learn, but did, was the sequence of events in a criminal trial. Basically, because the government bears the burden of proof, it gets to go first—and last.

The Sequence of Events at Trial

Once the jury has been selected, the trial officially begins. The first official event is the government's opening statement: an opportunity to describe the defendant's alleged crimes in lurid detail. The defense is prohibited from interrupting except to object to particularly inappropriate statements. The government may not call any witnesses at this time, but it may make generous use of exhibits to bolster its claims and imbed in the jury from the very outset a firm conviction of the defendant's guilt.

Next, the defense presents its opening statement. Knowing now what the government will claim, a quick-thinking defense team can target some of its remarks at refutation. The defense can also present evidence that the government may have found "inconvenient" (supporting the defendant's innocence). In our case, these statements took less than a full day.

Prior to the opening statements, the judge cautions the jurors that nothing the lawyers for either side say can be considered evidence and that their statements represent their own opinions only. Real evidence must be presented through witnesses.

The presentation of evidence begins when the government presents their case-in-chief. They can call as many witnesses as they believe appropriate, and the party who called the witness conducts a direct examination of each. Then the defense has the right to cross-examine the witnesses. The government can conduct a re-direct if it feels a need to "clarify" any points brought up on cross, and the defense then gets a chance to do the same in a re-cross. All government witnesses undergo this process, and then it is the defense's turn. The procedure is the same with witnesses for the defense—if the team decides to present a case.

The defense team is actually under no obligation to conduct a defense. They didn't in the recent stock option backdating case against Kent Roberts, general counsel for McAfee Inc.—and the jurors voted to acquit. Whether they intend to defend actively or not, it is standard procedure for the defense to file a motion to dismiss under Rule 29 of the Criminal Code. It states that the government has failed to provide sufficient evidence for any reasonable juror to be able to find guilt. Though almost always filed, it is virtually always denied. Judge Carney advised my defense team to save their energy and not bother filing our Rule 29 motion until after the case had gone to the jury, because he wasn't going to consider it until he had heard all the facts of the case.

Because the government gets to have the last word as well as the first, it has the right to present a rebuttal. It allows new witnesses and the recall of old ones to respond to strong points the defense may have made. The defense can cross-examine these witnesses, but does not get an opportunity to rebut the government's rebuttal.

The end of the presentation of witnesses concludes the introduction of evidence. The final act consists of closing arguments. As always, the government gets to go first. Once again the judge admonishes the jurors to remember that nothing the lawyers present in closing arguments can be considered evidence. The government attempts to recap all the damning points it made and claims it has clearly shown, beyond a reasonable doubt, that the defendant is guilty of all charges.

Then the defense stands up to present its best arguments that the government has not met its burden of proof, and present counter-arguments showing how most of the evidence presented by both sides points to the defendant's innocence. Finally, as its last word, the government gives its rebuttal to the defense's closing argument.

It is important to remember that the defense does not have to prove a client innocent. The burden is on the government to prove someone guilty beyond a reasonable doubt. The verdict is always "guilty" or "not guilty"—never "innocent."

Finally, the case goes to the jury. For every criminal count, the verdict must be unanimous for either guilty or not guilty. If there is even one dissenter in either direction, the jury is considered to be hung on that point.

The Government's Opening Statement: Inside / Outside

On Friday, October 23, 2009, the trial began in earnest. First came the government's opening statement. Two members of the prosecution team, led by Andrew Stolper, had had minor roles in the infamous Enron trial and seemed determined to give this one a similar aura of notoriety. Apparently, they borrowed its inside/outside theme too. The prosecutors proposed that Broadcom had told its investors one thing (outside), while its executives engaged in various deceptions (inside).

Mr. Stolper did all in his power to create a negative impression of me with the jurors. Before giving his opening statement, he recited some of the indictment's inflammatory allegations. Mercifully, the judge did not permit a dramatic reading of all sixty-five pages of its trash talk. In his opening paragraph, Mr. Stolper propounded, "We're here because the defendant"—I was always "the defendant" to him; never "Mr. Ruehle," as that might show some respect—"lied to the SEC, he lied to Broadcom's accountants, and, most importantly, he lied to Broadcom's investors, and there were thousands of them."

Later, he accurately described the options committee as consisting of only the two founders, Henry and Nick. That's not at all unusual.

In fact, I'm not aware of any company where the CFO is on the options committee. But Mr. Stolper had to make it look sinister as he said, "Even as the chief financial officer, the shareholders didn't trust him to do the grants." What an absurd statement! Shareholders have nothing to do with who is on the options committee. He was just trying to throw mud and say how untrustworthy I am.

He tried one last shot in his final remarks, telling the jury I refused to be interviewed by the special attorneys conducting the so-called independent investigation of Broadcom's option practices. As discussed earlier, declining such an interview is a standard response for a person in my position; my attorneys advised me to protect my Fifth Amendment rights. The defense later called an expert witness to attest to the appropriateness of my action. But Mr. Stolper insinuated that my refusal to take part in a rigged interview was evidence of my guilt.

By the time Mr. Stolper's opening statement concluded, a casual observer might have come away with the impression that Broadcom was a criminal enterprise and that I was the criminal-in-chief. Immediately after the opening, and outside the presence of the jury, Matt Umhofer, a counsel of the Skadden firm, raised his first of many motions for mistrial based on the prosecution's attempted introduction of inadmissible information. The motion was denied.

Not So Fast—Let's Hear from the Defense

By around 11:00 on Friday morning, it was time for Rich Marmaro, lead defense attorney, to make his opening statement. It was a critical juncture in the case. Although the fundamental rule in American jurisprudence is the presumption of innocence, the reality is often a little different. As a society, Americans tend to be law-abiding citizens with a healthy respect for authority. Of course, there are exceptions, but generally I think most Americans—and therefore most members of the jury pool—have a basic trust in authority and want to see criminals convicted.

Just the fact that someone has been indicted—i.e., accused of committing a crime—will cause a lot of people to presume that person did something wrong. This, compounded with a two-hour-long, inflammatory prosecutor statement, puts the defendant in a deep hole. The defense can then try to even the ground by raising enough doubt about the accusations that jurors will be motivated to at least listen to the rest of the case. Otherwise, they might simply mentally register a guilty verdict and spend the rest of the trial just going through the motions until they can mark their ballots at the end.

First impressions are critical. In the jury selection process, the jurors got to see my lead attorney, Rich Marmaro, in action. Granted, my opinion may be biased, but I believe he made a very favorable impression with his calm and respectful demeanor and his obvious knowledge of both the law and human nature. His opening statement would be the first opportunity for the jurors to form a positive impression of me.

Rich Marmaro—The Man Equal to the Task

In a case as complex as this one, both sides will use teams of lawyers. Any time Rich got a compliment on his outstanding job, he would credit the rest of his team from Skadden, Arps. They were terrific. In my entire business career, I have never seen a team with the applied intelligence and drive that they had. So, Rich was not a one-man band, but he was the team leader in every way, and he handled the bulk of the trial work. His very capable partner, Jack DiCanio, was also critical in the case. As I have remarked, the defendant's chair in a criminal trial is a very lonely place. Having Rich Marmaro and Jack DiCanio sitting on either side of me made it a lot less so.

Now for a little background on Rich. Talk about positive first impressions. Have you ever met a professional for the first time who you immediately concluded was no-nonsense and really knew what he or she was talking about? That was my impression of Rich, and from what others have told me, it was not unique.

Growing up in New York City, Rich did his undergraduate work at George Washington University, graduating *magna cum laude* and Phi Beta Kappa. He then earned his law degree at New York University. He clerked for a federal judge in New York and eventually made his way to Los Angeles. In the early 1980s, he served as an assistant United States attorney in the Central District of California. This was the same district that filed criminal charges against me in 2008. In 1984, he left the government side and began the next phase of his career as a defense attorney (a very common career path for defense attorneys).

I have worked with professional services firms where the big guns come in to make the initial presentations and show up for the high profile meetings but then delegate most of the work to underlings. Not Rich. I swear that Rich must have been intimately familiar with virtually all of the case's over six million pages of evidence. This was to serve him very well in cross-examinations of hostile witnesses who had been painstakingly coached by the prosecution team. It also served him well in his opening statement.

The Defense's Opening Statement: Inside = Outside; Then vs. Now

A criminal trial is very much like a war. In theory, it shouldn't be that way. Both the government and the defense should be on a search for the truth. I'm sure that practitioners on both sides would claim that that's what they're doing, but let's face it: both sides want to win. I knew I was innocent, and so did Rich and the whole Skadden team. As they said, a defense attorney's heaviest burden is to defend a client who they know, beyond any doubt, is innocent. We have all read of cases when innocent people were convicted.

The government sought to fight a very narrow case. Mr. Stolper hammered away in the opening statement on the point that this was not a case about accounting; it was not a case about business; it was a case about lying. This really made no logical sense. The foundation

of the government's case was that I had "lied" about the accou
If the case was not about accounting, how could I have lied about it?

In contrast, the defense sought to bring in as many facts as possible so the whole truth could come out. In our view, the case was about a team of technologists and business people building a world-class company from the ground up. We acknowledged that often, the pace of technology is much faster than the pace of underlying business processes. When a company grows in three years from $20 million in annual revenue to $1 billion in revenue, it puts real strain on the processes.

Rich laid out his themes early. He told the jurors they would hear witness after witness claim that I was "a good and decent man... [who] always tried to do the right thing; that he always tried to get the accounting right; and that he always tried to help the employees."

Then he asked, "Why is he sitting here?" He answered his own question. "We're here because this is a case involving two simple words: 'then' versus 'now'." He described the media-driven frenzy following the now-famous academic study of option pricing. He brought up the accounting opinion APB 25, which governed stock option accounting until it was abandoned entirely in 2005 after years of controversy.

In fact, APB 25 was issued in 1973 as a twelve-page document. After years of questions regarding its implementation in the changing business environment of the 1980s and 1990s, the accounting authorities issued FIN 44 in 2000 as "An Interpretation of APB Opinion No. 25." This interpretation was 96 pages long and was followed by 121 pages of appendices. Following the issuance of FIN 44, E&Y issued a "clarification" of the interpretation that was 83 pages long. It's no wonder financial and accounting professionals were confused!

Rich laid out five "truths" that he promised would give the jurors the real story: (1) Broadcom was and is a success story (it had no Enron-type bankruptcy); (2) I was an important part of its success;

(3) Broadcom's option program was integral to the company's drive to attract the best employees and assure their interests were aligned with those of shareholders; (4) Broadcom's rapidly exploding business growth caused its option program to be fraught with delays and frustrations, but there was never evil intent; and (5) APB 25 itself had been far less than crystal clear.

After the first hour of Rich's opening we broke for lunch. Our lunches, in a room reserved upstairs at Tommy Pastrami's across from the courthouse, were to become a well-worn ritual. These were not relaxing lunches. While we had our salads and sandwiches, we reviewed morning testimony and prepared for the afternoon.

After lunch, Rich was in peak form as he concluded his opening statement: "I'm going to summarize the evidence. I'm going to tell you what I believe the evidence has shown, why I believe the government has not come close to meeting its burden. And then, I'm going to ask you to set Bill Ruehle free. I'm going to ask you to walk him out that door a free man just as he is today."

Rich advised the jurors that his cross-examinations would probably take considerably more time than the government's direct, because the government gets to prepare its witnesses while the defense has no access to them. His voice of experience was right; cross typically took two to three times as much time as the government's direct examinations.

Rich wrapped up his opening by 2:30 p.m.; the judge wisely decided that the jurors had probably heard all that they could absorb after spending most of the week in the jury selection process and sitting through the opening salvos. They knew that nothing they had heard yet was evidence; the first witnesses would arrive the following Tuesday.

After the jury was dismissed, the Judge continued the hearing on the mistrial motion by Matt Umhofer. It was a very serious motion with a lot of contentious arguments on both sides. Had the prosecutors' opening statement included prejudicial comments in violation of pretrial rulings? The motion was denied, but the defense was granted some of the points we wanted.

It would have been appropriate to end for the weekend on that serious and rather somber note. Instead, in a jaunty tone, someone on the prosecution team offered an invitation: "We're all going down to our office for beers. Colleagues, everyone welcome." Needless to say, no one on the defense team had any interest. Our work was just beginning.

The Beginning of the End of the Ordeal

I felt a surprising level of serenity that first weekend. Julie and I had vowed that we would not allow our lives to be totally dominated by the case. In fact, we became a couple even as we knew criminal indictments were inevitable. We were engaged less than four months prior to indictment and married four months after it.

Clearly, we had to put a lot of things on hold so we could focus on our defense, but we were not about to allow the government to define who we were. We were actually relieved when the trial finally began. By then it had been over three years since I had left Broadcom. I was anxious to finally clear my name. Breaking for the weekend, the last thing the jury had heard was the defense's opening statement and that was a positive note for us. Rich did an admirable job of bringing me back to parity.

Some very dear friends had been in the courtroom with us that day. We invited both couples to join us at our San Diego home for the weekend. Of course, we rehashed the day's courtroom events, but we also talked about past joys we had experienced together and longed for a future free from the surreal experience of government prosecution.

Over the past three years, the government had made various announcements about charges filed and Broadcom officials had made some self-righteous statements, while we remained silent.

Finally, as Julie so appropriately remarked, the duct tape had been removed from our mouths. Now we could tell our side of the story. Initially that would be a real challenge, as the government would be eliciting well-coached testimony from carefully intimidated witnesses. We would have to pull the truth out from reluctant witnesses. But at least we now had a voice.

Chapter 9

The Government Case—
A Study in Revisionist History

In a normal trial process, the side presenting its case must notify the other side in advance of who their next few witnesses are going to be. These disclosures are always done with a lot of caveats that they are estimates: that circumstances could change or out-of-town witnesses may not be available at a predicted time, and so forth. In other words, each side wants to keep the other guessing about who their next witnesses may be. This offers a short-term tactical advantage, as the opposing side must prepare for multiple witnesses, preventing them from putting full focus on anyone specific.

Prior to trial, the government had given us the names of over forty potential witnesses. We responded with a similar number. As trial drew closer, the Court required a more specific list of witnesses for the next few days.

The defense still had to prepare for several witnesses. We expected the government to try proving their case through three key witnesses. Foremost was Nancy Tullos, who had cut a plea deal in exchange for probation if she was sufficiently "cooperative." Then there was Carol Prado, former Manager of Shareholder Services (thus the employee stock options record keeper). We believed she had been at least tacitly promised immunity from the government. The third we expected was Gail Patton, who had held several senior accounting positions at Broadcom, including responsibility for reporting financial statements to the SEC.

Ms. Tullos and Ms. Prado showed up on the government's early lists, so members of the Skadden team were constantly preparing for them. I should point out that there are two main types of witnesses. The first, "percipient witnesses," includes those who were present when alleged crimes were committed or had some form of connection with the company. The other type includes "expert" witnesses who know a particular subject area but have no firsthand knowledge about a company or its employees. Among other differences, expert witnesses are paid by the side that hires them; percipient witnesses cannot be paid.

First Government Witness—Donna Levy of the SEC

For all the government's snarling so far, it was a little surprising that they started out with what was essentially a neutral witness. Donna Levy was an expert witness; she was special counsel in the SEC's office of enforcement. By her testimony, she had no direct involvement with the SEC charges against me or other Broadcom executives.

Basically, she presented a neutral tutorial of the SEC's role in ensuring that publicly traded corporations adhere to certain reporting guidelines. She took only a couple of hours and consumed only fifty-seven pages of transcript (out of a trial total of over eight weeks and 5,200 pages).

The government's biggest disappointment was probably when they tried to lead her to say that the final responsibility for the accuracy of a corporation's financial statements rested solely with the CFO. They did everything but put the words in her mouth. Her actual statement was "Certainly he is the chief financial officer, so he has a lot of responsibility for that. I mean, ultimately, I think it's him and the upper management and the board of directors." She told the truth: the responsibility is shared with the CFO, the CEO, and the board of directors.

Compared to what was to come next, Ms. Levy's testimony was only a warm-up.

Second Government Witness—Carol Prado

One of the many things that saddened me about this case was to see trusted former colleagues cave in to the government's pressure and turn against me. These were often people I had relied on, mentored, or even people I had brought into the company and presented with the finest opportunity of their careers. Others, who had preceded me at Broadcom, I had looked up to.

The government's first percipient witness was Carol Prado. I had hired her shortly before the IPO because I needed an experienced person to oversee the stock options administrative processes. Carol was about my age and was nearing the end of her career. In fact, during her tenure at Broadcom, she "retired" two or three times, but would come back at least part time to lend her expertise.

From the FBI 302s and other pretrial notes, I knew that her recollection of events had morphed over the many months from her first interview with the independent attorneys to her most recent with the prosecutors. My defense team would internally classify this kind of progression as "flowering." Anyone who studies the results of any kind of survey knows that respondents' answers depend a lot on how the questions are asked. Try to put yourself in this situation: your questioner has the power to deprive you of your liberty if he or she doesn't like your answers.

In trial, it came out that Carol had been interviewed at least a dozen times by the independent attorneys and the prosecutors and had testified before the grand jury. She was then "rehearsed," by her own recollection, two or three times immediately before testifying. Her recollection of events changed most dramatically somewhere after all her meetings with independent attorneys and well into her many meetings with the government.

Obviously, I can't get inside the head of a witness and determine whether they are sincere in their testimony. Everyone is aware that perjury is a very serious crime; no reasonable person would inten-

nmit it. I also believe the power of suggestion is very
rticularly when one's liberty is at stake. Therefore, if a
is a little gray and the prosecutor would obviously rather
it be fined as black than white, a person could be influenced in
that direction.

As described earlier, the emotive buzzword in this case was backdating. This refers to option dates being determined at a later date
than what is shown on the documents. In all the years I worked at
Broadcom I don't recall ever having heard anyone use the word
backdating. I certainly never heard Carol use the word.

I have not counted from transcripts how many times she used it in
her testimony, but it was almost comical to hear her use it in response
to almost every question in direct examination. I even recall a question about whether the options committee could approve a grant if
only one of the two members had been present. It had nothing to do
with whether or not options had been backdated, but she nevertheless responded, "They would be backdated, yes."

One of the more startling comments in her testimony was that she
had approached me in "1998 or 1999" to advise that our options
process was wrong and that we should change it. She claimed
that I acknowledged the fact but said, "it was for the good of the
employees." In her direct testimony, she simply reported this as a
fact. Since we had reviewed all her pretrial statements to attorneys
and government officials, we knew this was part of her "flowered"
recollection.

On cross-examination, Rich probed her on it. Among other documents, he presented a timeline of all of her interviews, including
multiple sessions with the attorneys at Irell & Manella, Kaye Scholer,
and the USAO and SEC. He asked, "And it was at this meeting, the
ninth time you had an opportunity to give all your information about
Broadcom's stock option program that you suddenly remembered
a conversation that allegedly happened eight years before you had
never mentioned before. Am I correct?"

She answered, "It was not at the meeting. It was—in the middle of the night I woke up and remembered the meeting."

A little later in Carol's testimony, Rich characterized the incident as her "middle-of-the-night epiphany," and the name stuck. He also showed Carol a copy of the documentation from her exit interview at Broadcom. At exit interviews, departing employees have no need to be politically correct. Carol acknowledged that she had not commented about any concern over improprieties in Broadcom's option program.

In general, Carol handled her testimony very professionally, which is what I would have expected of her. She did not get emotional and she generally came across as credible, although clearly well rehearsed. The absurdity of the middle-of-the-night epiphany seemed to rattle her a little bit, but she recovered.

The only time she appeared flabbergasted was when Rich asked her if she believed she was a coconspirator in criminal activity with twelve other current and former Broadcom employees. She was shocked. The color drained from her face and she literally gasped for words. Apparently, the prosecutors who so carefully rehearsed her for testimony did not think it important to inform her that they considered her a coconspirator.

Carol's testimony was interrupted several times for various motions and to allow another witness who had some time constraints— Werner Wolfen—to testify, but the ratio of time on direct versus time on cross was in line with what Rich had previously predicted.

When someone has been well rehearsed and is being questioned by a friendly attorney, it can go pretty quickly. When that same person is being questioned by an attorney with adverse interests, it can take a much longer time to unearth the truth.

In addition, the government has the power of subpoena. They can and do demand that all possible defense witnesses appear before the grand jury. The SEC also has subpoena power. However, the USAO cannot *require* an interview without someone from the defense present, but they can and do request them. These requests are almost always granted because no one wants to appear uncooperative. It came out in Carol's testimony that she believed the government could subpoena her to talk with just their side.

The one-sided power of the government to compel witnesses (either formally through subpoena or informally through intimidation) is so significant that I want to include some testimony that brings home the point.

Rich showed Carol a copy of a letter from the previous year in which he politely requested just one interview. Carol, through her attorney, had refused. Carol said, "I said if I didn't have to do it, I would rather not. No. My answer would be no."

Rich Marmaro: Okay. Now, I couldn't force you to meet with me; right?

Carol Prado: Right.

Q: Okay. Bill Ruehle was your boss?

A: Yes.

Q: He was fair to you at all times?

A: Yes.

Q: You knew that all I wanted to do was meet with you one time, right?

A: That's what the letter said, yes.

Q: You had already agreed to voluntarily meet with the government probably ten times by that point; right?

A: It was my understanding if I didn't cooperate, they would subpoena me, so I felt I had to.

Q: But you knew I couldn't force you to do anything?

A: That was my understanding.

Q: So you said no?

A: Yes. I had enough meetings.

Q: You had none with me.

A: Right.

There are a couple of important lessons from this exchange. First, the playing field is clearly tilted in favor of the government as far as access to witnesses or potential witnesses. Second, here, the witness—Carol—was under the mistaken impression that even if she didn't want to grant the interview to the government, they could subpoena her to give one anyway. Although her belief was inaccurate, the government has a major intimidation factor going for them. They never promised Carol they would not prosecute her. She knew the defense could never prosecute her, because the defense has no such power.

Third Government Witness—Werner Wolfen

I first met Werner Wolfen in the spring of 1997 during my interviews for the CFO position at Broadcom. Werner was the lead attorney for the Los Angeles law firm, Irell & Manella. He was also one of two independent directors of Broadcom (Lanny Ross was the other; Nick and Henry were the two inside directors then).

Werner and I met in his Century City office and immediately formed a bond. He often worked with high-net-worth individuals, including many from the entertainment industry, looking for investment opportunities. In 1994, Werner assembled a group of mostly showbiz types who had been clients of his firm to make a $2 million investment in Broadcom. He was then invited to join the Broadcom board.

I want to establish that Werner was a key figure in the early development of Broadcom. He was to become the lead independent director. He served on both the audit and compensation committees. Werner retired from the Broadcom board in 2007, having reached the then-mandatory retirement age of seventy-six.

At Broadcom I interacted with Werner frequently. Besides the board and audit committee meetings, we often talked by phone, usually because he desired updates on happenings at the company or because I solicited his input on various strategic matters. We had a very open and professional relationship based on what I thought to be a high level of mutual respect.

That relationship appeared to crumble during a relatively short interview Werner had with the Kaye Scholer law firm in the independent investigation of the options matter. As I've noted, when the investigation had to choose between speed and accuracy, speed invariably won. I believe that Kaye Scholer's investigation was very slanted, aimed not at uncovering truth but at producing culprits.

Taking a handful of potentially damaging e-mails out of context, they convinced Werner that the CFO with whom he had shared a very open and respectful relationship for nearly a decade was really a scoundrel. This opinion came through clearly in the pretrial interview notes we had seen, as well as on the stand.

The moment the prosecution was waiting for came when they were able to elicit the comment that though Werner had trusted me in earlier days, he could no longer do so after exposure to the information he had been shown in the course of the case. The comment would come back to haunt Mr. Stolper later.

In deference to Werner's age, his recollections were often a little confused. For example, he insisted that the general counsel, David Dull, reported to me for the duration of my time at Broadcom. I can understand that Werner would not necessarily be aware of who my direct reports were or weren't in general, but for the seventeen years before he joined Broadcom, David had worked for and with Werner at Irell.

Under cross-examination, Werner made the surprising admission that even though he was chair of the audit committee and therefore had to approve all Broadcom SEC filings, he never actually read them. Judge Carney later expressed surprise over this.

It was also clear from the government's case that they were doing as much as they could to denigrate Nick. Werner jumped right on that bandwagon and claimed that although Nick had once been a dynamic leader, his leadership ability fell off dramatically after a time. When asked when that time was, he replied that it was at Broadcom's IPO. We have already calibrated the dynamic growth of Broadcom post-IPO, which clearly did not reflect ineffective leadership at the top.

Werner's testimony was at least mercifully brief. It took only part of one afternoon and part of the next morning. His testimony pretty much left a lot of people shaking their heads and wondering how accurate his recall really was.

Bizarrely, on the morning of the second day of his testimony before the jury entered the courtroom, Werner approached me as I stood by the defense table and shook my hand. Coming from a former trusted colleague who had done the best he could on the stand the previous day to do a hatchet job on me, I found this really strange. It felt like a mafia movie where the don approaches his former colleague and says, "Nothing personal. It's just business," just before he whacks the guy. The rest of Werner's testimony was neither friendlier nor more hostile than before.

Following the Wolfen testimony, Matt Umhofer made the second of seven motions for mistrial. This one was based on pretrial motions where the judge had granted a defense motion to exclude certain hearsay allegations from the Broadcom restatement and related comments by the Broadcom audit committee. The defense alleged that the government had craftily led Mr. Wolfen to bring in "evidence" that had been specifically excluded in a classic end-run play. The motion was denied.

Fourth Government Witness—Ken Venner

The government tried to make a big deal of the peripheral issue that for a small number of strategic positions, Broadcom had hired candidates through companies we were thinking of acquiring. This allowed the candidate to receive options in the target company that would have a good upside to them if the acquisition were consummated. Though, as always with stock options, there was no guarantee that the upside would still be there by the time the options vested.

One such hire from 2000 was Ken Venner as chief information officer (CIO). Though Ken was brought in to report to Nick, I took the lead role in his hiring. The government thought they had a juicy case against me on this one. The problem is, it was a nonissue. Ken's options did have more potential upside than those of a direct Broadcom hire: they were effectively granted at below-market prices because they were priced based on the value of the company that was targeted to be acquired before the acquisition was firmed up. They were also all accounted for correctly.

The government tried to make it look like this was a shady process, done in secret. The cross-examination of Ken was done by Skadden attorney Matt Umhofer. Matt walked Ken through his hiring process with a focus on his negotiations with me.

Matt Umhofer: Now, when Bill talked to you about this process, he told you how that – how the options were going to work, didn't he? He told you that you were going to be hired through an acquisition; isn't that right?

Ken Venner: Yes.

Q: What did you understand that to mean at the time?

A: That they were acquiring a company and that I would pass through there and then join Broadcom as an employee.

Q: So Mr. Ruehle didn't hide from you the fact that when you came on board, you weren't going to be at Broadcom – formally at Broadcom from day one. You were going to be with an acquisition at first; isn't that right?

A: Correct.

Q: You felt comfortable with the offer; isn't that right?

A: After I got past the passing through another company, yes.

Q: Okay. And Mr. Ruehle assured you that everything was above-board; isn't that right?

A: Correct.

Q: He didn't tell you to keep quiet about this. Keep it on the down low?

A: He did not.

Q: And you realized that even though the options were potentially valuable, there was a risk that they would be eventually worth nothing?

A: Correct.

In fact, the options did turn out to be worthless as the tech meltdown left all of Ken's first option grant deeply underwater.

Any time either side in a trial calls a witness, there is always the risk that the witness might help your opponent more than help you. I think that turned out to be the case with Ken. He sat up on the witness stand and responded directly and professionally. He did not attempt any spin. Though the government had interviewed him and the defense had not, he presented a factual and emotively neutral testimony. It was refreshing to see a government witness present based on his own recollections rather than those the government wanted him to have.

The defense was able to establish that all facts pertaining to hiring new employees through acquisition had been thoroughly documented to and by the auditors and attorneys. It further was brought out that, due to the tech meltdown, all of Ken's initial options turned out to be worthless by the time any had vested. So the whole scenario the government tried so hard to make look like a criminal conspiracy was much ado about nothing.

Fifth Government Witness—Nancy Tullos

Nancy Tullos was to be the government's star witness. If ever a person was subjected to the heavy hand of the government, it was she. She had left Broadcom in 2003 under less-than-ideal circumstances. Within six months of Nick's departure in early 2003, Nick's interim replacement, Lanny Ross, decided Nancy was not the appropriate long-term vice president of HR. After some contentious negotiations, Nancy and Lanny agreed on a termination settlement.

Sometime after that, she landed a dream job as VP of HR for QLogic, another fast-growing semiconductor company in Orange County. That is, it was her dream job until the federal prosecutors were able to get her fired. In 2007, Andrew Stolper called the general counsel of QLogic and advised him that he may have disclosure obligations related to Nancy as a person of interest in the case against Broadcom. He asked what QLogic's policy was for dealing with executives who refused to cooperate with a government investigation. I don't know exactly what happened next, but the very next day, Nancy "resigned" from her dream job. Prior to this, Nancy had rebuffed the government's attempts to interview her. Now the message was clear: you can't hide from us!

When a person is under threat of indictment in a criminal case and wants to cut a cooperative deal with the prosecutors, that person presents a "proffer" to the government: the value they believe they can bring to the government's case in exchange for an agreement not to be prosecuted—or, if prosecuted, to be granted leniency in sentencing. When the government tries to convince a reluctant target that cooperation would be in that person's best interest, it presents a "reverse proffer."

The reverse proffer is designed to scare the potential cooperator into submission. In Nancy's case it worked. It didn't work right away, because she didn't think she had done anything wrong, but eventually she made a plea agreement with the government. But this wasn't handed to her out of the kindness of their hearts. They insisted that she plead guilty to a felony.

As we learned much later in the trial, the prosecutors told her attorneys that it had to be a felony, because a misdemeanor would not carry enough weight with the jurors. The government wanted to present a Broadcom executive who had confessed to a felony, hoping to convince the jurors of felonious doings at the company.

Nancy pleaded to the "crime" of obstruction of justice, based on a 1999 e-mail response to an HR subordinate asking to "please delete" it. Ironically, if you don't want someone to put something in e-mail, it makes more sense to say so verbally. And Nancy copied her "please delete this e-mail" message to another subordinate without a request to delete it. Finally, she did not delete the e-mail herself.

But wait—it gets worse. Destruction of evidence (and e-mail has certainly become a prime form of evidence) is a crime if one knows an investigation is in progress. The Broadcom investigation began in 2006, but the offending e-mail was from 1999. Are we to believe that in 1999, Nancy Tullos had the prescience to know that this e-mail could potentially be relevant in an investigation begun seven years later? In fact, the statute of limitations on an obstruction charge is five years. To plead guilty to it, she would have had to agree to waive the statute of limitations.

It was significant that, even with all their pressure, the prosecutors could not induce Nancy to plead guilty to securities fraud. In fact, when she was asked the same question about participating in a criminal conspiracy that Carol Prado had been asked, she provided the same answer: absolutely not.

Nancy's testimony was very painful to listen to. It was long. Her direct took about a day and a half. Then Rich had to probe and prod and display e-mails that belied the heavily coached statements she was making under direct. Her cross lasted four full days. The redirect and re-cross together consumed another day. But the painful part wasn't the length; it was the content. Talk about revisionist history! The Broadcom Nancy recalled on the stand was not the one I recalled from my nine-plus years there.

For example, several of us—led primarily by David Dull and me—constantly strove to improve our administrative processes. Under Nick's leadership, we had only limited success, as that was not his main area of concern. Once he left, we were able to implement very solid processes. The most tangible evidence of this was that after mid-2003, no more option grants had to be restated because of faulty paperwork. By this time, both Nick and Nancy had left the company. Even before that, we had made progress in reducing the time to complete all the option documentation. When she was questioned about this on direct and on cross, rather than acknowledge that there had been a good-faith effort to improve the processes, Nancy claimed instead that I was leading an effort to be "more careful" so we could do a better job of fooling the auditors.

My lowest emotional point in the case was after the first morning of the Tullos direct. I knew her testimony was manufactured. At this early stage, she appeared sufficiently credible that I think she actually believed what she was saying. I was concerned that the jury would believe her version of what had happened and who was responsible.

The prosecution was determined to win their case with Nancy. They worked real hard on her. It came out later in the trial that the government had conducted at least twenty-six sessions with her to elicit her testimony and to make sure it comported with their view of the case.

During her testimony we got to see some disturbing patterns in the government's presentation of the case. If an e-mail is potentially incriminating, take it out of context. (Our cross-examination needed a lot of time to show dozens more e-mails to put the offending one in context.) On the other hand, if an e-mail were potentially exculpatory, the prosecution would say the writers were speaking in code. If internal controls were not put in place, call it recklessness; If controls were there, call it a cover-up. Whatever happened to the search for the truth?

In the end, Nancy's testimony was completely discredited by Judge Carney. He actually ordered it stricken from the record. But back in mid-November, we didn't know that was going to happen. Rich did a particularly brilliant job of showing how misleading her testimony was. When it was his turn to cross-examine, he came out swinging. The polite (but firm) demeanor he showed in the Carol Prado cross was gone. Nancy's testimony was so obviously geared to one result: to earn her a sentence of probation for being so helpful to the government. Rich had to pry the truth out of her like an oral surgeon extracting a tooth.

His first opportunity to discredit Nancy's testimony came in the first half hour. A key point the government tried to establish through Nancy was that the options committee (Nick and Henry), vested with the sole power to grant options to all but corporate officers, never actually met. In her direct, Nancy had repeatedly made the claim that she "knew" that the committee never met but rather selected favorable pricing dates after the fact. In fact (under obvious government pressure), she claimed that I was the one who selected all the dates even though I was never on the options committee.

There were a couple of problems with her assertion. The most glaring is that she was dead wrong. Later, Henry Samueli testified under oath that the options committee met regularly and did, in fact, determine the grant dates. The other problem was that Nancy's assertion on the stand directly contradicted her sworn statement to the SEC from 2007.

Because all prior official statements by witnesses must be available to both sides in a trial, we had full transcripts of Nancy's SEC statements. In one, she said she had no way of knowing whether the committee was meeting or not. This is certainly far different from her testimony at trial that she "knew" there were no meetings.

The courtroom had a large movie-size projection screen for displaying evidence such as e-mail and SEC statements, and both sides made liberal use of it. When Rich questioned Nancy about the apparent discrepancy between her SEC statement and her trial testimony, he dramatized the point by projecting the statement and had Aaron, our technical support guy, highlight the appropriate passage.

After her contradictions were pointed out, Nancy called one particular statement she had made to the SEC "not accurate." The next part of the testimony unfolded:

Rich Marmaro: It's a lie?

Nancy Tullos: Yes, it's a lie.

Q: How did you feel about lying to the SEC in 2007?

A: Mr. Marmaro, I didn't know that that's what I was doing.

Q: You didn't realize you were lying at the time?

A: No, I did not.

Q: Okay. But after your meetings with the government, you came to a different mind-set about whether you were lying; right?

A. Well, the best I can explain to you is that when I started this process, my entire focus at Broadcom on the option granting process was to do the best thing I could for the employees, because I felt it was the responsibility and duty of others in the company

106

who had the knowledge and experience about the securities far more than I did to be taking of the financial reporting.

Nancy hemmed and hawed, knowing she was stuck. Just a few yards away sat the government prosecutor team who could recommend that she be sentenced either to probation or to jail time as a result of her plea agreement. Rich wasn't about to let her squirm out of it.

Rich then asked, "Ms. Tullos, my question is very simple: were you lying to the SEC in August of 2007? Yes or no?" This brought a hush to the courtroom.

Then looks of astonishment appeared on jurors' faces when she answered meekly, "Yes." Looks of extreme anguish crossed the faces of the prosecution team.

The defense relied on an important distinction: "then versus now." Certain accounting guidelines were interpreted differently over the 1998–2002 time frame than they were by 2006. The Sarbanes-Oxley Act from mid-2002, which wasn't fully implemented until 2004, influenced these changes.

For consistency in financial reporting, companies are expected to follow what are known as Generally Accepted Accounting Principles (GAAP). Note that "principles" are not necessarily "rules," and that principles are subject to interpretation. The most important accounting principle in this case was published in the Accounting Principles Bulletin (APB) Opinion 25, from 1972.

APB 25 was modified significantly many times over the years, but then abolished altogether in 2005. The important point is that the interpretation of this (or any other) accounting principle is subject to the facts and circumstances at the time. During the frenetic technology boom of the late 90s and early 2000s and before the classic meltdowns of Enron and WorldCom, there was far less scrutiny on the finer points of stock option accounting.

Following those well-documented corporate frauds and the hastily enacted Sarbanes-Oxley legislation, the world's viewpoint changed. Analogous to what can happen to the presumption of innocence in a criminal case, financial statements had generally been presumed accurate before all the turmoil, while in the political environment that ensued, they were suspect as inaccurate at best and fraudulent at worst. In other words, it became politically correct to assume the worst about corporations and the way they reported their numbers.

This point was key in the case. Given how obvious it was that Nancy's testimony was being viewed through a 2006 prism, we spent a fair amount of time trying to figure out how to demonstrate it. Then, on the third day of her cross, Nancy handed it to us on a silver platter.

During a brief pause in Rich's cross, Nancy volunteered an incredible statement. By this time she was worn down and hating Rich, so she was going to give him a piece of her mind. He hadn't even asked her a question, though his most recent theme had been to contrast her earlier statements with her current ones. Nancy offered, "Mr. Marmaro, the facts for me haven't changed. What has changed over time is my opinion of those facts." If Nancy had been a friendly defense witness, she could not have made a more helpful statement for our side, though it was clearly not her intention. Thank you, Nancy!

The consummate professional that he is, Rich resisted any temptation to do a fist pump or make any other show of glee. He looked Nancy directly in the eye and said, "And so, based on your education from the government, you have a different opinion than what you felt at the time, right?" She agreed.

With surgical skill, Rich would make an effort to put e-mails in context to neutralize the government's effort to cherry-pick them so they could present a very narrow case. Part of this was to pull e-mails out of context. Rich would then have to take a series of e-mails that preceded and followed the government's cherry-picked e-mails. A good example of this is fully illustrated in Appendix B regarding a particular option grant that the government had alleged was back-dated.

When Rich developed the context with surrounding messages onscreen in the courtroom, suddenly the government's "smoking gun" e-mail looked very benign. He prepared to apply the exercise to one of Nancy's e-mails, asking if she recalled its context. She responded, "No, Mr. Marmaro, but I'm sure you have some e-mails to refresh me." This actually brought a chuckle to the courtroom.

Another exchange centered around the Broadcom practice of making some selected new employee hires through companies Broadcom was contemplating acquiring. This practice was previously highlighted during the Ken Venner testimony. In her direct testimony, government attorney Andrew Stolper began:

Andrew Stolper: Did you express your displeasure with the practice to the defendant?

Nancy Tullos: Yes I did.

Q: What did the defendant say, and then what did he do?

A: He agreed with me. I think he thought it was a bad practice, too, but he did not help me shut it down.

Q: In addition to telling the defendant about hiring through acquisitions, did you attempt to get support to shut down the practice from Broadcom's general counsel?

A: Yes, I did.

Q: How did that go for you?

A: Pretty much the same way it went with Mr. Ruehle: everybody nodded wisely but no one helped me.

So here was Nancy trying to make it appear that she was single-handedly trying to prevent the company from continuing with a practice that she felt was wrong. During her cross, Rich displayed a couple of emails that absolutely contradicted her testimony.

In an e-mail dated October 12, 2000 that Nancy sent to three executives (which was displayed in court and entered into evidence) in one of the Broadcom business units, Nancy included the statement:

> *To be clear I have been told by David Dull and Bill Ruehle to "shut down" all hiring into acquisitions. Of course, in my effort to help Broadcom with some difficult hires, I have violated what was a pretty clear message from David and Bill. She concludes her e-mail with the statement, "Please delete this email immediately after you read it."*

It is important to note that initially when this email was produced by the government to the defense the section where Nancy states she had clear instructions to stop the process of hiring through acquisition had been redacted. The redaction issue was brought up during the trial and government denied that it had anything to do with its redaction. The content of the email speaks for itself: it was very important exculpatory evidence for the defense to show my mind-set. I wanted to shut down the process not because it was "wrong" but because it was inherently unfair in that it allowed some employees preferential treatment over others.

Rich also produced a series of e-mail exchanges Nancy had with Henry Samueli in July 2000 where she is proactively urging Henry and other senior managers to hire a high value potential employee through an acquisition. For a process that she found so distasteful, Nancy was a pretty strong advocate of continuing the practice.

With our strategies working as we'd hoped, I felt by this point that we had largely neutralized the government's star witness. It was tedious for everyone. Pulling the truth out of an uncooperative witness was an arduous process, but boy, was it worth it!

Sixth Government Witness—Bruce Stump

Bruce Stump had been the engagement partner (the most senior E&Y auditor) on the Broadcom audit from 1997 through 2003. He reviewed junior auditors' work and interfaced with company executives and board and audit committee members on big-picture items—not the details.

I had worked very closely with Bruce from his start on the Broadcom account shortly before our IPO. (Bruce had retired from E&Y in 2007 when he reached the mandatory retirement age.) He always seemed to have a good grasp on the dynamics of the business as well as technical expertise in accounting, but his revisionist view of Broadcom also surprised me.

Bruce's recollection of detailed events was understandably blurred by the passage of time as well as the fact that he was not generally the person on site. In a couple of instances, though, he seemed to have perfect recall of conversations that had taken place eight or nine years before the trial. Naturally, these were conversations that the government thought could be harmful to me.

As Rich cross-examined him, he seemed to suffer a sudden attack of amnesia. He didn't seem to be able to recall much of anything other than the carefully rehearsed points elicited by the government. Nevertheless, Rich kept pounding away, trying to bring out the truth. At one point, when the jury was out of the courtroom, the prosecutors complained about the tediousness of Rich's cross-examination. To his credit, Judge Carney admonished Bruce's attorneys to advise their client to stop being so evasive and just answer the questions. If he would do that, said the Judge, the process could go much faster.

Early in his cross-examination, Rich asked Bruce:

Rich Marmaro: Did you provide any written material entitled "determining measurement date for stock-based compensation" prior to 2006?

Bruce Stump: I don't personally remember delivering that.

Q: Did you personally advise Dr. Nicholas or Dr. Samueli of the importance of contemporaneous documentation of granting decisions?

A: No, I don't remember that discussion at all.

Q: To your knowledge, did any Ernst & Young auditor personally advise the option committee of the importance of contemporaneous documentation of granting decisions?

A: No, I don't specifically recall any discussion like that.

Near the end of his cross, Rich probed Bruce on some of the changes in the accounting world from the 1998-2003 time period that was charged in the case, to the present day. This was critical to our "then vs. now" theme.

Rich Marmaro: Now after 2006, or at least after late 2006, Ernst & Young started advising its clients on how best to avoid Opinion 25 measurement date problems, right?

Bruce Stump: Yes, I believe that's correct.

Q: That was a little late, wasn't it sir?

A: Well, that was after a number of years where there were a lot of questions, a lot of situations that come to light. There were a lot of new interpretations of the literature, so a lot of things that happened between then and 2006.

Q: The documentation problems had happened in 1998 to 2003, correct?

A: That's correct.

Q: And your advice on how to fix documentation problems occurred in 2006, correct?

A: That was the firm's recommendation. I think we talked a little bit about a management letter, what we talked about getting the minutes more timely getting them signed off, things of that nature.

Q: The truth is, sir, that back then no one, including Ernst & Young and including Broadcom, was focusing on the stock option documentation to support the accounting; isn't that right?

A: I don't think there was much emphasis on documentation, yes.

Q: As there is today?

A: Yes.

Q: And no one was focusing on concepts like measurement date like they are today. Isn't that true?

A: There is a lot more literature today on different questions that arises to measurement date.

Q: The fact is, when unusual issues of stock option accounting arose at Broadcom, Broadcom's accounting department consulted with Ernst & Young?

A: If there were questions as to how to account for a – particularly related to business combinations, yes.

Q: The fact is, they consulted with Ernst & Young on how to handle options to consultants?

A: Yes. I believe that's true.

Q: They consulted with Ernst & Young on how to handle options to part-time employees?

A: Yes. I believe we saw something related to that.

Q: They consulted with Ernst & Young on how to handle options accounting for vesting on leave of absence?

A: Yes, I believe we discussed one situation on that.

Q: They consulted with Ernst & Young on how to deal with the whole underwater options issue?

A: I believe that there were some situations where we did discuss underwater options.

Q: The fact is, Mr. Stump, Ernst & Young was not asleep at the switch at that time, were they?

A: I don't believe we were.

Q: The fact is, that Ernst & Young did its best to give the best advice it could under the applicable standards of the time?

A: Yes. We tried to make our clients aware of what the accounting literature was saying and any changes that we foresaw.

Q: At a time when the world of stock option accounting was much different than it is today; isn't that right?

A: Yes, it is much different today.

Q: The fact is, that since 2006 hundreds of companies have come under scrutiny for options-granting practices which at the time seemed reasonable?

A: Yes. I think we did discuss if there were over 120 companies.

Q: The fact is that new sets of auditors and new sets of lawyers in 2006 and 2007 started interpreting Opinion 25 in a very strict way and looking back several years to see how companies' options paperwork matched up to that new strict interpretation. Isn't that a fact?

A: I wasn't part of the restructure team. I had already left the Broadcom account. My understanding is that from reading different accounts of it that they had a problem with documentation.

Q: Sir, the SEC staff says it intends to recommend securities fraud charges against you. But if they do, isn't the fact that you will fight those charges?

A: That's correct.

Q: Because you don't think you did anything wrong, do you?

A: That's correct.

The profound effect the Enron case had on how people behaved in accounting matters must be acknowledged. As part of that case, the government brought charges against Arthur Andersen, Enron's independent public accounting firm. As a result, Arthur Andersen was forced to liquidate. At the time, they were one of the Big Five—that is, the five largest and most reputable public accounting firms in the world. They appealed their indictment and eventually the charges were reversed by the US Supreme Court—two years too late. All 26,000 of their employees had been put out of work.

All companies, but particularly professional services companies, learned: don't become the next Arthur Andersen. Do whatever you can to accommodate the government so they don't bring charges against you. This mentality infected corporations also: rather than defend their innocence, it was much safer to throw a few sacrificial lambs to the wolves and say they were the source of any wrongdoing.

Seventh Government Witness—Paul Amlong

The next government witness was flown in from Baltimore, but he may as well have flown in from Mars. Paul Amlong was introduced as an investor who had briefly owned some Broadcom stock in 2006. He was not designated as an expert, which means he was not paid to testify. He was a percipient witness, though with absolutely no firsthand knowledge of Broadcom.

Most people's image of an investor is that of a professional money manager from some respected firm like Fidelity or JP Morgan or the like. This was not Mr. Amlong. He was a day trader. By his own testimony, he had about a $30,000 investment account provided by his parents (Mr. Amlong was probably in his 40s). He had invested some of it in Broadcom in 2006, before the news broke on the alleged backdating issues.

As so often happens with day traders, his timing was unfortunate, and his Broadcom stock declined. The government tried to imply that it had declined due to backdating, but they were never able to prove that. (In fact, at each of three public announcements about the restatement and investigation, the stock price had gone up.)

Mr. Amlong provided some unintended comic relief when he was probed on his investment style. It turns out that he had attended a seminar (or maybe more than one) led by some self-styled investment advisor named Gary. Many of Mr. Amlong's answers included the words "Gary said." When shown excerpts from Broadcom's annual financial statements and asked to comment on the significance of the item "stock-based compensation," Mr. Amlong admitted he didn't have a clue. In fact, he admitted he never read financial statements, because that was not what Gary said to do.

To give a flavor for this witness, early in his cross-examination, Jack DiCanio began:

> Jack DiCanio: Now, sir, before the government flew you out from Maryland to testify here, did they ask you whether you reviewed Broadcom's public filings just before you invested in April of 2006?

> Paul Amlong: I don't remember.

> Q: Let me ask you now, sir, before you invested in Broadcom in April of 2006, there was a 10K that was issued by Broadcom just a few months before your investment. Did you know that?

A: I'm sure – I know it now, but I'm not saying I knew it in 2006. I don't know.

Q: Understood. But, sir, it's your testimony today that before you invested in April of 2006, you did not review that 10K filed by Broadcom just a few months before you invested; is that right?

A: I would have reviewed just the earnings reports. So that's what I would – and I wouldn't have literally read what Broadcom issued as the internal report. I would have looked at the results of the report.

Q: That's the press release that sometimes gets issued along with their earning statements?

A: Right

Q: And it gives just the top line result of the company?

A: Yes. And that was all I really was concerned about.

Q: You didn't dig down, as you testified on direct, into the particular line items on any public statement?

A: Right.

A little later, Jack probed Mr. Amlong on the level of financial analysis taught by Gary.

Jack DiCanio: When you took the course with Gary, did he explain to you what those kinds of numbers mean in real life?

Paul Amlong: No. We didn't discuss that. That is – he is teaching trading and looking at more current information.

Q: More current information meaning what the company is doing today?

A: Today.

Q: Because what happened in the past to investors like yourself are not as relevant; correct?

A: Yes.

Later on, the defense introduced a real professional investor, and the contrast was like night and day. I don't think Mr. Amlong's testimony did anything to help the government's case.

Eighth Government Witness—Bob Tirva

Because evidence can only be introduced into a trial through witnesses, some are called solely for that purpose, like Bob Tirva. At the time of the trial, he was vice president and corporate controller of Broadcom; he had been promoted to that position after I left. The previous corporate controller also had left.

Bob was a good, solid guy who was really just there to allow certain Broadcom financial statements to be entered into evidence. The government prosecutor was clueless about how stock options worked. In one line of questioning, he tried to get Bob to acknowledge that if an option were priced below market, the company would have to "kick in" the difference. Bob looked a little perplexed at the nonsensical question and responded that, no, there was nothing to "kick in."

His testimony was quite brief and, in my opinion, it neither helped nor hurt the government's case.

Ninth Government Witness—Professor Christopher Jones

Some expert witnesses accept their roles and present a very straightforward explanation of their subject. Others bask in their fifteen minutes of fame and do their best to convince everyone that they are the smartest person in the room.

Professor Jones proudly described his advanced degrees, including a PhD in finance from Wharton. He was an associate professor of finance at the University of Southern California. His mission was to prove that Broadcom's option grant dates had about as much chance of being chosen at random as the probability of lightning striking a particular place at a particular time.

Professor Jones acknowledged that he had no firsthand experience with Broadcom, which is standard practice for an expert witness. Upon cross-examination by Jack DiCanio, he testified that the option dates he had studied had been supplied by the prosecution and did not represent all Broadcom grant dates.

The defense did not disagree with his conclusion that the favorable dates chosen for option grants were unlikely to have been random. We never claimed that they were. At the time, the process for granting options was not the rigid one in use by 2006.

It was hard to judge the impact of Professor Jones on the jury. He certainly didn't help the defense case, but he also did not present a slam-dunk for the prosecution.

Tenth Government Witness—Paul Bonin

Any federal criminal case is assisted by one or more FBI agents, who help gather evidence and attend all interviews of potential witnesses with prosecuting attorneys. You'll remember that their notes at those sessions result in official Form 302 transcription records. No court reporter is present, so the quality of an interview record depends on the accuracy of the FBI agent's notes.

Two FBI agents were assigned to the Broadcom case. Paul Bonin was called as the government's so-called summary witness. This standard procedure is another way to assure both sides that all desired documents are entered into evidence through a witness.

After all the earlier drama, Mr. Bonin's time on the witness stand was anti-climactic. It seemed his main objective was to bring into evidence all of the option exercises and stock sales I had made while at Broadcom. He was clearly trying to build a case that I had a motive to underprice Broadcom options for my personal financial benefit. Of course, he failed to mention that virtually all of my transactions were from options I had been granted prior to the IPO, and those were never alleged to be "backdated." Jack DiCanio brought this out on cross, as well as the fact that approximately 20 percent of all my stock proceeds had been donated to charity. That was inconvenient for the government's theory that I was motivated by greed.

Later, as we'll see, Mr. Bonin was called as the government's only rebuttal witness and sparks flew between him and Rich Marmaro.

When Mr. Bonin's testimony was completed on Tuesday, November 24, the government rested its case. It was two days before Thanksgiving and the judge excused the jury for one week.

Decision Time: Do We Put on a Defense Case?

Once the government rests a case, the defense has to declare whether or not they will be putting on defense. The burden of proof is on the government and if the defense is convinced it has not met the burden, they can decline to put on a case and leave it completely in the hands of the jury. We decided to put on a defense.

Broadcom IPO day – April 16, 1998. Henry and Nick in foreground

Official "tombstone" announcement of Broadcom IPO

House in suburban Cleveland where Bill grew up

Bill and his wife and baby daughter rented the second floor of this house when he was a student at Allegheny College in Meadville, PA in the early 1960's

Bill's family, including wife, his son, two daughters, two step-daughters and all six grandkids. All at Disneyland the month after the indictment in 2008 - The source of all my strength!

Julie with two of her friends from high school at the Caspian Sea in their native Iran in 2006

Julie and Bill on the road in upstate New York in 2007

Julie and Bill's sister, Barbara in upstate New York in 2007

Julie and Bill in New York City in 2007

The day of our engagement – Valentine's Day 2008

ulie and Bill's engagement party in San Francisco, 2008. From left,
Glenn's wife Kate, Bill, Julie, Julie's Dad and Mom, Bill's son Glenn,
Bill's daughter Janine

Our wedding in October 2008 - The trial would start in one year

Day of acquittal - Rich Marmaro and Bill leaving courthouse

Day of Acquittal – Henry Nicholas (Nick) leaving courthouse

Day of Acquittal – Henry Samueli leaving courthouse

Day of Acquittal – Julie and Bill with Skadden team leaving court house. Skadden team, left to right, includes Rich Marmaro, Patrick Hammon, Ryan Weinstein, Matt Sloan, Matt Umhofer

A little celebration the evening of December 15, 2009 (Day of Acquittal) - From left, David Dull, Nick, Bill

New Years Eve 2010 with our supportive friends Terry and Russ

Julie and Bill outside the White House in June 2011

Chapter 10

A Trial within a Trial

Some members of the defense team were sufficiently confident that the government had not met the burden of proof that they advocated not putting on a defense case and going directly to the jury. Why would a defense not want to put on a case? Remember, every time a witness takes the stand for either side, there is always a possibility the witness could be harmful to the side that called them. Even with the massive government coaching of Nancy Tullos, I believe her testimony helped us more.

However, I, Rich, and most of the Skadden team believed we could mount a very effective defense case. Because we did have the truth on our side. Deciding not to is a more conservative position; there is a reasonable chance that at least some of the jurors also believe the prosecution has not met its burden. Since a jury's verdict in a criminal case has to be unanimous, even one juror who is not convinced the government has met its burden of proof results in a hung jury. The government can decide to retry the case, but if most jurors vote for acquittal, they are more likely to drop it.

On the other hand, if the defense does mount a case, it is more likely the jurors will reach a unanimous verdict in one direction or the other. If mounting no defense increases the chance of a hung jury, it means that there would be a lower probability of a unanimous "guilty."

Although in practice, a hung jury is as good as "not guilty," we wanted a clean victory. The idea of a hung jury with a possibility of a retrial a year or two down the line was not at all appealing. (Obviously, a guilty verdict was even less appealing.) Having spent over three years on the case already, and having seen how the government witnesses' carefully scripted stories collapsed on cross-examination, we went for the clean kill.

Our Most Important Decision—Which Witnesses Should We Call?

We knew we would not call anywhere near the forty potential defense witnesses we had listed during discovery, but we could not choose intelligently until we had heard the government case. We knew early that we wanted Henry Samueli and David Dull, and that I was a highly probable witness as well.

Henry could counter Nancy Tullos's claims that the options committee never met. Likeable Henry was also a good speaker and, as one of Broadcom's founders, he could be counted on to provide the larger context of its story. We had seen the transcript of Henry's SEC testimony: his recollection of events was consistent with mine. And David had been intimately involved in Broadcom's administrative processes as a senior executive and general counsel; his SEC testimony meshed as well.

You might ask, "So what's the big deal? Just call these two guys." The big deal was that both men had been thoroughly intimidated by the government prosecutors. Henry had even been cajoled into pleading guilty to lying under oath to the SEC. David had been left on ice as the prosecution remained intentionally vague about whether he would be criminally indicted or not.

Even if we had not been able to call Henry and David, we would have put on a defense case, because Rich and I were not willing to leave anything to chance.

I myself really wanted to testify for a number of reasons. First, I had been forced to remain silent in public for three long years while all sorts of horrible things were said about me. I wanted to set the record straight. Second, I was *there* at Broadcom and could provide a firsthand account of what really happened, not the revisionist one he government bullied out of their witnesses. Finally, I believed I owed it to the jurors, who had seen me only as a stoic figure on the other side of the courtroom. I had to believe they were dying to hear what I had to say.

Henry Samueli's Plea Agreement

Henry's plea was as highly questionable as Nancy's. The false statement he had pleaded to was ambiguous at best. Less than a page later in his transcript, he corrects it. The prosecutors promised him that if he pled guilty to one count of lying under oath to a federal agency, they would recommend a sentence of probation and a fine of $12 million. For most people, that fine would be impossible. For Henry, recognized on the Forbes 400 as one of America's billionaires, it was affordable. The government had originally asked for a much larger fine, but were refused.

As in Nancy's case, it is important to note that Henry did not plead to any form of securities fraud. From the government's point of view, his plea bought them two things. It assured them that Henry could not testify adversely to them under threat of an increase in his recommended sentence. It also served to cast doubt on his credibility with the jury if he did decide to testify. After all, who could believe a confessed liar?

The Icing of David Dull

David Dull was the only other Broadcom executive charged by the SEC besides Nick, Henry, and me, so some speculated that he would also be indicted when Nick and I were. Although he was not, the prosecutors were careful to leave a very strong impression that they could change their minds at any time—for instance, if he volunteered any cooperation with the defense. This is putting a person on ice, or "icing," a standard bullying tactic for anyone in authority. Stepping off the ice, someone just might get burned.

Our Plea for Fairness

The Sixth Amendment to the US Constitution, among other guaran-tees, allows a defendant to call any witnesses he or she chooses. The court can compel them to testify. That's all good in theory, but if we were to call Henry or David as reluctant (read "intimidated") wit nesses, their testimony could not be expected to be as fulsome as i they had not been influenced by government pressure. They would be within their rights to invoke the Fifth Amendment in response to every question, and their attorneys told us that they would.

The defense can request that the government grant so-called "use immunity" to the witnesses—that is, agree not to use any of the witness's testimony against him or her. That would have nullified the government's carefully orchestrated strategy to keep these gentlemen off the stand. However, the defense can make immu nity requests directly to the Court. Rich and the Skadden team had already written up the immunity requests.

As soon as the jury was excused for Thanksgiving break, Rich stood up and made a verbal request for use immunity while hand-ing written copies to the prosecutors (knowing full well they would deny) and the judge (hoping he would be reasonable) As expected, the government huffed and puffed and claimed the request was inappropriate. As we had come to expect, Judge Car-ney took a more reasonable position and scheduled a hearing for the following Monday.

Will My Sixth Amendment Right Be Preserved?

The Thanksgiving break was very welcome. Julie and I traveled to the San Francisco Bay Area to spend Thanksgiving dinner at the home of my son, Glenn. Julie's daughters, two of my three children and five of my six grandchildren were able to join us. Basking in the love of family was a major contrast with the hostile courtroom atmosphere!

We had to carefully consider who our witnesses would be if the court did not grant immunity. A defendant rarely testifies on his or her own behalf—and not because of guilt. We do have the constitutional right not to testify. But there is a risk that a skilled prosecutor will twist testimony and evidence, whether from the defendant or others, to make the defendant appear guilty. If the immunity requests were to be granted we knew I would not have to testify, because Henry and David, as long-time senior executives, would be able to provide all the context and the truth. In case immunity was not to be granted, I spent part of the Thanksgiving weekend preparing to testify.

Judge Carney opened the immunity hearing with a tentative ruling in our favor. The government would make its arguments first, then the attorneys for Henry and David, and finally, Rich Marmaro.

As expected, the government attorney was bitterly opposed. He trotted out every argument he could think of to say that granting immunity would set a dangerous precedent for other cases. As he blustered his way through his arguments, he even threatened to appeal the Court's decision as being without legal basis. I think that he was just frightened that Henry's and David's testimony would contradict his carefully coached witnesses and blow up his case. That is exactly what happened.

Incredibly, he declared that defendants are "not entitled to perfect trials; they're entitled to fair ones."

In response, Judge Carney said, "...every week I look at defendants in this chair and tell them they have a constitutional right to call witnesses. And so, if that means anything—if that means anything—I have got to have a reason when I tell a defendant who is fighting for his reputation and maybe the remaining of his adult life. I have got to tell him why Dr. Samueli and Mr. Dull are not going to testify, even though they're not subject to the same charges."

Judge Carney challenged the prosecutor, asking how he would feel if he were the defendant and the two people who were best able to

attest to his innocence were not permitted to testify. The goverr
ment attorney sort of harrumphed his way past that one.

In a little sideshow, Henry Samueli's attorney objected to the immu
nity request because he feared the government would still some
how use Henry's testimony against him and upset the agreement
that were already in place. Judge Carney did his best to establis
that Henry's testimony could not hurt him and could very well hel
him. The judge advised Henry's attorney that if the Court did grar
immunity and if Henry refused to testify, the courtroom marshal
would take him into custody. Henry did the right thing and agree
to testify.

Judge Carney stuck with his tentative, but before his final ruling h
made a most memorable comment in response to the government'
vehement objections. He acknowledged that a lot of people woul
probably disagree with his ruling, and said, "I was appointed to thi
position to do the right thing, and sometimes the law is not caugh
up to speed as to what the right thing to do is."

His final ruling was as follows:

> A defendant in a criminal case has a constitutional right to ca
> witnesses in his defense. If that right is to have any true meaning
> there must be a compelling reason for not requiring a witness t
> testify. I see no such compelling reason in this case, so I'm goin
> to grant use immunity to Dr. Samueli and Mr. Dull. I believe suc
> use immunity is necessary here, to avoid distorting the fact-find
> ing process and denying Mr. Ruehle his due process right to ca
> witnesses and have a fair trial.

> Ms. Tullos, a cooperating witness and the beneficiary of a ver
> favorable plea deal, has given incriminating testimony agains
> Mr. Ruehle. If they testify consistently with their Securities an
> Exchange testimony, Dr. Samueli and Mr. Dull will give very favc
> rable testimony to Mr. Ruehle that contradicts Ms. Tullos' versio
> of events.

Neither Dr. Samueli nor Mr. Dull, however, were willing to testify, out of fear that they might be incriminating themselves, even though the government has agreed not to prosecute Dr. Samueli for any crimes relating to stock option backdating, and decided not to seek charges against Mr. Dull for any of those alleged crimes.

Under these exceptional circumstances, there is an intolerable air of unfairness and denial of justice if Dr. Samueli and Mr. Dull do not testify for Mr. Ruehle. I believe the jury must hear both sides of the story.

That's the final order of the court.

The Drama Continues...

As we left the courtroom for the day, we on the defense team were feeling very good about our case. We believed we had defused the government's witnesses and that we could now call to the stand the two people most intimately familiar with what had actually happened.

We were totally unprepared for what happened next: the government's Foot Shot #3. (It may have been more of a head shot.) Later that evening, we learned that David Dull's attorney, Jim Asperger, had received a call earlier in the evening from Andrew Stolper. Jim and a fellow defense attorney on the call both heard what they characterized as an overt threat. Of course, the government insisted the call had been harmless.

The call had not been recorded, so no one could testify to its exact words, but David's attorneys found it so incredible that they immediately documented their recollections of it. The government apparently said that they believed David had testified inaccurately before the SEC, and Mr. Stolper advised David's attorneys that if David now testified the same, he could still be charged with perjury and the immunity he had just been granted would not do him any good.

141

Mr. Stolper allegedly added that if David would echo Werner Wolfen - that he no longer trusted me after seeing certain documents, then David would be subject to a "soft cross." The clear implication was that David would be torn apart in cross-examination otherwise. Mr Stolper then alleged that any progress the defense could make with the jury in three hours of technical discussion on accounting issues could be undone with three minutes of testimony like Werner Wolfen's because it was the kind that resonated with jurors.

Also in the now-infamous phone call, Mr. Stolper asked the Dull attorneys if they had cautioned Rich Marmaro about the dangers of calling David to the stand. In their opinion, Mr. Stolper was trying his best to influence David's testimony.

The defense had begun the previous day with an expert flown in from the East Coast; his cross-examination was scheduled to start the next morning. Before the court opened, Jim Asperger and his colleague presented their written recollections of Mr. Stolper's call to the Court, the government, and the defense.

Judge Carney was appalled. He was also very conscious that twelve jurors and three alternates patiently waited in the jury room to continue the case, so he decided to let the first defense witness proceed on schedule and scheduled an evidentiary hearing for the lunch break. After two hours, the hearing was not complete, so its continuance was scheduled for after court the next day.

The hearing process was very interesting. The three "witnesses" were Jim Asperger, his colleague Seth Aronson, and lead prosecutor Andrew Stolper. The judge, another government attorney, and Rich Marmaro would all be questioning them. How often does a defense attorney get an opportunity to examine the lead prosecutor on his case? This was unprecedented.

Per normal protocol, any witness not on the stand had to remain outside the courtroom to avoid being influenced by others' testimony. Messrs. Asperger and Aronson's independently told stories that were virtually identical. Not surprisingly, Mr. Stolper's was a little different.

To give a flavor of Rich's examination of Mr. Stolper, here is part of the testimony regarding Rich's probing on the issue of whether Mr. Stolper tried to influence David Dull's attorneys not to call David to the stand.

Rich Marmaro: Mr. Stolper, isn't it a fact that it was you who brought up the notion that Mr. Dull's testimony could hurt Mr. Ruehle's case?

Andrew Stolper: As I said, I don't recall who brought it up. I recall there being a discussion on the topic.

Q: Isn't it a fact, Mr. Stolper, that your purpose in bringing up that conversation was to try to discourage Mr. Asperger or to encourage Mr. Asperger and/or Mr. Aronson to discourage me from calling David Dull to the stand?

A: To encourage Mr. Asperger, Mr. Dull to encourage you to not call David Dull to the Stand?

Q: Yes.

A: Was that my purpose?

Q: Yes.

A: No.

Q: But you will agree that that subject matter came up and was discussed by you?

A: It was discussed by all of us, yes.

Q: You will agree that you gave Mr. Asperger and Mr. Aronson reasons that you thought David Dull's testimony could hurt Mr. Ruehle?

A: As I said, we all participated in a discussion about how Mr. Dull's testimony may hurt Mr. Ruehle's case and how it may hurt the government's case.

Q: Mr. Stolper, try to answer my question if you could. Isn't it a fact that you raised, with Mr. Aronson and Mr. Asperger, your views on how David Dull's testimony could hurt Mr. Ruehle's case?

A: Did I raise my views – repeat the question.

Q: I want to remind you you are under oath.

A: Thank you.

Q: Isn't it a fact that you were the one to raise with Mr. Asperger and Mr. Aronson what your view was as to how Mr. Dull's testimony could hurt Mr. Ruehle's case?

A: As I said, Mr. Marmaro, I certainly had a view about that as did they. It was part of a discussion.

Q: It wasn't my question. My question was did you express that view to counsel for Mr. Dull?

A: Did I express what view?

Q: The view of how Mr. Dull's testimony could hurt Mr. Ruehle's case?

A: It wasn't a view. It was a factual discussion.

Q: Mr. Stolper, did you discuss factually your belief on how the facts, according to your view of the facts, could hurt Mr. Ruehle's case if Mr. Dull testified to them?

A: I think, yes. As I said before, we all participated in the discussion on that topic.

Q: Mr. Stolper, did you say to Jim Asperger and Seth Aronson that you were surprised that I would call Mr. Dull as a witness for Mr. Ruehle?

A: Yes.

will certainly not claim to be an unbiased observer. With that caveat, gathered from the hearing that the government attorney had made an unabashed attempt to intimidate a key witness. I believe this was a major reason for Judge Carney's eventual decision to dismiss the case without even sending it to the jury.

But Wait, There's More...

In a subsequent hearing, Henry Samueli's attorney presented evidence of further government misconduct. It had leaked information to the press about Henry's alleged failure to cooperate with the investigation in 2006 and 2007; and in 2008, comments about his appearance before the grand jury had found their way to the press. Now, who could possibly have been motivated to do this? This is a really serious issue. Grand jury proceedings are secret by law. Anyone guilty of violating the rule of secrecy is committing a crime.

These allegations caused Mr. Stolper to take the witness stand once again (outside the presence of the jury). When Rich asked him if there were other cases when he leaked information to the media, Mr. Stolper was unable to recall. Henry's attorney was able to further undermine the credibility of Mr. Stolper when he established that the USAO had affirmed in 2008 that Mr. Stolper would not be involved in any aspect of the case involving Henry.

Judge Carney became so uncomfortable with some of the prosecutor's behavior that he ruled that Mr. Stolper could no longer have a speaking role in my trial. As the lead prosecutor and by far the most familiar with the case of any of its attorneys, this was a serious blow to the government.

Yet one more outside figure would be brought into the case: Nancy Tullos's attorney. In a hearing before the judge it was learned that the government had conducted 26 interviews with Ms. Tullos in a thinly disguised effort to shape her testimony.

How Do You Remedy That?

In an impassioned plea, Rich requested—in fact, practically demanded—that the case be dismissed. The way he saw it, the government's misbehavior was so egregious that dismissal was the only appropriate remedy. By this time, the defense's first two expert witnesses had testified – one an accounting expert who testified to the rampant confusion regarding implementing APB Opinion 25 and one a sophisticated investor who testified that noncash charges are irrelevant to investment decisions.

Rich's comments to the Court were so powerful that I want to display them here:

> Everyone says that Mr. Stolper talked about whether or not Mr Dull testifies consistently with his SEC testimony; and if he does that he could be prosecuted.

> Your Honor, that's an extraordinary statement for a federal prosecutor to make to a defense witness on the eve of his testimony Mr. Stolper had no business making that statement. None.

> Mr. Stolper says it was not his intent to suborn perjury, or to intimidate a witness, or to color his testimony in any way. But, your Honor, the only reasonable view of those statements is just that But you don't have to go that far to get the remedy or get to the remedy that I'm going to urge the court to do.

> Mr. Stolper says that "if Mr. Dull testifies a certain way, there would be a soft cross." And if he testified a different way, the implication is there would be an aggressive cross. That's an extraordinary thing for a federal prosecutor to say to a defendant's main witness' lawyer on the eve of his trial testimony. Extraordinary.

> Mr. Stolper's testimony, I submit, your Honor, in large part, should be rejected because all he did was split hairs to save his skin. Mr Solper referred to that call as a typical call.

Your Honor, I respectfully submit that if that's a typical call from our United States Attorney's Office down here, then they need some serious training.

Your Honor, Jim Asperger has been a lawyer for almost as long as I have. I served in the U.S. Attorney's office with him. He clerked for the chief justice of the United States. He told your Honor that it was the most extraordinary call that he had ever received as a lawyer. Mr. Stolper calls it "typical."

Mr. Aronson and Mr. Asperger both said that the effect of Mr. Stolper's statements was that they were concerned and troubled. They both believed and took away the same message from Mr. Stolper; that David Dull was trying to be intimidated. Two experienced lawyers came into your court, your Honor, and testified they were shocked and intimidated.

But what makes this terrible and what makes this irreparable is what happened next. Because as responsible lawyers, they reported that to their client. Their client is our number one witness in this case. What you saw the last two days, your Honor, established that whatever misstatements were made on Broadcom's books were immaterial to reasonable investors and further that it was mass confusion in the application of APB 25.

But our main witness – and I told your Honor this from the moment we started talking about this – was David Dull. I told you he would be number one. And Mr. Stolper knew that. Your Honor, what happened here – and forgive me for getting excited about this. But what happened here was both a fifth and sixth amendment violation of my client's right. A fifth amendment violation because he has a right to due process. A sixth amendment violation for the reason that the court granted immunity. Because he has a right to compulsory process. He has a right to put Mr. Dull on the stand unfettered, unintimidated by Mr. Solper. And that right has been denied forever.

You can't give a limiting instruction. You can't give an intermediate sanction. You can't just remove Mr. Stolper from this court room forever. That won't do it.

You can't ask Mr. Adkins to cross-examine. That won't do it.

This witness has been irreparably harmed. Now, he may say tha he will ignore it. But your Honor, I got a client to defend and he' the number one witness in Mr. Ruehle's defense. And in his mind now is that Andrew Stolper is out to get him; that Andrew Stolpe is watching every word to determine whether or not he has com mitted perjury. And in fact, the audacity of the government to say *if you testify consistent with sworn testimony to the SEC, that we have not prosecuted to date, if you do that, you could be subjected to perjury.*

This is not an issue of could, would, will. Those words don't matter. In fact, the case law is that if he says "could be subjected to perjury," that's enough to get the relief that I will ask for.

There was no reason, your Honor, no legitimate reason for tha conversation to have occurred. The purpose was to ask for an in terview which is a fair reason to talk to a witness' lawyer. Every thing after that, your Honor, was intended – but more importantly had the effect of chilling a defense witness.

Yes, I'll be able to call him, but I'll never be able to call him as was Monday evening when your Honor granted him full immuni ty. You took an extraordinary step, your Honor. You took a coura geous and extraordinary step to immunize the two key witnesse in this case.

Now, for the first one, Dr. Samueli, he already got his treatmen from the U.S. Attorney's Office when they leaked information tha he wasn't cooperating, and they embarrassed that man in the press. So he already had his bit of Mr. Stolper. But it wasn't unti Monday night that Mr. Dull got his case, and I can't ever get tha back, your Honor. I cannot unring that bell. And no matter wha remedy you try short of it, it will be insufficient to protect M

Ruehle's right to a fair trial to Mr. Dull's evidence, because Andrew Stolper knew that David Dull would exculpate Bill Ruehle. He knew it in his bones. That's why they fought the immunity motion. That's why they put him on ice for the last two years, and that's why they didn't want him anywhere near this court. And that's why Mr. Stolper said to him, *does Marmaro really know what he's in for? Does he really know that David Dull won't help him?*

Who is the prosecutor to tell a defense lawyer or to ask a defense lawyer whether I know what I'm doing?

The only purpose for those comments is to try to discourage me from calling David Dull. Your Honor, we took a courageous act by asking for immunity. Your Honor was more courageous in granting it. And now all that is down the drain. And look at the context, your Honor.

This comes moments after the Court had a hearing where you agonized over immunizing people in an extraordinary thing. You said you had never done it before. You said you had never seen such an extraordinary case for it. And you said to these gentlemen, *now, you are free to testify so the jury can hear your testimony unfettered.*

Mr. Stolper interfered with that. He had no right to do that, and he did it. Whether he intended to do it – which I submit he did, or whether the effect of it was to interfere, that has no place in this courtroom, your Honor.

And you said something at the immunity hearing. You said that you are effectively like a gatekeeper. You said that – put the law aside. What you want is fairness. And if the law catches up later, so be it. The law has caught up, your honor. In the last year courts around the country have dismissed indictments over conduct just like what Andrew Stolper did today. And they do it for a reason, your Honor, and the reason is: there's a bigger message here than Bill Ruehle. Bill Ruehle's rights to a fair trial are important. But how many times is this going to happen, if it goes unchecked?

In the dark recesses somewhere, how many times is this going to happen, unless courts say, *you can't do that*. And even if it requires a man to go free – which I submit he should anyway, but that's a different argument. Even if it involves a defendant going free, your Honor, that's what our system of justice is about. Because prosecutors have to behave themselves. They have to apply the rules, they have enormous power. We have seen your Honor many instances in this case that I'm not going to argue to the court now where there has been questionable conduct. We raised them in the prosecutorial misconduct motion, and the court denied it. But we have seen a witness get fired or lose her job based on a call by Mr. Stolper to her boss. We have seen Dr. Samueli's information being leaked to the press, embarrassing that man. We have seen Sue Collins' lawyer write a letter to the government complaining about Mr. Stolper's coercive practices. That's all background, your Honor. All of that is just background.

This is not a one off situation, your Honor. But this is the most egregious example of government misconduct I have ever seen. have been doing this, your Honor, for 30 years.

Your Honor, the case law is quite clear. If a prosecutor tells a potential witness that he could be prosecuted for perjury, that is threatening, coercive conduct that warrants and justifies a dismissal of the indictment.

Rich then went on to cite several cases that supported his assertion that such behavior by prosecutors had indeed resulted in dismissal of indictments. He then wrapped up:

Your Honor, the government's conduct here was intentional. It wasn't inadvertent. It's the culmination of a pattern, I would submit, of misconduct, but I'm not asking to dismiss based on the pattern. It was intentional and not inadvertent. And as a result we are the ones who are harmed. Mr. Dull is not harmed any more than he obviously feels, but he won't bear that harm. The only person that's harmed by this conduct is Bill Ruehle. We are now in a box. What do we do? Do we call our main witness and worry that in the back of his mind is Mr. Stolper's threat and that I have

150

to – if I testify consistent with my prior sworn testimony, which the government has not prosecuted him for, that I will then be subject to perjury? Or what do I do?

Do I change that testimony to please Mr. Stolper; but if I change that testimony, I may subject myself to perjury because it's different than my prior testimony?

If I were Mr. Dull, your Honor, I don't know what I would do. I really don't. Because he's got Mr. Stolper's threat in his head. That bell can't be unrung.

Your Honor, a dismissal of an indictment and a Rule 29 grant – let me start again.

A dismissal of an indictment does not happen every day. A grant of judicial immunity happens less frequently than that. But there are occasions – and this is one of them, your Honor – that to do the right thing is to do the extraordinary thing. And the only right thing here, your Honor, the only thing that will absolutely protect Mr. Ruehle's rights, that will unquestionably protect them is to grant a Rule 29 motion or to dismiss this indictment. There is no remedy short of that.

A curative instruction will not work. An expulsion of Mr. Stolper from this courtroom will not work. Even a statement to the jury that Mr. Stolper misbehaved and he tried to intimidate Mr. Dull will not work. It will not work to give me latitude to cross-examine my own witness.

What an awful position to put a defense lawyer in that in order to correct the damage that was done by the prosecutor, I have to take my own witness on cross-examination on his SEC testimony if he departs from it, because he was warned by Stolper that if he's consistent with it, Mr. Stolper will view him as a liar. What an awful thing. What a terrible burden on me to do that.

So that doesn't work, your Honor. Your Honor, Mr. Asperger has maybe said it best. Mr. Asperger is a measured, conservative lawyer. Mr. Asperger told your Honor under oath that it was the most extraordinary conversation he ever had with a prosecutor. Mr. Aronson, who is a civil lawyer, even a civil lawyer knew that it was wrong. Your Honor, anyone hearing what happened in this court today and hearing Mr. Stolper's explanations was left with a very uneasy feeling about what happened that night. But the most uneasy feeling is Bill Ruehle's, because if you do nothing, or if you do anything short of a dismissal, it's Bill Ruehle's life that may be hanging in the balance. No one else's. Not Mr. Stolper's. Not anyone else's. They come and go and cases come and go to them. This is the case of his life. We have fought this case fairly, aboveboard and on the merits and honorably, and I think the court has seen this. This was a low blow, your Honor, and there's certain low blows in prize fights which actually result in declaring the person who is victimized as the winner.

I won't feel like a winner if you grant this motion, your Honor. This is something that needs to be done. I will feel awful if your Honor gives us a remedy which your Honor believes might help us but is short of what I have asked for. I can't think of a remedy that's fair. I can't think of a compromise here, your Honor.

I'm happy to answer any questions that the Court has of me, but – and I apologize for going on. And I apologize for speaking as fervently as I have. But, your Honor, this is an issue that when I first heard about it, literally, knocked me off the floor. It was that substantial. And I don't say that lightly, your Honor.

I have been around the block and you have, too. This is something where I said you can't play that way. You can't do that with the defense's main witness, and they did that, your Honor. I submit they did it intentionally. You don't have to go that far to dismiss this case. But I submit that's exactly what happened.

Judge Carney did not agree at the time, but he did say the following:

All right. Here's going to be my ruling: I'm going to deny the ruling to dismiss the indictment without prejudice. That can be raised again. My preference would be to raise it after the jury returns a verdict, if there's a guilty verdict on any one of the counts. But I really think it's going to be important for me to hear exactly what Mr. Dull has to say.

I do believe there was government misconduct, but I cannot tell from the testimony of the witnesses whether there was an actual threat to Mr. Dull if he did not testify consistently – if he testified consistently with the SEC testimony, that he would be prosecuted for perjury.

'his was a very consistent position for Judge Carney to take. He was bsolutely dedicated to learning all the facts of the case before ren-ering a final decision.

'he View from the Defendant's Chair

fter suffering through several weeks as a piñata for the govern-ent prosecution team and their highly coached witnesses, I felt profound sense of relief after these latest developments. Finally, e truth was being allowed to shine through. I would be allowed to all the witnesses who could speak most knowledgably about the ruth of what really happened at Broadcom. And the dirty tricks and timidation tactics the government used so indiscriminately had at st been exposed.

y no means did it mean that I was ready to relax and assume vic-ry—on the contrary. It motivated me to work even harder with my efense team to assure we were ready to capitalize on the advan-ges we had just been granted.

Chapter 11

The Defense Case—Now It's Our Turn

1 the courtroom I maintained a log of key points that came out
1 testimony so I could compare notes with my attorneys during
reaks, but also just to make my own observations.

lso, each morning in the courthouse, Julie would write a very ten-
er, brief note and have it handed to me as I sat in the defendant's
hair waiting for the judge and jury.

n Tuesday, December 1, Julie's note began as follows:

> Today begins with a full moon and so does our defense case. I
> feel energized yet very conscious of not allowing myself to feel
> over-confident. I am still in awe of Judge Carney's words from
> yesterday. His words echo in my head, "I am now focused on Mr.
> Ruehle's rights."

he full moon reference resonated with the time my oldest daugh-
er, Janine, had told us that a full moon had presaged some positive
vents in her life. (In fact, the evening she flew in to sit in on some of
he defense portion of my trial, she mentioned that a full moon was
1 view during her entire flight.)

uring the trial, that morning before receiving Julie's note, I had
ritten:

> Finally our turn to put the truth up front, instead of having to ex-
> tract it like a dentist pulling teeth. Knowing we have Henry and
> David queued up is good. Seeing the gorgeous full moon this
> morning is good. Having a strong opening witness today is good.
> Please God, be with us.

Finally, It's Our Turn

By the end of the trial, the record would show that the government case consumed seventeen court days and called ten witnesses. The defense case required seven court days and seven witnesses—of whom one, Jim Asperger, only became a witness due to extraordinary circumstances.

The government had done their best to paint a very narrow picture and had carefully coached their witnesses to stay within the lines. It was the burden of the defense to show the jury the context of all the witnesses' statements and to drag the truth out of them. Remember that most of the witnesses faced the very real prospect of government retribution if their testimony strayed.

We had no concerns about how our own witnesses would testify. It had been a long trial, and we knew the jury was getting restless. Judge Carney was sending signals that he hoped to send the case to the jury before Christmas—less than four weeks away. We wanted to present a thorough defense, but as crisply as possible, since the jurors were getting weary and we didn't want to lose their attention. We also wanted a crisp defense because the truth should be simple: if explanations are too long and complicated, many people become suspicious. We believed the truth *was* simple, and we were determined to tell it that way.

We decided to use only two witnesses from Broadcom: Henry and David could tell the whole story. We brought in one very sophisticated investor who, through the fund he managed, had owned large blocks of Broadcom stock. We had an accounting expert who had once been the deputy chief accountant of the SEC. Finally, we brought in a summary witness who looked like a kindly, middle-aged mom, but who happened to have a PhD in applied mathematics from Harvard and who was very articulate but not at all arrogant. We also had the benefit of Jim Asperger as a surprise witness.

We Wanted the Jury to Hear the Real Story

Listening to the government's twisted version, you would think that Broadcom was a criminal enterprise instead of a great American success story. We had to overcome that. I always believed that our defense needed to go farther than just raising a reasonable doubt as to whether I was guilty. I believed we had to prove that I was innocent, even though that is technically not required by law.

Our defense rested on five major themes. First, the guidelines governing the accounting for employee stock options were not fixed rules but principles subject to interpretation. Second, the $2.2 billion of noncash charges that we did not originally take (in accordance with the current interpretation of APB25), were not material to investors. Third, because I was not a professional accountant, I consulted regularly with accounting experts inside and outside Broadcom when I was unsure of a proper accounting treatment (including that for stock options). Fourth, I always acted in what I believed to be the best interests of the shareholders and employees of Broadcom. Fifth, that over two hundred other companies, including many that were well known, had made similar interpretations of the APB Opinion 25 that were only later considered incorrect. Many of these companies also restated their financials in response to the changes in interpretation.

Because of all the froth the government stirred up, we had to defuse a number of secondary issues as well—for example, my refusal of an interview with so-called independent lawyers in 2006, on the advice of counsel. And to hear the government, you would have thought that Broadcom's sole function from 1998 to 2003 was to grant employee options—and to backdate them at that! They completely ignored the part where we grew the company to a multi-billion dollar revenue level in that time—in spite of the horrendous 2000–2001 crash in the technology sector.

We wanted to make sure we clearly articulated our five major themes and help the jurors understand the context: how Broadcom had thrived and created thousands of jobs worldwide, including over two thousand in Orange County—within a few miles of th courthouse. At the time of the trial, Broadcom was a major player ii the technology sector, and it still is today.

First Defense Witness—John Riley

Our first witness, John Riley, was an accounting expert who ha passed his CPA exam in 1979; since then, he spent many years i public accounting. For eleven years, he worked as an accountant fo the SEC, eventually rising to the position of deputy chief accountan its number-two accounting position. More recently, he had been senior executive at Navigant Consulting, a Boston-based firm tha advised clients on a wide range of accounting issues.

Navigant's advisory work included stock option accounting issue similar to Broadcom's. Navigant had been senior advisors in ove sixty such cases—and Mr. Riley himself in at least twenty-seven.

I've noted that the accounting guidelines regarding stock option were vague and subject to interpretation. On September 19, 200 (ironically the very day of my forced retirement from Broadcom the SEC's Office of the Chief Accountant (OCA) published a length letter providing, for the first time, guidelines for interpreting th stock option accounting principles. I had been familiar with that let ter in 2006, but from Mr. Riley's testimony in 2009, I learned tha much of it had been based on a letter he himself had written to th OCA. This guy knew his stuff. Rich showed the letter to Mr. Riley an asked him to describe what it was.

> John Riley: It's a letter written by the then chief accountant, Con rad Hewitt, regarding the – providing some guidance into th stock option issues.

> Rich Marmaro: So let's first talk about whether or not this i somewhat extraordinary for the office of the chief accountant t write a letter like this in the middle of this kind of an issue. Is it?

A: I have never seen anything like this before.

Q: So that would make it highly unusual.

A: Yes.

ater Rich asked Mr. Riley about some of the differences between ow APB Opinion 25 was interpreted pre-2006 vs. how it was now eing interpreted and how this could have led to so many restate- ents.

Rich Marmaro: That includes a belief that Opinion 25 afforded flexibility to select grant dates with some degree of hindsight or within a certain period of time?

John Riley: Yes.

Q: And that's based, in part, on your personal knowledge from the investigations and in part on your study?

A: Yes, that's correct.

Q: As-of dating was used as being felt to be sufficient to establish measurement dates?

A: Yes.

Q: I want to drill down a little bit more on the newfound rigor in applying Opinion 25. What did you mean by that?

A: Well, I believe that in connection with the investigations or re- views, whatever we want to call them, that took place in the 2006, 2007 time frame, I think people took, investigators and auditors, both took a very conservative position with respect to the appli- cation of APB 25 in determining whether adjustments to meas- urement dates were required.

Q: I want to ask you whether in taking that conservative position, in your opinion did that result in higher amounts of restatements at these various companies in terms of the dollar amount of the noncash expenses restated?

A: Well, I believe that had there not been a conservative positio
taken in many of these matters, there may very well not hav
been any restatement at all.

Q: The fact that there were large numbers in some of these re
statements, including Broadcom, of 2.2 billion in noncash e:
penses, did that in any way affect any of these companies' cas
positions or cash flows?

A: No.

Q: Did that in any way affect any of these companies' core bus
ness?

A: No.

Q: In fact, the companies that we have reviewed – Bed, Bath an
Beyond, Cheesecake Factory, Barnes & Noble, Microsoft – ar
companies that are still in business and quite solvent?

A: As far as I know, yes, they are.

With Rich's skillful questioning and Mr. Riley's considered an
plainspoken answers, the jury was educated on the complexitie
of accounting for stock options. They were also made aware of th
other 220 United States companies who had publicly disclose
options accounting issues. These included such well-known, house
hold names as Apple, Microsoft, and Barnes & Noble.

Companies Announcing Stock Option Investigations and Restatements

99 Cents Only Store
ACI WORLDWIDE, INC.
Actel Corporation
Active Power
Activision
Adobe Systems, Inc
AES Corp
Affiliated Computer Services (ACS)
Affymetrix
Agile Software
Alkermes
Altera
American Italian Pasta Co
American Technology Corp.
American Tower
Amkor Technology
Aon Corporation
Apollo Group
Apple Inc.
Applied Micro Circuits
Applied Signal Technology
Arbinet-thexchange, Inc.
Aspen Technology
Asyst Technologies
Atmel
Autodesk
Avanir Pharmaceuticals
Back Yard Burgers, Inc.
BakBone Software
BEA Systems
Bebe Stores, Inc.
Bed, Bath & Beyond
Bell Microproducts, Inc.
Biomet
Black Box
Blue Coat Systems
Borland Software Corp.
Broadcom
Brocade Communications Systems
Brooks Automation
CA Inc.
Cablevision (CSC Holdings Inc)
CEC Entertainment
Central European Media Ltd.
Ceradyne
Children's Place
Chordiant Software
Cirrus Logic
Citrix Systems

Clorox
CNET Networks
Cognos Inc
Coherent, Inc.
Columbia Laboratories Inc
Computer Sciences
Conlilian Corp
Corinthian Colleges
Costco Wholesale
Crown Castle International
Cyberonics
Cymer Inc
Cytyc Corp
Dean Foods
DesCartes Systems Group Inc
Digital River
Ditech Networks
Dot Hill Systems
Dycom
Eclipsys Corp
EDCI Holdings, Inc.
EGL Inc
Electronic Clearing House
Electronics for Imaging, Inc.
Embarcadero Technologies
Emcore
Epix Pharmaceuticals
Eplus
Equinix
Extreme Networks
F5 Networks
Family Dollar Stores
Finisar Corp
First American
FLIR Systems
Forrester Research
Fossil, Inc.
Foundry Networks
Fuel Systems Solutions
Gap
Genesee & Wyoming
Gensym Corporation
Getty Images
Greater Bay Bancorp
GSI Group Inc
Hain Celestial Group Inc
Hansen Natural
HCC Insurance Holdings
Home Depot
iBasis

Insight Enterprises
Insituform Technologies Inc
Integrated Silicon Solutions
Internap Network
Interpublic Group of Companies
Interwoven
J2 Global
Jabil Circuit
Juniper Networks
Jupiter Media
Kangaroo Media
KB Home
Key Energy Services
King Pharmaceuticals, Inc.
KLA-Tencor
Knobias Inc.
Kopin Corporation
KOS Pharmaceuticals
Kratos Defense & Security Solutions, Inc.
KV Pharmaceutical
L-3 Communications Holdings
Landry's Restaurants
Macrovision
Management Network Group
Marvell Technology Group
Mattel
Maxim Integrated Products
McAfee Inc.
Meade Instruments
Medarex
Mercury Interactive
Michaels Stores
Micrel
Microlslet Inc.
Microsoft
Microtune
Mills Corp.
Mips Technologies
Mobility Electronics
Moldflow Corporation
Molex
Monster Worldwide
MRV COMMUNICATIONS INC
msystems
Nabi Biopharmaceuticals
Nabors Industries
Newpark Resources
Novell
Nvidia
Nyfix

OI Corp
Omnicell Inc.
Openwave Systems
Orbital Sciences Corporation
PacificNet
Parametric Technology Corp.
Pediatrix Medical Group, Inc.
Peet's Coffee & Tea, Inc.
PMC-Sierra
Power Integrations
Progress Software
Quest Software
QuickLogic
Radio One
Rambus
ReGen Biologics
Research in Motion, Ltd.
Restoration Hardware
Sanmina-SCI
Sapient
SBA Communications Corporation
ScanSource Inc.
Selectica
Semtech
Sepracor
Sharper Image
Shaw Group
Sigma Designs
Silicon Image
Silicon Storage Technology
Skins Inc
Sonic Solutions
Sonus Networks
Sotheby's
SPSS Inc.
Staples Inc.
Sunrise Senior Living
Sunrise Telecom
Sun-Times Media
Superior Industries
Sycamore Networks
Symbol Technologies Inc.
Synopsys Inc
Sysview Technology Inc
Take-Two Interactive Software
TeleTech
Tesco Corp.
Tetra Tech Inc.
The Cheesecake Factory
Third Wave Technologies

Thomas Group Inc
THQ
Trident Microsystems
Turbochef
Tyco International
UnitedHealth
UTStarcom Inc.
Valeant Pharmaceuticals
VeriSign
ViaSat
Vitesse Semiconductor
Western Digital
Wet Seal
Wind River Systems
Witness Systems
World Air Holdings
Xilinx
XM Satellite Radio
Zarlink Semiconductor
Zoran

At the conclusion of his direct, Rich began:

Rich Marmaro: Just a couple of final questions, Mr. Riley. In your opinion was Opinion 25 simple?

John Riley: No, it was not.

Q: Was it straightforward?

A: No.

Q: Was it easy to apply?

A: No.

Q: Was it, in fact, widely misapplied by some of the leading companies in America during the period 1998 to 2006?

A: Yes, it was.

Q: Mr. Riley, based on your years at the SEC, based on your consulting work, based on all of the reviews of the public disclosures of companies that you did not consult with, please tell the ladies and gentlemen of the jury what your opinion is of what happened here with regard to Opinion 25 and its application?

A: Again, my opinion is that companies developed broad-based stock option granting programs as part of their compensation program with their employees. There was no guidance in APB 25 as to how to specifically how to apply that standard to a broad-based option granting program and diversity in practice developed.

People believed that they had some flexibility so that administrative processes wouldn't lead to an accounting charge. So, for example, if – I think there was a common belief that if an option committee or a compensation committee or a senior executive who had the requisite authority, decided to make a grant and selected a price and had an approximate number of options in mind, that you could carry out an administrative process and that wouldn't effect the original decision.

Likewise, I think that people believed that the use of as-of dating would give you some ability to go back and effect a transaction as of an earlier date, and as long as the dates and the prices matched up, that that was consistent with a fair value approach to granting the options under APB 25.

The government attorney crossing Mr. Riley did his best to dirty up the process by bringing up cases where executives at other companies had been convicted on some sort of backdating charge. This provoked Judge Carney to instruct the jury that this was not evidence that *I* should be found guilty. (To be fair, the judge also instructed them that just because many other companies had followed accounting practices similar to Broadcom's, it did not prove that I was not guilty.)

The government witness most similar to Mr. Riley in expertise was Bruce Stump, the former E&Y audit partner, but that was the only

imilarity. Mr. Riley was direct and articulate and provided a broad
erspective of accounting practices at American companies, dozens
f which he had worked with personally.

y contrast, Mr. Stump was evasive, inarticulate, and focused solely
n Broadcom and its alleged misdeeds. It should be noted that E&Y
ad also been charged in plaintiffs' lawsuits against Broadcom and
ad to have a major concern that they could be "the next Arthur
ndersen." It is also important to note that after Broadcom com-
leted their restatement in 2007, they had fired E&Y as their audi-
ors and filed an arbitration brief against them. This all served to
ut Mr. Stump in a very difficult position. If he had acknowledged
hat his interpretation of the accounting guidelines was consistent
with Broadcom's over the 1998–2003 time period, he would put his
irm at great risk.

felt very positive after the Riley testimony. I felt that he had pro-
ided a good education for the jury and had thoroughly supported
he defense position, even though he had no motive to do so. He had
he proper gravitas and not a hint of arrogance. In the battle of the
ccountants, I scored the defense as a decisive winner. I felt that our
irst theme, that the accounting guidelines were subject to interpre-
ation, had been proven.

econd Defense Witness—John Peavy

Ve called John Peavy as a percipient witness because he had been
n owner of Broadcom stock—in fact, a lot of it. The defense paid
is travel expenses from Texas, but he received no compensation.

Ir. Peavy's background, too, was very impressive. He provided a
are combination of impeccable academic credentials and demon-
trated success in the real world of investing. His education included
n MBA from Wharton and a PhD from University of Texas. He was
 Chartered Financial Analyst (CFA). This is to a financial expert as
 CPA is to an accounting expert. He had been a finance professor at

several universities, including Southern Methodist University an
the University of Virginia.

At the time of the trial, he was running an investment firm he ha
founded, managing over $500 million for large institutions. Prior t
that, he had been the chief investment officer managing over $8
billion (with a "b") in retirement funds for Texas teachers and othe
state employees. While at Texas Teachers, Mr. Peavy's fund bega
investing in Broadcom. At its peak in 2002, it owned over 1,000,00
shares.

I don't recall ever having dealt with John Peavy during my year
as a CFO. I do recall having dealt with a number of very smart an
sophisticated investors whose investment outlook was very simila
to Mr. Peavy's. My point is that although he may have had a stronge
academic background and have been more articulate than most, hi
views were reflective of a large proportion of institutional investor

He argued very persuasively that GAAP earnings were far les
important to investors than cash flow. In other words, the $2.
billion of noncash charges included in the Broadcom restatemen
were of no significance to an institutional investor. He was also ver
helpful in educating the jury about the differences between GAA
financials and so-called pro forma, or non-GAAP, financials. The lat
ter show what the company's operating results would be withou
noncash charges and without unusual one-time charges or credit
The latter more closely tracks the real cash flow of the company an
therefore, according to Mr. Peavy, is a more important measure fo
the serious investor.

When Rich asked him if the GAAP bottom line had any effect o
whether Texas Teachers would buy, sell or hold Broadcom stock, M
Peavy responded:

> Well, no, not the bottom line GAAP, because that's an accountin
> historical number. I will certainly say that we looked at that a
> a starting point to come up with our cash flow. But as far as us
> ing the so-called, as you called it, the bottom line number, the ne
> income or net loss number that's reported by GAAP, particularl

when you have a lot of noncash items, as you do in the case of Broadcom, that number becomes almost meaningless in my ability to value the future prospects of the company and, thus, assign a value on the company.

Later in his direct examination, Rich probed directly on the point of whether in-the-money options would have any impact on his valuation analysis, Mr. Peavy said:

No. Because the thing that we're looking at is the information is the two key things: what are the numbers of shares that are out there under option and the exercise price on them. Whether they were granted in-the-money, out-of-the-money, on-the-money is totally meaningless to the evaluation to future cash flow.

Finally, Rich asked Mr. Peavy how his analysis of a company would be affected if the company was found to have misstated the accounting for its employee stock options. Mr. Peavy replied:

We saw there's dozens of companies that had options issues. None of those issues, even though they had to go back and restate them, none of them, in my opinion, it certainly didn't affect the way I value a stock. It was immaterial information that, yes, it had to be restated. But did it have any effect on my valuation of the company? The answer is absolutely no.

The government attorney who cross-examined Mr. Peavy was totally out of his element. He tried to dumb down the financial analysis in a way that showed he did not begin to understand it. When the government attorney did not like Mr. Peavy's answers about the irrelevance of noncash charges, he tried to make a distinction between "short-term investors" and "long-term investors." Mr. Peavy calmly responded that people who made only short-term stock trades were speculators, not investors.

Although Mr. Peavy was only on the stand for part of a day, I believe he convincingly demonstrated the truth of our second theme: noncash charges are not material to investors' decisions about whether to invest in a particular stock. Then there was the huge intangible of credibility. Jurors can't be expected to internalize all of the arguments propounded in an eight-week trial. They rely heavily on their intuition of the credibility of witnesses. Here we had an almost laughable comparison. Take John Peavy, PhD economist, manager of billions of dollars of retirement funds, respected college professor, author of several books and dozens of articles, and compare him with Paul Amlong, a forty-something day-trader waiting for "Gary" to tell him where to invest about $30,000 of his parents' money.

I felt good about our defense after the Riley testimony and even better after Peavy. These men of class clearly and convincingly underscored two of our critical defense themes.

Third Defense Witness—David Dull

By the time David took the stand, we had been through the drama of the witness immunity grants, the infamous Stolper call to David's attorneys, and the evidentiary hearing that exposed government dirty tricks.

David was a partner at Irell & Manella and Broadcom's principal outside attorney on all business transactions issues. Shortly before the IPO, he left a very lucrative career with the law firm to join Broadcom as our own first general counsel.

My first interactions with David happened immediately upon me joining Broadcom in 1997. David was extremely well qualified. He held undergraduate and law degrees from Yale and had even done post-graduate work at Oxford University in England. He had spent virtually his entire pre-Broadcom career with Irell, spanning some seventeen years. He had a deep understanding of the law and applied it intelligently to business. We shared a great mutual respect and worked very closely together, particularly in the early years. While Broadcom was rocketing to a billion-dollar annual revenue level in record time, David and I scrambled as best we could to help enable the growth and to keep the administrative processes in sync with it.

n direct examination, Rich skillfully walked David back through
he history of Broadcom. I could sense the jury connecting with this
.arrative. The piecemeal Broadcom history that the government
ttempted to orchestrate with their witnesses would have left the
mpression that Broadcom was a losing enterprise, but the com-
any's actual continued growth and market presence put the lie to
hat. David described a company with a lot of challenges but with a
trong technology base and a devoted employee base, starting at the
op. It has consistently been a top performer in its industry.

)avid was also able to put into context the informality with which
3roadcom "meetings" were conducted. This was particularly impor-
ant as it related to meetings of the stock option committee that the
overnment tried to portray as a sham and part of a "cover story."

Rich Marmaro: Why don't you tell the ladies and gentlemen what
"meeting" is, according to the Broadcom type of meeting?

David Dull: We haven't really talked about this, but it probably
isn't a surprise, based on everything I have said so far. The way
the company was managed in those days was a very informal
management environment and management style. And I inherited that when I came to the company. As a lawyer, I had an interest in a certain level of order and processes for doing things and
so forth. It was quite an adjustment for me, frankly, to be in such
an informal environment.

But Broadcom was definitely a company where we did things the
way that Nick and Henry and the Board wanted them to be done,
not the way the lawyers might have liked. And so I adjusted to
what was quite an informal decision-making process.

What I mean by that is, that we didn't have, for example, formal
noticed meetings of the option committee. The decisions on options, to my knowledge, were made by Nick and Henry, meeting
on a very informal basis, and the informality didn't have to mean
they would be together sitting in the same room. It would be sufficient that they could talk in the hall or on the telephone.

In addition to – obviously they were spending a lot of time with eac other in those days, so I do believe that many of the grants were ar proved where they were physically together, but there were othe situations where it would have been easy for them to decide on grant over the telephone, or even just talking in the hall.

David was also able to talk from first hand knowledge about th continual improvements that he and I in particular were strivin to make. In response to a question from Rich about our efforts t improve the administrative processes, David responded:

> As the company grew, we found the need to put more processe in place. When the company was 150, or even 300, employees i was very easy for managers to talk to each other, make decision on the fly, and go implement them. And you are only talking abou a handful of people being involved in the whole process. That wa easy to do on a very informal basis.

> As the company grew, it became more important to put in plac more elaborate processes which would be more comparable t the processes that existed in larger public companies.

> In addition, the finance group, I think in particular, and the lega group, to some extent, also saw and took opportunities to put i place better controls and processes where – I wouldn't say the were deficiencies before, but there were areas that had not bee addressed before.

David was there at the time of many of the e-mails the governmen had tried to use against Broadcom executives. Because his immu nity meant he didn't have to kiss up to them, he was able to put ther in context.

One particularly moving moment was when Rich walked Davi through a lengthy e-mail by Nick about Broadcom's hard-won cour room victory in an intellectual property suit in 2001 that had bee brought by Intel. We felt it was an example that would help the jur to understand Nick as a leader and not as the shady character th government portrayed him to be.

y 2000, Broadcom was growing quickly and taking market share
om large players, including Intel. We became a frequent target of
itellectual property (IP) litigation, which is standard procedure in
ie tech industry. Companies spend large sums of money and man-
ower developing IP and acquiring patents on it. Much of this is for
ie legitimate purpose of assuring that those who create IP can ben-
fit from it. Much IP litigation, though, is frankly used for harass-
ient, particularly against early-stage companies, who with highly
iotivated and intensely focused engineers can often out-innovate
lder, slower organizations. Therefore, the older, slower guys often
se the legal system to try to regain their losses of market share.

itel had filed a cease-and-desist suit against Broadcom in 2000,
aiming infringement on three Intel patents. Had Intel prevailed,
iey would have been able to shut down much of Broadcom's busi-
ess. As often in litigation like this, a settlement was attempted
'here Broadcom would pay a large sum and Intel would allow it a
mited use of "their" technology. As negotiations continued, Intel
radually chipped away at the extent of the use they would allow.
ventually, the limits became so narrow and the demanded sum so
utrageous that Broadcom rejected the offer and risked a trial. Had
ie jury decided against Broadcom, the consequences to the com-
any could have been devastating—possibly even fatal.

o everyone's relief (except Intel's), the jury found in favor of Broad-
om. Nick immediately e-mailed Broadcom employees, commend-
ig everyone involved for their perseverance in the face of possible
itastrophe. I was moved almost to tears as Rich had David read it
loud on the stand. This was the leader we had all followed to build
 great company—the opposite of the government's portrait of him
s a drug-addled criminal out to deceive investors and anyone else.
could sense the jurors' reactions as they saw clear evidence of the
erson Nick really was.

ny good trial lawyer will acknowledge that, while facts are the most
nportant thing in a case, often the most effective way to introduce
iem and to cement impressions is through a little drama. Rich was
ertainly up to that task. To conclude David's direct, Rich walked

him through the report of the Stolper-Asperger phone convers.
tion. The transcript records David's reaction to it: "Initially surpris
shock, fear, and then—excuse me. A profound disappointment as
lawyer that such a thing would be happening." What the transcri
did not show was the choked-back sob before the "excuse me." Th
entire courtroom sat in stunned silence. Had someone asked me 1
speak at that moment, I would have been too choked up to do so.

The government cross on David was pretty weak. To be fair, th
judge had ruled their lead prosecutor out of a speaking role, bt
more important, truth telling is much easier than lying. A witnes
allowed to speak from direct recall is much more credible than or
who is trying to remember what he or she was supposed to say 1
avoid the ire of prosecutors. David was obviously very smart an
low-key. He projected the avuncular air of a kindly college profe
sor. It would be hard for a juror to imagine him as part of a crimin
conspiracy, as the government had charged.

We now had had one of our two key witnesses testify. I felt that Da
id's testimony had resonated very positively with the jury. Amor
other points, he stood up strongly for me, establishing that I had n
hesitated to contact experts inside and outside the company whei
ever I was unsure of the proper accounting or legal answer to a
issue.

I would say that the scope of subjects covered in David's testimor
was most similar to Carol Prado's, but the contrast between the wi
nesses was striking. David was very relaxed and confident, whil
Carol was nervous, constantly looking toward the prosecutors du
ing her cross-examination in an apparent effort to see if she wa
testifying according to script. David appeared spontaneous, whil
Carol seemed rehearsed.

Fourth Defense Witness—Jim Asperger

Judge Carney had been so visibly shaken by the Stolper phone ca
incident that he agreed to allow Jim Asperger, chief defense cou[n]

sel for David Dull, to appear as a witness and to be subject to both direct and cross-examinations. He repeated his recollection of the phone call in the presence of the jury.

I don't know if there is any precedent for a witness's attorney to take the stand, but from my read, it had a very sobering impact on the jury. They were exposed to the government's dirty tricks by someone whose client was an intended victim. By this time, I was a little dazed. I had very experienced attorneys telling me that they had never seen anything like this. They had never seen witness immunity granted, they had never seen a prosecutor cross-examined, and they had never seen a defense attorney take the witness stand. At each one of these steps, I could see the jurors shaking their heads in disbelief. I still refused to allow myself to get too encouraged.

Fifth Defense Witness—Steven Molo

Steven Molo, admitted to the bar in 1982, was an expert in white-collar criminal and civil matters. My defense team retained him for his expert opinions on internal corporate investigations and his experience in advising clients of their rights in them. This was important, because the government tried to make a big deal out of my refusal to talk to the purportedly "independent" Kaye Scholer attorneys.

Mr. Molo had very strong credentials. He had been a professor at Northwestern University Law School, had been a government prosecutor, and had many years of experience as a defense attorney. When Rich asked him if he had written a book on corporate internal investigations, Mr. Molo, not prone to excess modesty, replied, "I wrote what I think most people would consider to be the definitive treatise on this topic of corporate internal investigation."

The Molo testimony, though often verbose, provided a pretty good overview of the internal company investigation process. He referred to the government standards for measuring the level of cooperation from targeted companies, including their propensity to disclose large volumes of privileged material. In this environment, he opined it is often in the client's best interest not to talk to the investigators. A client has to anticipate that anything said to the investigators can and will be turned over to the government prosecutors.

Mr. Molo countered effectively the government attorney's characterization of my refusal to talk to the investigators as an admission of guilt. He stood up strongly for the client's wisdom in following attorney recommendations, as I had.

On re-direct, Rich reminded the court that another person at Broadcom had refused to talk to Kaye Scholer: Nancy Tullos. However, the advice had come not from her own attorneys but from the government prosecutors. Rich produced the letter from the USAO to Nancy's attorneys requesting that she "decline the invitation to speak with your investigators." When asked whether he had ever encountered such a request, Mr. Molo replied that he couldn't ever "recall a circumstance, either reading about it or, for that matter, in any case that I have been involved in, where a prosecutor has sought to effectively impede or obstruct the company's internal investigation."

The Molo testimony was mercifully short. Once again, I felt the defense had presented a strong witness. We were now partway through the fifth day of the defense, and I felt we had effectively countered most of the seventeen days of prosecution testimony.

Sixth Defense Witness—Henry Samueli

This was a big day in the courtroom. Henry is very high profile in his own understated way, if not as colorful as Nick. First, he was a billionaire. Second, he was a renowned philanthropist who had donated tens of millions of dollars to support the schools of engineering at UCLA and at UC Irvine (both bear his name). He had funded the construction of a Jewish temple in the Irvine area. And in his spare time, he was the owner of the Anaheim Ducks professional hockey team.

ecause of his notoriety, the courtroom was packed with spectators
nd media. In fact, any time the case was written up in the media,
.e story always featured the two billionaire founders of Broadcom.
ven though I was the one on trial, often I was not mentioned at all.
hat was fine with me.

s the jury listened to Henry tell his classic rags-to-riches tale, they
ere enthralled. This man epitomized the American dream.

nowing the government would do their best to impeach his cred-
ility by focusing on Henry's guilty plea for rendering his so-called
lse statement to the SEC, Rich had Henry address it right out of
e box. He put the plea in context. He showed graphically on the
rge screen Henry's statement from the SEC testimony that he had
o involvement in option granting decisions for corporate officers.
elow, about seventeen lines later, was his correction of it.

enry's testimony on the plea agreement began with Rich asking
m the question:

Rich Marmaro: And what did you plead guilty to?

Henry Samueli: I pled guilty to making one false statement to the
Securities and Exchange Commission.

Q: Do you remember whether that statement involved whether
or not you were involved in granting options to officers of the
company, which was the job of the compensation committee, and
that you indicated that you were not so involved?

A: Yes. I recall the question was about my involvement in the
granting process of options to Section 16 officers, who are the
highest executives of the company, and, as you point out, that is
the purview of the compensation committee.

And I replied that I wasn't involved in the granting process, which
was not truthful because, in fact, I was involved in making recommendations to the compensation committee.

But ironically, the thing that bothers me most about that, is th
there is nothing wrong with being involved in the process of ma
ing grants to Section 16 officers. I'm perfectly allowed to ma
recommendations.

So why I would say I wasn't involved just escapes me.

Q: Have you searched your mind about why that answer came
your head at that time?

A: I thought long and hard about it because that is not my sty
I would never do something intentionally wrong under norm
conditions. So my gut feel is, because I was asked about a compe
sation committee issue, my instant reaction was to say no, I was
involved because I wasn't on the compensation committee.

But I apparently didn't think through that question carefully b
cause the question wasn't whether I was on the compensati
committee, it just asked about my involvement in the process
grants to Section 16 officers.

I made that false statement and I accept it, but I bang myself
the head for making such a stupid statement.

Q: In fact, there was a document, wasn't there, which show
your involvement in at least one aspect of the process?

A: Oh, yes. There are many examples of e-mails and discussio
that show my involvement in this Section 16 granting process.

Q: Okay. So I want to ask you about your state of mind at the tin
and what went into your decision as to whether or not to ple
guilty to that single question and answer.

We went over at some length the events of 2007. You have d
scribed those to the ladies and gentlemen quite clearly yesterd

What, if any, impact did the events of 2007, and Mr. Stolper's co
duct towards you at that time, what, if any, impact did that ha

on your state of mind in terms of wanting to get all of this behind you?

A: It had a significant impact on my state of mind.

I was quite afraid at the time because there was a lot of pressure being put on me. The company was doing an internal investigation which I cooperated willingfully and gladly with.

The SEC had done this independent investigation, called me in to testify, and I gladly went in to testify with them.

And I had, independently, the U.S. Attorney's Office after me and trying to pressure me into coming in and testifying to them – or interviewing with them with no pre-conditions whatsoever.

So I felt enormous pressure, and I was very worried, very worried at the time.

Q: Would you share with us a little bit more about what you were worried about at the time, and what you thought could happen to you if – just – if you didn't give in at that time and plead guilty and if you decided to try to fight the government?

What were you worried about?

A: Well, prior to me actually agreeing to the plea agreement, an indictment was, in fact, filed against Dr. Nicholas and Mr. Ruehle. And it was very public, made the headlines, massive indictment. And I saw that indictment. It was in the public domain. And that indictment named me personally as an unindicted coconspirator, HS.

And it was my understanding that coconspirators are not supposed to be named in an indictment, but my initials were clearly there, it was obvious it was referring to me, dozens and dozens of times in that indictment.

So I could clearly see hanging over my head the pressure of an indictment against me because I was even given the impression that I was going to be indicted.

And I just couldn't see myself putting my family through that because I'm a very visible member of the Orange County community, the national community, and while, in this courtroom, you're innocent until proven guilty, in the press, you are guilty until proven innocent. And I could see that headline there, "Samuel faces 300 years in prison if convicted." I just couldn't put my family through that.

So, based on that alternative, I was comfortable pleading guilty to a single false statement with the assurance of a probationary sentence in that plea agreement. That was the agreement we came to.

Q: Were you afraid that if you fought the government, and for some reason things didn't go well, that you could face years and years in prison away from your family?

A: Yes. Particularly, over 300 years in prison, is what I saw that could face there. And that was truly frightening.

Q: Did you have a young family at the time?

A: I have three daughters, yes.

Q: You decided to accept the government's offer to resolve your case by that one single question and answer, with the government agreement for probation, you felt that was a rational business decision at the time?

A: It wasn't a business decision. It was a personal decision, taking into consideration what I would have had to put my family through in the alternative. And, yes, I made that very difficult decision of picking the lesser of two evils.

Q: Do you remember how many questions you were asked at the SEC testimony for two days?

A: Hundreds and hundreds of questions, if not over a thousand questions. It was a lot.

Q: If I represented to you that the SEC asked you 1,360 questions over those two days, would that sound about right?

A: That certainly wouldn't surprise me.

Q: Were you shown literally tens of pages, if not hundreds of pages, of exhibits?

A: Hundreds of pages of exhibits is my recollection.

Q: And you pleaded guilty to one question and one answer about the compensation committee?

A: That is correct.

Q: Were you afraid, if you didn't go for the government's deal, they would throw the book at you?

A: I was convinced of that.

n a half day of direct testimony, Henry helped the jurors not only nderstand the Broadcom story; he allowed them to feel it. Here vas the technology guru whose passions were academia, interact- 1g with brilliant and motivated students, and the challenges of eveloping cutting-edge technologies. He was almost an accidental illionaire.

[e also helped negate the impression of me as a devious person and abitual liar that the government worked so hard to create. Obvi- usly, it was important to establish my credibility with the jury. I 1ink Rich had already done a great job by dissecting the govern- 1ent witnesses' inconsistencies. Now there was an opportunity to licit firsthand testimony from a senior Broadcom executive with vhom I had worked closely for many years.

n a typical interchange, Rich would ask, "Did you observe how peo- le related to him? Did you observe, for example, whether—well, vhat did you observe about how your colleagues related to Bill?"

Henry answered, "I believe my colleagues related very much lik
I related. They viewed him as a man of high integrity. A man the
could trust. Someone they confided in. We're very open and con
municated with him very openly. I think it was a pretty univers
feeling around the company about Bill."

In a few hours, he was able to undo Nancy Tullos's convoluted st
ries about the sham options committee meetings and how I mac
after-the-fact option pricing decisions. Henry said, "She testifie
that the option committee...was not meeting. That it was really a fi
tion; is that true? I'm actually amazed that Nancy said that. Becaus
we worked very closely together. She knew what was going on i
the company at that time and, quite frankly, the Nancy Tullos I kne
back then would not have said that."

The functioning of the stock options committee was a pivot
point for the prosecution. In Andrew Stolper's opening statemer
he said:

> In a nutshell, those two gentlemen at the top, Henry Samueli an
> Henry Nicholas, would have option committee meetings. They'
> meet on Friday. And, according to the cover story, they would loo
> at the stock, and they would say to themselves, is the stock goir
> to go up, or is the stock going to go down.

> They'd look into their crystal balls, and if they believed the stoc
> was going to go up, they would grant stock options. And if the
> believed the stock was going to go down, they would wait.

> That was the cover story that these two folks were meeting in re
> time, having meetings in real time, and making decisions abou
> whether the stock is going to go up, whether the stock is going t
> go down, and then they would decide grant or not grant.

You will recall that when Nancy Tullos testified, she swore that sh
knew that the options committee never actually met, thus reinfor
ing Mr. Stolper's so-called "cover story." You may also recall that
was on that point that Rich pointed out during her cross-exam
nation that she had made a very different comment when she wa

nterviewed by the SEC. That was the comment that prompted her o begrudgingly admit that she had lied to the SEC.

'he prosecutors theory, as supported by their friendly witness, Nancy Tullos, was totally debunked by Henry, the person who was ctually there as a member of the options committee. In response to question by Rich on his direct examination, Henry described the nformal and sometimes chaotic option granting process:

Well, we knew that we were constantly hiring people, so that wasn't a surprise that week-to-week we would be hiring people. So really the primary decision we would make post-IPO, it was different pre-IPO versus post-IPO, the post-IPO we would gather up the employees who started up for the week, and we may not even know their names, it might be that we just assume that we knew ten people joined this week, and we'd have to grant them shares on a Friday, for example. So we would either bump into each other in the hall or at the end of some other meeting we had, we'd say, *do we want to grant these employees their options this week or maybe do we want to wait till next week?* So it would just be a casual conversation that I would have among the ten times a day that I would run into Nick.

So I would just catch as catch can, so to speak, and I'd either be in another meeting with him on a business topic, and at the end of the meeting, the topic might come up, *Nick, do we want to grant this week?* Or I might just run into his office, or he might be in my office for some reason. So it's just a casual conversation much like we did for the seven years prior to the IPO.

Later, Rich asked Henry to describe how their granting decisions were made. Henry responded:

Well, typically Nick would carry the ball on that and communicate that most likely to Bill, since Bill's office was right next door to Nick, and Bill reported to Nick, so he had the most direct communication with Bill. So the typical process would be we would decide that we're going to make a grant this week, and then Nick would then go off and inform Bill somehow, I don't know exactly

how, and then Bill would then start the process of putting every
thing in place, getting the paperwork done, getting the data er
tered into the computer systems and so forth. He would assig
those tasks to other people. There's a lot that happens post th
granting decision by Nick and I. We view that as kind of the star
of the process and that gets the ball in motion. And typically the
shareholder services would have to generate paperwork for th
employees on giving them their actual grants. They would hav
to communicate that to the various finance and HR people. S
there's a lot going on below the executive level to implement th
grants.

Henry detailed the operations of the options committee and contex
tualized the granting of stock options as a very small part of Broac
com's activities. He was able to explain how Broadcom's equity
based compensation packages worked as employee incentives.
they worked hard, investors could favor them with a better stoc
value, which would also benefit stockholders. It is common know
edge that employee ownership interest in a business can improv
productivity, because there is no incentive to improve a compan
that pays a static salary whether it does well or not.

Rich switched his focus to government leaks to the press about Her
ry's level of "cooperation," copies of government letters to Broac
com directors implying that Henry should be fired, and requests fo
Henry to submit to an unlimited number of interviews with goverr
ment prosecutors.

On the large screen, Rich dramatically displayed a side-by-side com
parison of the government letter to the Broadcom directors and a
article that had appeared in the *LA Times* shortly thereafter. Th
wording was so consistent that it was painfully obvious that the *Time*
article information had to have come directly from the government.

Rich asked, "How did all that make you feel about the good faith c
the federal government in how it was conducting its investigatio
of you?"

In one of the more memorable statements of the trial, Henry responded, "I felt like I was being strong-armed by my own government. I felt unbelievably depressed about it, because I had faith in the criminal justice system, faith that people do things the right way. I literally felt like I was dealing with the Mafia."

Now it was time for Henry's cross. In my trial notes I expressed my hope that it would go well, since I knew that a skillful cross-examiner can make the most honest person appear guilty. But Henry's narrative was completely believable, because it was all true. It was very helpful to my case. In my notes I wrote, "My heart rate has accelerated for the first time in this trial. This could be the clincher."

The government was clearly outmatched by Henry's intellect, not to mention his intimate familiarity with what went on at Broadcom. Henry calmly and consistently rejected the misleading impressions the government was trying to create for the jury. Out of frustration, the government attorney at one point blustered, "Isn't it true that the one person at Broadcom who could orchestrate the backdating of options and the improper accounting for them is the defendant?"

Henry responded, "I'm not comfortable making a statement like that. It's just not fair to me."

The government attorney compounded his bluster with the outrageous comment, "Well, we're not here to be fair to you, sir. You're here to answer my questions." Rich Marmaro objected that this was argumentative, and the judge sustained his objection, ordering the comment to be stricken from the record.

The re-direct closed as Rich asked Henry: "Did you ever intend to commit any crime at Broadcom?"

Henry replied, "Of course not. I would never commit a crime against a company that I loved so much, the company that I founded; my baby. I felt like that was my family there. The employees were my family. I can't even imagine such a statement."

"Forgive me," said Rich, "if I ask my last question about Bill Ruehle in your examination, but to your observation, what credit do you give Bill Ruehle in terms of the success that Broadcom enjoys today?"

"Bill Ruehle is a good man. He worked very hard to make Broadcom a successful company. I trusted him. I had implicit faith in his integrity, and he was an important part of the success of the company."

Dismissal of the Samueli Guilty Plea

The last few hours of the cross, to the government's dismay, failed to produce much of value to the prosecution.

In fact, as soon as the jury was dismissed that day, Judge Carney asked Henry to step up to the podium, where he made this astounding statement: "I'll just get to the point of it. Dr. Samueli, I'm going to set aside your guilty plea. I'm going to dismiss the information against you. I've looked at the plea agreement. I've listened to your testimony, and you didn't make a false material statement."

Judge Carney then spoke of how disturbed he was by the government's conduct. He also advised us that he would be setting hearings on our Rule 29 motion for dismissal and on the defense's expected motion based on prosecutorial misconduct.

Once again, the contrast between the government's witness and ours was striking. Nancy Tullos' scope of testimony most closely paralleled Henry's. On our side was Henry, cofounder of the company, member of the options committee, pillar of the community, legend in the industry, able to speak his mind without fear of government retribution because of his immunity grant. On the other side was Nancy Tullos, senior HR executive for five years, not a member of the option committee that she claimed never actually met, testifying with the knowledge that only afterward would the government decide whether she would serve prison time or not.

The next evidentiary hearing followed. Nancy's attorney had verbally told some of our defense team about the government pressure on his client, but when he actually took the stand, he waffled. He never came right out and said that the government's behavior troubled him. Nevertheless, he did shed enough light on the process to show how the government's misconduct was obvious. He also provided color on the government's requirement that she plead guilty to a felony charge in order to influence the jury.

Setting Up for the Grand Finale

Judge Carney's body language showed that he was deeply disturbed. At the conclusion of the government's case he had advised the defense to hold off our motions until after the jury deliberated. This was now a Wednesday afternoon. Judge Carney asked both sides to submit their motions to him by noon on Monday and to restrict them to no more than twenty-five pages.

He told us the Rule 29 motion should concentrate solely on criminal intent and that "the rules are not clear. There are standards. There is judgment. And Bill Gates, Steve Jobs are doing this." Also, he said, the independent public accountants pretty clearly had known what Broadcom was doing and that its lawyers were certainly paid enough that they should have known. He questioned whether there was sufficient evidence of criminal intent in light of all these facts. He also referred to the government misconduct, not as hypothetical, but as a fact. He told us that he assumed we would be addressing the cumulative effect of all this."

This was all obviously very positive news to me. Still, I could not afford to let my hopes rise lest they be dashed. Better to keep expectations low and not risk disappointment.

Judge Carney said that the next day, the jury would hear the final defense witness and what he decreed would be the briefest of government rebuttals—limited to one witness. We had a day to debate

183

the Rule 29 and prosecutor misconduct motions and another, if nec essary, to agree on jury instructions. The day after that, both side would begin their closing arguments. This was a major departur from the judge's announcement that he would only entertain th Rule 29 and misconduct motions after the case had gone to the jury

It was pretty hard to dampen enthusiasm at this point, but we dic My trial notes comment at that point read, "Talk about an emotiona moment! Now we have to count the hours until 9:00 a.m. Tuesday.

We continued to prepare for our closing arguments. On Friday morn ing my trial notes read, "Last day of evidence. God willing, mayb last day of trial. Should be no new fireworks today. Media shoul lose interest now that Henry the Star is no longer here."

Seventh Defense Witness—Barbara Luna

As I noted earlier, each side in a criminal case presents a summar witness whose main purpose is to complete the appropriate intro duction of any desired evidence. FBI Special Agent Paul Bonin ha been the government's; the defense called an unassuming-lookin woman named Barbara Luna.

Ms. Luna was a classic example of how appearances can be mislead ing. Rich walked her through her background: she had an under graduate degree in physics from Wellesley College and a master and PhD in applied mathematics from Harvard. She had also picke up a CPA somewhere along the line. Her career included work a an investment banker, a consultant with multiple public accountin firms, a litigation partner in various law firms, and finally, a princi pal in her own litigation advisory firm, where she was in charge o the forensic accounting practice. She also somehow found time t teach at the UCLA graduate business school, at Cal State Northridge and in the Pepperdine MBA program.

By the time her credentials had been laid out, the members of th jury seemed to be paying her the full attention she deserved. Unlik

184

Mr. Bonin, an integral part of the government's case and therefore expected to see everything through a government lens, Ms. Luna was an independent practitioner. She acknowledged, in response to a question from Rich, that her compensation would be the same whether her conclusions supported the defense position or not.

Rich had her address data about movements in Broadcom's stock price around option grant dates and around various announcements in 2006 at the time the internal investigation began. Among other things, the government had tried to build a case that my May 2006 sale of Broadcom stock had been in reaction to bad news I somehow knew was coming and that I was trying to bail out ahead of it. The number of shares I sold then—fifteen thousand—put the lie to that. At the time, I owned over two million vested, in-the-money shares. If I was trying to "bail out," why did I only sell less than 1 percent of my holdings?

The direct examination was concise and, I believe, effective. The cross was relatively ineffective, because it's pretty hard to dispute facts, but the government tried to sway the jury anyway. The defense had stated that in all routine quarterly calls with securities analysts held as each quarter's financial results were released), no one ever asked about noncash stock-based compensation charges. The government countered that analysts would not have been able to ask about charges the company had "concealed" because they would have no way of knowing about them.

Ms. Luna very effectively pointed out how all of the charges were called out in various sections of Broadcom's financial disclosures. By the end of her testimony, I felt the defense team had presented a clear and simple case—the direct opposite of the government's convoluted charges.

Comparing our summary witness, Ms. Luna, to the government's, Mr. Bonin, I would judge it a clear win for Ms. Luna. She appeared objective, knowledgeable, and independent. By contrast, Mr. Bonin had a clear vested interest in the outcome of the case, because he had been an integral part of it for over three years. On summary witnesses, I would say, "Advantage: defense."

Government Rebuttal Witness—Paul Bonin

We know that since the burden of proof in a criminal case is on the government, they get to go first and last. My understanding of the law is that the rebuttal case is not intended as an opportunity to pull out surprises in an attempt to sway the jury with shocking new evidence. A rebuttal is limited to responding to the arguments the defense has presented through its witnesses; Judge Carney made it clear to the government that he would hold them strictly to these guidelines.

The government's only witness was Special Agent Paul Bonin, and his testimony was limited to his claim that he was not involved in the case until after the alleged press leaks about Henry. He acknowledged that he had been copied on e-mails prior to that, but said it was common practice and that he really had had no direct involvement then.

In his cross, Rich displayed no less than eleven instances over a six month period preceding Mr. Bonin's alleged start time on the case that demonstrated that he had been present during interviews of potential witnesses. Mr. Bonin acknowledged that all the statements were accurate and clearly became agitated. As Rich summed up, Mr. Bonin interrupted him belligerently. When Rich calmly tried to get him back to the questions at hand, Mr. Bonin lost it and snapped "I'm not going to create a false impression, because I have seen what you have done with that."

Rich immediately moved to have the comment stricken, saying, "I think that's outrageous, Agent Bonin. We have seen the conduct of the government in the case."

Not backing down an inch, Mr. Bonin began, "I think it's outrageous that you—"

Judge Carney intervened with, "Stop it sir. That's enough." What a display for a jury to witness!

Finally, Rich asked Mr. Bonin whether it was important for him to provide context for the e-mails predating his official start on the case. Mr. Bonin readily agreed that it was, saying "That's why I'm testifying, to make sure that people understand that and I can provide that context." I'm sure Mr. Bonin thought he was making an important point for his credibility. He was, but even more important, he was making a key point for the defense, as Rich pointed out to the jury: e-mails taken out of context can indeed be very misleading. The government's entire case had relied on that.

By the end of Mr. Bonin's very brief rebuttal testimony, I was feeling pretty good. Once again, a government witness had inadvertently helped the defense more than he helped the government. The emotional outburst of the witness—an FBI Special Agent, no less—gave the jurors valuable insight into the bullying mentality of the government in this case.

Time to Wrap It All Up

At the conclusion of the court day, Thursday, December 10, Judge Carney dismissed the jury for a week, after which they would receive instructions and begin to hear closing arguments. He never hinted that the case would be dismissed before they returned; I suspect that he wasn't sure that it would be yet, but his actions clearly showed that he was at least considering dismissal.

One sign of this was in his handling of yet another defense motion for mistrial by Matt Umhofer, our designated technical expert on points of law. In one of the last court sessions of the defense case, Matt once again stepped to the podium. Before he could even open his mouth, Judge Carney remarked, "You're not going to move for mistrial, are you Mr. Umhofer?" Matt sat back down.

Once the jurors were out of the courtroom, Judge Carney reiterated to defense and government that he wanted the Rule 29 and Pros Misconduct briefings by Monday—but by earlier than his original noon deadline. The defense readily agreed, but the governmen objected to simultaneous briefings because that way, they could no counter the defense's arguments. The Court denied their objectio and repeated the request.

The stage was set.

Chapter 12

Free at Last

he weekend was welcome downtime for Julie and me as we left our
range County hotel and returned to our San Diego-area home. Not
o for our Skadden defense team, who were refining the motions
nd working on closing arguments.

pening statements and closing arguments are like the bookends
f a case. In closing, the attorneys for each side recap what they
elieve are the most compelling pieces of evidence supporting their
ase. This is the chance for all the attorneys to be at their dramatic
est. The government will try to portray the defendant as a threat
o society. The defense will try to portray their client as the victim
f a wrongful prosecution. From my "unbiased" position, I would
ave to say the defense had the correct argument in this case. The
efense team had prepared what I believed to be a very credible and
onvincing closing argument based on all the facts of the case. But in
ne end, that package was never unwrapped.

: was a very positive sign for us that the Court wanted the motions
ubmitted prior to even closing arguments, since he had repeatedly
aid he wanted them after the jury had deliberated. Over the week-
nd, we learned that Judge Carney had requested the presence of
ick, Henry, David Dull, and all their respective attorneys for the
notion hearings. It didn't sound like a cast of characters called to
vitness a routine hearing. We all did our best to rein in our opti-
nism, but it really looked like the case might be dismissed.

Vhile the Skadden team worked through the weekend, I took one
f our twins to a holiday party hosted by a company for whom I was
oing advisory work. (Our other twin was sick, so Julie stayed home
vith her.) Most of the party guests had been following the case, and

they all tried to congratulate me. I fended them off, saying that wasn't over yet and that anything could happen. *Don't let your hop* *get inflated,* I kept telling myself.

Prosecutorial Misconduct Motion

Misconduct by prosecutors is not just an idle charge leveled b defense attorneys. We live in a competitive environment. Attorney are always seeking to win for their clients. Plaintiff attorneys striv to win so they can collect large—sometimes outrageously large-contingency fees. Government attorneys are not immune to th sense of competition. Although their ultimate responsibility is search for the truth, it unfortunately sometimes becomes second ary to winning.

Why would prosecutors want so badly to win? The loftiest answer that they are defending the law and protecting innocent people fro predators. That is a good and honorable reason, and I believe that truly is the major motivator. There are, however, other motivatior less honorable. Some may prosecute hard because of political amb tions. A former mayor of New York City and a former governor New York State both captured the public eye with their hard-nose prosecutions.

Financial gain is another strong motivator. By this I don't mea bribes or anything that sordid (though such cases have occasior ally occurred). Most defense attorneys spent early career years prosecutors. It's a great place to learn. A junior government atto ney will get far more trial experience than a junior defense attorne Prosecutors who win a lot of their cases are more likely to come the attention of the high-end defense law firms and land high pa ing gigs in the private sector.

Then there is always the issue of ego. Prosecutors are no differer from anyone who likes to boast about career successes and choose to say little or nothing about their failures. (This one is rather pe

erse, since prosecutors can count the conviction of an innocent
person as a "success.")

The vast majority of criminal and civil cases proceed without any
misconduct on the part of prosecutors. However, Pulitzer Prize-
winning journalist, Maurice Poseley, initiated a study sponsored by
the Northern California Innocence Project and recently published
a comprehensive report of prosecutorial misconduct in California.

Of the thousands of federal and state criminal cases prosecuted in
California from 1997 through 2009, over four thousand cases of
prosecutorial misconduct were claimed. After judicial review, three
thousand claims were rejected outright, 282 reached no decision,
and 707 cases found misconduct. That's an average of about one
misconduct case per week during this period. In 159 cases, the misconduct was found to be so profound that the guilty verdicts were
set aside.

Sadly, less than one percent of the prosecutors who committed misconduct were ever disciplined, and most of those who were received
light punishment such as a "public reprimand." The most serious
discipline recorded during this time was a four-year suspension for
a Santa Clara County prosecutor who had been found guilty of misconduct in multiple cases over a decade.

Our final motion, authored primarily by Matt Umhofer, ran the maximum twenty-five pages Judge Carney had allowed us. There was a
lot of misconduct to document.

Its introduction stated:

> Sadly, in this case, the government has failed to observe its own
> laws and shown utter disregard for its charter, the Constitution,
> through a pattern of misconduct that began early in its investi-
> gation and continued throughout the trial. As a result, William
> J. Ruehle's rights have been trampled, and the integrity of these
> proceedings has been irreparably compromised.

You might be tempted to ask: "What else would you expect a goo defense attorney to say?" True enough. But in this case, well-docu mented facts backed up the assertions.

Those facts were highlighted in the following bullet point summar from our motion:

> There is now clear and convincing evidence that the govern ment in this case:

- attempted to dissuade a witness from testifying on Mr. Ruehle's behalf;

- threatened an immunized witness with a perjury prosecu- tion if he testified consistently with prior sworn testimony;

- suggested how defense and prosecution witnesses should testify;

- pressured two witnesses into dubious and invalid plea agreements;

- leaked information directly related to an ongoing grand jur investigation in an effort to gain cooperation;

- discussed adverse employment consequences for witnesse who did not cooperate;

- elicited false and misleading testimony from witnesses;

- committed serious violations of *Brady* and *Giglio*; [cases that describe the government's obligation to disclose infor- mation that they discover that might be exculpatory to the defendant and to disclose any special "benefits" they have promised to witnesses] and

- gave false and misleading testimony to this Court.

All of this was outlined on Page 1 of the defense motion. The next 2 pages went into detail on each of the allegations. The beauty of thi presentation is that the truth of all of our misconduct allegation ame out in courtroom testimony— some in the presence of the ury; some not—but all was in a formal court of law and under oath.

After recounting details of the misconduct and citing over two dozen cases where misconduct resulted in dismissal, Matt's text concluded:

More concerned with securing a conviction than doing justice, the prosecution in this case attempted to transform accounting errors made in good faith at hundreds of companies by thousands of individuals into a conspiracy to commit securities fraud at a single company, perpetrated by a single man. As a result, Mr. Ruehle and his right to a fair trial have suffered great and incurable prejudice, and the integrity of our criminal justice system has been tarnished. Under the circumstances of this case, only dismissal can undo the damage the prosecution has wrought.

Rule 29 Motion

Rule 29 is very powerful. Essentially, no criminal case can be presented to a jury if the judge decides that the government has fallen so far short of its burden of proof— guilt beyond a reasonable doubt—that no rational juror could convict. It is standard practice for the defense to file a Rule 29 motion as soon as the government rests its case. It is also standard practice for the motion to be denied. Not so in this case.

From a defendant's point of view, Rule 29 is much more powerful than pros misconduct. Since a case can be retried if dismissed for pros misconduct, it often is. A Rule 29 dismissal has the same legal effect as a unanimous jury acquittal, and under the Constitution's double jeopardy provision, no one can be tried twice for the same crime. As I've said, Judge Carney's interest in moving up our filing of the motion gave us great hope.

Matt Sloan, one of the senior Skadden attorneys, wrote our motion brilliantly:

- The government's proof is deficient on virtually every sub-stantive element of every count of the indictment.

- Not a single witness has testified that he or she entered into an agreement or scheme with Mr. Ruehle to falsify Broad-com's financial statements. Indeed, the government's two cooperating witnesses—as well as Dr. Samueli and Mr. Dull whom the government alleged were coconspirators—have all denied under oath that they engaged in any scheme or conspiracy.

- Not a single witness has testified that he or she acted with criminal intent to cheat or deceive Broadcom or its share-holders.

- Not a single witness has testified that Mr. Ruehle knew or believed that Broadcom's financial statements were false or misleading in any way, or that Mr. Ruehle ever directed them to falsify Broadcom's financial statements.

- Not a single witness has testified that Mr. Ruehle know-ingly lied to Broadcom's auditors, Ernst & Young (E&Y), or intentionally concealed information from them. Indeed, the testimony has established that Mr. Ruehle repeatedly urged the finance department to openly discuss issues with E&Y.

- Mr. Ruehle established that Opinion 25 was widely misap-plied throughout corporate America, causing 220 compa-nies, including industry leaders such as Microsoft, Apple and Barnes & Noble, to restate or correct their financial statements.

The motion then described how the government had pressured witnesses into providing testimony favorable to their theory of the case, had done their best to render key witnesses unavailable, and in spite of all that, had not come close to meeting their burden of proof.

In our motion, we stated:

In order to prevail, the government must prove beyond a reasonable doubt that Mr. Ruehle (1) had a specific intent to defraud, or to cheat and deceive; and that he acted (2) "willfully" and (3) "knowingly." The government has failed to adduce sufficient evidence for a reasonable jury to find any of these elements beyond a reasonable doubt. To the contrary, the evidence has established that Mr. Ruehle acted in good faith with respect to every aspect of Broadcom's stock option process.

Our motion detailed each of the elements the government failed to prove, including the accusations of choosing specific option grant dates. It showed the government's failure to prove criminal intent on any of them (because there was no criminal intent!). We cited case law (points and authorities, in legal parlance) and drove home how contrived the evidence was.

The government had complained about having to present their rebuttal simultaneously. The rebuttal case they presented was a rehash of some of the trial transcripts of their carefully scripted witnesses. It was not very effective.

Having observed Judge Carney for nearly a year and a half I was confident that he would give a thorough reading to all the motions filed by the defense and by the government. I had the further confidence that he would do the right thing.

Walking into the Courtroom on December 15

Julie and I recorded our feelings on the fateful day of the motion hearings.

As I sat in my defendant's chair, I penned:

This could be it—or not. It's a bit of a circus. Nick, Henry and David were all requested to be here. Could make some history today—or could go back to closing arguments on Thursday. News

truck outside—then it disappeared. Need to stay focused. Juli
gives me strength. I am prepared to accept whatever is decide
today. Every available seat is taken. Reporters are sitting in th
jury box. An adjacent courtroom is handling overflow with a vid
eo feed. There is way too much drama in the setup for this to b
just a routine hearing. Remember—the truth is on our side.

In the same moments, Julie was writing her own thoughts, as sh
did every morning in the courtroom. Her note to me read:

My hands are shaking. I am rather speechless but I have a stron
urge to write you. We have come here for many days and no mat
ter what the Judge decides we are grateful to him to have allowe
the door to the truth to get unlocked. Thank God for Judge Carne
Thank God for the truth. Thank God for Rich and his team. If i
weren't for Rich and his team, Henry would have had to live wit
a lie he didn't tell for the rest of his life as a felon. If it weren't fo
Rich and his team David would have to live in fear of prosecu
tion for a long time. If it weren't for Rich and his team Nick woul
have had to endure this grueling ordeal of trial. And if it weren
for Judge Carney opening and unlocking the door to the trut
Rich and team would not have been able to execute like they did
Thank God for Judge Carney. No matter what his decision is toda
he has done a lot for us.

On most days of the trial, more spectator seats were empty than no
Today, there was standing room only. There was even an overflov
room. The sixteen seats in the jury box were all occupied by mem
bers of the media. No one wanted to miss this one.

Every morning, the Skadden IT guy would raise the large projectio
screen. Since we expected to be arguing our motions that mornin
we naturally assumed it would be raised. The screen was very clos
by me. My heart skipped a beat when Aaron started to raise it an
the court clerk came over to say we wouldn't be needing it toda
No screen meant no arguments. No arguments meant there was
pretty good chance the judge had already made up his mind.

The Dismissal

Having sat through twenty-four days of court proceedings, I knew the opening routine really well, but as I've just described, today's opening was like no other.

Judge Carney entered behind his bench, as always. He began by greeting all the attorneys for the government and for the defense. There were four sets of defense lawyers instead of just one. After the greeting, he declared that he would read his decision into the record and then open it for everyone's comments. Talk about a good sign! There would be no reason for him to set up all this drama just so he could read into the record that he had ruled against the motions. Still, I wasn't 100 percent certain he was going to dismiss, so I still had to stifle my enthusiasm. I couldn't see Julie from my seat, so I couldn't read her reactions.

By the time the judge had read his first three paragraphs, even I was able to breathe a deep sigh of relief and realize my ordeal was finally over. They read:

I heard all the evidence present at Mr. Ruehle's trial and at the evidentiary hearings. I now know the entire story of what happened. This decision supersedes any prior findings, rulings or credibility determination that I had made on a partial record without the benefit of all the facts.

Based on the complete record now before me, I find that the government has intimidated and improperly influenced the three witnesses critical to Mr. Ruehle's defense. The cumulative effect of that misconduct has distorted the truth-finding process and compromised the integrity of the trial.

To submit this case to the jury would make a mockery of Mr. Ruehle's constitutional right to compulsory process and a fair trial. The Sixth Amendment to the United States Constitution guarantees the accused the right to compulsory process for witnesses in its defense. For this Constitutional right to have true meaning, the government must not do anything to intimidate or improp erly influence witnesses. Sadly, government did so in this case.

Wow! Let's just dissect that for a moment. In the first paragrap Judge Carney notes that he has paid careful attention to *all* the ev dence—from the government and defense. He acknowledged tha he had made prior rulings in the case based on incomplete know edge.

The three witnesses critical to my defense from the second para graph were Henry Samueli, David Dull, and Nancy Tullos. I inter preted this to mean that even Nancy might have been able to giv a more accurate testimony without the sword of government pros ecutors hanging over her head.

The third paragraph provides the Constitutional basis for his dis missal of the charges against me. It was clear throughout the tria in many comments made by Judge Carney, that he held an unwaver ing respect, even reverence, for the Constitution and for the wisdor of the Founding Fathers. In this ruling he applied that reverence i a most tangible manner. This was his prelude to dismissal of a charges against me in accordance with Rule 29.

Always thorough, the judge then presented his full rationale, recit ing the many instances of intimidation that the government ha applied against Nancy Tullos. His last two paragraphs about her sa it all:

> Not surprisingly, Ms. Tullos' testimony at trial came off scripte and not consistent with the extensive email trail brought out dur ing cross-examination.

> I have absolutely no confidence that any portion of Ms. Tullo testimony was based on her own independent recollection c events as opposed to what the government thought her recollec tion should be on those events.

Nancy Tullos was on the witness stand for a total of six days; Ric Marmaro methodically dissected her government testimony fc ur of them, provided context to defuse her potentially damaging omments, exposing her as "scripted and not consistent with the xtensive e-mail trail." Judge Carney never implied that she had lied n the stand—that, of course, would be a federal crime—but he elieved her comments had been made selectively in favor of the overnment.

udge Carney also remarked, "In effect, the government left Mr. Dull anging in the wind and uncertain of his fate for almost two years." e recounted the infamous Stolper phone call and said, "The lead rosecutor somehow forgot that the truth is never negotiable."

he judge concluded, "There was no evidence at trial to suggest that r. Samueli did anything wrong, let alone criminal. Yet, the govern- ent embarked on a campaign of intimidation and other miscon- uct to embarrass him and bring him down." He then recited six ifferent injustices, capped off with how the government "crafted a unconscionable plea agreement pursuant to which Dr. Samueli ould plead guilty to a crime he did not commit and pay a ridicu- us sum of $12 million to the United States Treasury." He concluded at the government's actions were designed to pressure Henry to icriminate me, or, failing that, to destroy his credibility as a defense itness.

udge Carney, my hero as a wise and courageous man, issued the fol- wing order (see full transcript of his order in Appendix C):

- Dismissed, with prejudice, the stock option backdating indictment against me and entered a judgment of acquittal, based on both prosecutorial misconduct and insufficient evidence (Rule 29). He ruled that Nancy Tullos' entire tes- timony "is unreliable and must be stricken." He noted that the Rule 29 dismissal prevented the government from ever again bringing charges against me for options practices because of "the double jeopardy clause of the Fifth Amend- ment."

- Dismissed, with prejudice, the stock option backdating indictment against Nick. He based this on the fact that the same three witnesses necessary for my exoneration would also be necessary for him and because of the government's improper behavior Nick would not be able to receive a fair trial.

- Ordered the government to show cause why the drug-related indictment against Nick should not be dismissed. He based this on, once again, the need for the same witnesses to allow him a fair defense.

- Dismissed, without prejudice, the SEC complaint against the four of us—Nick, Henry, David and me—relating to the stock options issues. Without prejudice means the SEC can still bring the case. He ordered them to decide whether or not to move forward with their case within thirty days.

Not only was my criminal case dismissed, a total of three criminal cases and four civil ones were dismissed with a stroke of Judge Carney's bold pen.

The government dropped Nick's drug-related indictment before the judge's deadline for them to decide whether to press it. The SEC asked for a three-week extension on their deadline, but they ended up dropping as well. A clean sweep!

At the end of his ruling, before opening the floor to the always loquacious defense attorneys (and the by-now not-so-loquacious government attorneys), the judge quoted from a US Supreme Court case regarding the responsibility of government attorneys:

The United States Attorney is the representative, not of an ordinary party at a controversy, but of a sovereignty whose obligation to govern impartially is as compelling as its obligation to govern at all, and whose interest, therefore, in a criminal prosecution is not that it shall win a case, but that justice shall be done. As such he is in a peculiar and a very definite sense the servant of the law, the twofold aim of which is that guilt shall not escape nor innocent suffer.

He may prosecute with earnestness and vigor. Indeed, he should do so. But while he may strike hard blows, he is not at liberty to strike foul ones. It is as much his duty to refrain from improper methods calculated to produce a wrongful conviction as it is to use every legitimate means to bring about a just one.

One by one, the defense attorneys had their brief say. Rich was choked with emotion as he praised Judge Carney for his unquenchable desire to hear all the evidence, even to the extent of granting unprecedented defense immunity to key witnesses. Rich said that in his thirty-four year career, he had "never been more proud to be a lawyer."

Next up was Nick's lead defense attorney, Brendan Sullivan, famous in his own right as the defender of Oliver North in the Reagan-era Iran-Contra case and of Senator Ted Stevens. (The Stevens case resulted in conviction, but it was overturned after findings of serious prosecutorial misconduct.) In other words, Brendan had been around the block a few times.

Brendan referred to Rich as a "young lawyer" (his own career spanned forty-two years). He then commented on Attorney General Eric Holder's remarks about the overturn of the Stevens case. He concluded, "The message delivered by this court today had been heard throughout the country by all who enforce the law, and we are all better off and the system of justice will be better off for the courage demonstrated in this court on this date."

The government attorneys said, "I hope you understand we disagree with your ruling and we will need to decide what we do next."

Mr. Ruehle, You Are a Free Man

The judge thanked everyone. He turned to face me and spoke the words that will forever echo in my soul: "I don't think that anything needs to be said further other than, Mr. Ruehle, you are a free man."

I somehow managed to find my voice long enough to speak the onl
four words I said aloud in the entire trial: "Thank you, your Honor.

With that, the defense side of the courtroom became a love fest. Th
government side was morose.

Leaving the courtroom, I was besieged by reporters. The most com
mon question was, "How does it feel to be free?" I answered the onl
way I honestly could: I really didn't know yet. I said that after thre
and a half years of scrutiny, culminating with a criminal trial tha
could have resulted with the rest of my life in prison, I wasn't able t
just throw a switch and go back to feeling "normal."

That evening, we had an impromptu celebration back at our Orang
County hotel, but it was somewhat subdued. Everyone had worke
so hard and had such an intense emotional investment in the cas
that we all had a little trouble letting go. That's not to say ther
weren't a lot of very broad smiles and a lot of hugs and handshake:
The workaholics on the Skadden team were profoundly relieve
and were finally able to admit to themselves how tired they wer
From the time we had all moved into our hotel in early Octobe
most of the Skadden team had spent only Thanksgiving night hom
with their families. Julie and I, at least, had had most of our wee
ends off.

December 15 will always be a day that Julie and I celebrate. Davi
Dull, who has a rather encyclopedic mind, actually informed us tha
December 15 is Bill of Rights Day. On that day in 1791, the Bill c
Rights—the first ten amendments to the US Constitution, includin
the Fifth and Sixth that were so important in my case—was ratifiec
We now affectionately refer to that date as Rights of Bill Day.

On that date in 2010, and again in 2011, we sat in on Judge Carney'
courtroom just for nostalgia. The cases he was hearing were fa
afield from the one we had suffered through, but we saw the sam
thoroughness and thoughtfulness from the judge we had come t
know and respect so deeply.

ime to Meet the Jurors

'e still had one more scheduled day of court. As we waited there
n December 17, 8:30 came and went, but still no judge and no jury.
hey arrived about forty-five minutes later: Judge Carney had been
ading his December 15 order to the jurors.

e had also told them that they needed to reassemble in their nor-
al seats so he could officially dismiss them. He explained that the
rocess would be quite brief and that they would be required to file
ut in the direction of the jury room as they had done many times
efore. He then told them that if they wanted, they could reenter the
ourtroom and meet me and anyone else associated with my case.

o my delight, most of the jurors availed themselves of the opportu-
ity. Most of them had deduced that Julie and I were a couple, and
ome gravitated to her in the gallery immediately, some to me at the
efendant's chair. There were congratulations, handshakes, hugs,
g smiles, and many a well-meaning comment. It was exhilarating.

y this time we should have been immune to surprises, but there
as still one more in store. In what we later learned was an unprec-
dented move, Judge Carney came down off the bench and stepped
to the "well" where Julie and I were standing (the area on the
ourtroom floor surrounded on four sides by the bench, the govern-
ent tables, the gallery, and the defense tables, and where few ever
ead).

lie and I had told each other how much we would love to be able
 shake his hand. The judge walked directly over to me, shook my
and, and wished me well. I simply told him that of all the many
ousands of words I had heard in that courtroom, the most memo-
ble were his saying he had been appointed to do the right thing
d that the law sometimes had to catch up. He thanked me and
en stepped over to Julie to give her a big hug. Julie's face lit up as
ough she had just been hugged by God—which, we both agreed,
as probably exactly what had just happened.

Julie's Poignant Posting

You've already read some of Julie's courtroom messages to me. Sh writes with great insight and passion. Early in the case, she ha maintained a website called *Justice for Bill* where she would po status reports on the case, always very careful to not say anythir the prosecutors could use if they were able to gain access to th site.

For extra caution, all her postings were vetted in advance by or defense team. One day, we learned that the prosecution team ha indeed found a way into the site. We learned that they would rea the site every morning in search of something juicy. That was enoug for us. We stopped posting until the end of trial.

Following our acquittal, Julie wrote the most touching story I hav ever read. We were introduced to Arianna Huffington through friend, and Julie's narrative was published on the Huffington Po website. It reads:

This story began in 2006 when a professor from a Midweste *university published a statistical analysis suggesting that mar* *corporations must have used hindsight in selecting dates to gra* *stock options to their employees. The media quickly jumped c* *board and applied a label of "backdating" to the practice. It turr* *out backdating is not illegal per se, as long as it is accounted f* *properly. At last count over 220 companies have filed amende* *or restated financial statements to correct their accounting. Or* *of the companies who corrected their accounting was Broadco.* *Corporation, a very successful technology company that make* *semiconductor chips for everything from cable set-top boxes* *Bluetooth headsets to iPhone chips. As a result of this restate* *ment two of the company's officers—including Bill Ruehle—wei* *charged criminally by the DOJ. Throughout the pretrial period, B* *Ruehle's wife, Julie, wrote to family and friends about the procee* *ings. The following is Bill's wife's personal account for the fir* *stage of this ordeal.*

ndeed, Bill has received justice.

was a long journey with astounding intensity that could have had potentially disastrous outcome. There were times that Bill and I elt we were standing on very shaky ground and we had to keep our alance no matter how strong the jolts were. Or sometimes it felt ke riding a monumental wave that could crash down and sweep ur dead bodies to the shore. The intensity and difficulty taught us omething very important. We learned that the very shaky ground nd the tumultuous wave that could sweep us to our demise could lso be the means to our survival; an anchor to hold on to as long s we learn how to keep our balance and stay centered. We did it hile holding each other's hand very tightly and with our relentless efense team that would not give up. And most importantly, we had ou cheering us along all the way.

he Trial

he trial began with Nancy Tullos, the Vice President of Human esources at Broadcom, who had many misleading things to say bout Bill. During her cross-examination by our lead defense law- er, Rich (I refer to him as God sometimes in this context) she dmitted to lying to the SEC and was confronted with many incon- istencies in her statements. Rich and his team (I refer to them as ur angels in this context) knew all 6 million plus pages of emails nd documents in this case inside and out and they were able to xpose her for her lies. I have to say, her testimony stressed me ne most.

hen it came time for us to put on our defense case. We really idn't have to do it but something in our gut told us we should. We anted Henry Samueli and David Dull on the stand and as it turned ut, the judge did also. He granted them immunity to testify for us nd the government objected and pleaded against it. Judge Car- ey always said he wanted the whole story to come out, and it was e who unlocked the door.

And it was that night, November 30th, when the immunity wa granted that Andrew Stolper, the lead prosecutor, made conta with David Dull's attorney threatening him and encouraging him t incriminate Bill. You know the rest of the story from there. In shor all of his misdeeds were exposed—coercing Nancy Tullos to shap her testimony, leaking information to the press, etc.

Once Henry and David testified, the rest was history. Judge Ca ney saw the case for what it truly was. Bill Ruehle and the goo people of Broadcom did not defraud shareholders—they behave appropriately and conservatively within the boundaries they fe were allowed. In an attempt to criminalize this business behavio the government had to resort to unbecoming means to secure conviction—the conviction of an innocent man.

We had the truth on our side, but if it weren't for Rich and his team brilliant execution the truth might not have flown through the cour room the way it did. If it weren't for Rich and his team, Bill woul not have been exonerated. If it weren't for Rich and his team, D Nicholas would have had to endure the ordeal of trial like Bill and did. If it weren't for Rich and his team, Henry Samueli would hav had to live with a lie he didn't tell for the rest of his life as a felon. it weren't for Rich and his team, David Dull would have lived in fea of prosecution for more years to come. If it weren't for Rich and hi team, the government would not have been exposed for its mis conduct. And if it weren't for the incredible courage and dedicatio to the truth of Judge Carney, the door would have stayed locke and truth would have remained hidden.

Acquittal

I can't even begin to describe to you what went on on Tuesda December 15, 2009. You can read Judge Carney's order/transcri for that day by clicking here and I strongly encourage everyon who believes in the justice system or has had doubts about it t read it. Bill and I read it as if it's our favorite poetry piece. Judg Carney saw what this case was about and what it was not abou

206

nd he issued an order so eloquent and on point that I could not ave even dreamed about in my wildest imagination. He asked or Rich and the defense attorneys of Nick, Henry and David (he eferred to them as the "titans of the legal profession") to comment. hey did and all of that is in the transcript attached. He acquitted ill of all charges and dismissed the indictment due to prosecutorial isconduct for Bill and Nick. My favorite quotes are:

To submit this case to the jury would make a mockery of Mr. Rue-le's Constitutional right...to a fair trial;

he lead prosecutor somehow forgot that truth is never negotiable;

he government embarked on a campaign of intimidation and other isconduct to embarrass [Henry Samueli, Broadcom's co-founder nd witness in the case] and bring him down...The government's reatment of Dr. Samueli was shameful and contrary to American alues of decency;

m sure there are going to be many people who are going to be ritical of my decision in this case and argue that I'm being too ard on the government. I strongly disagree...You only have three vitnesses to prove your innocence and the government has intimi-lated and improperly influenced each one of them. Is that fair? Is hat Justice? I say absolutely not.

Mr. Ruehle, you are a free man."

ost-Trial—Meet the Jurors and the Judge

Ve woke up on Wednesday in a state of disbelief about what ad transpired. For three years, we had to be in fight mode and ontinuously reminding each other the importance of staying ocused. For three years, we viewed the world and its offering s temporary events and never truly counted on much other han each other's love and strength. For three years, we had ur fences up and all of a sudden, on Wednesday, we had to ake them down. It felt very unreal: how do we live without this dark cloud that's been hanging over us? We had lived with the expectation of thunderous showers and rain for three years and now it was gone. We felt the ground was removed from under our feet. It was then that we realized we drew strength from this difficult thing we were fighting. We became very strong because we had to. I cried when a truck pulled up to our driveway and took away a mountain of binders and papers we had to read and study for our defense at trial. I felt a part of me was being moved away. It felt somewhat therapeutic, but also brough fears. How or what are we supposed to feel next?

On Thursday, we went in for the judge to dismiss the jury (you can read juror interviews here). It was a truly blissful experience. To tell you the truth, I was looking forward to going in to see the judge and quietly, in my mind, thanking him and saying good bye. I had this extreme need to express my gratitude to him and I knew there was no way I would be allowed to talk to him. But then he did the unbelievable thing again. He allowed the jurors to come back to the courtroom to see us, and every single one of them gave Bill and me a hug or a handshake. I sobbed in the arms of one of them as she did, too. They all believed in Bill's innocence. And then the unbelievable thing happened. Judge Carney stepped down from the bench and shook Bill's hand as Bill gave him one of his favorite Judge Carney quotes back to him ("I was appointed to this position to do the right thing"). He then leaned over and gave me a hug. I finally had closure.

Epilogue

It's Finally Over, Right?

Well, not exactly. The criminal case was over and, because of the double jeopardy law, it could never be brought again. The SEC case was dropped in another six weeks. There was still one more civil case: a derivative suit.

A derivative suit is supposed to be an action on behalf of a corporation against the officers and directors who allegedly caused it harm. The logic is a little strained, to say the least. All corporations of any stature have indemnification agreements that require the corporation to bear any defense costs the officers and directors may incur as a result of criminal or civil charges. So, accordingly, Broadcom paid ours—defendants, witnesses, and potential witnesses alike. Broadcom has publicly disclosed that all the lawsuits over stock options cost it well over $100 million.

Legal costs and settlement costs are normally paid by a corporation's directors' and officers' liability insurance (D&O insurance). Just before my acquittal, Broadcom and the attorney for the plaintiff who brought the derivative case had agreed on a settlement: Broadcom's D&O insurance carrier would pay the corporation a large sum. The settlement applied to all eleven charged officers and directors except Nick, Henry, and me, because we were all involved in the criminal case. In effect, the eleven were paying themselves. Under the terms of the settlement, this exhausted their D&O coverage, so the corporation had to pay all legal costs out of pocket.

Perversely, this also meant that the derivative suit, theoretically for the benefit of Broadcom, was going to cost the company possibly tens of millions of dollars more to pursue the claims. In my opinion, Broadcom would only have agreed to such a settlement if they were

convinced that I and/or Nick would be found guilty—which coul
have voided all of the D&O insurance.

Once we were acquitted, the committee of the Broadcom board c
directors responsible for pursuit of the case filed a motion to have i
dismissed because it could produce no conceivable financial advan
tage to the company. The plaintiff's attorney naturally resiste
because he wouldn't be paid his contingency fee. The prevailin
judge, a different federal judge in Los Angeles, rejected the motior
so the case took on a life of its own. Judge Carney's wisdom coul
not be applied.

The three of us reached a final settlement, which the court approve
in May 2011—five years to the month from the first eruption of th
"business scandal of the century" in the media. Half a decade wit
this issue as the center point of my life—it's just not fair!

Now Is It Over?

We certainly hope and pray that it's all over. One of many lessons w
have learned from this experience is not to believe "it could neve
happen to me." It could. Thanks to a wise and courageous judge,
brilliant and tireless defense team (and the financial resources t
put it in place), and, finally, Julie's courage and mine to stand up t
the awesome power of the federal government, we prevailed. If an
one of these pieces had not been in place, the outcome could hav
been entirely different.

Notes on Post-Trial Conversations with Jurors

We have stayed in contact with some of the jurors. In April 2010, w
hosted a dinner for them and their spouses. To our delight, almos
all attended.

First, I want to credit one juror with a memorable comment from th
last day of court. The woman I had felt during jury selection woul

kely be favorable turned out even more so than I imagined. She old us she took copious trial notes to help with later deliberations, ut that during the government's presentation, her notes became ore than just a memory refresher. She had become so convinced f my innocence that her notes were now aimed at bolstering her rguments for a not-guilty verdict in case other jurors saw it differntly.

he defense team had been concerned about a potential gender gap. he government's two most damaging witnesses were both women, hile the defense trial team was entirely male. We knew we would ave to do hard crosses, particularly on Nancy Tullos, because they ad been so heavily coached and intimidated. We were concerned at the female jurors might be offended by this. To our surprise, t the dinner we learned that two male jurors were disturbed by ow "harsh" Rich was with the female witnesses, while several of e female jurors were totally unconcerned with it. They remarked at Rich had given them a real education on how to try a case and at, thanks to him, they were able to hear the whole story.

here was one disturbing comment made to Julie. One juror said e really didn't pay much attention to the defense case, being ore concerned about her young children at home. She thought the efense took too long with their cross-examinations and wanted e case to be over with so she could go home. I suspect that, even efore the trial began, she believed I was guilty. I don't think she ven understood the charges. However, she did say that she hadn't ad a strong opinion and would have gone along with the others they wanted a not-guilty verdict. Then she had the audacity to equest a picture taken with me.

o, there was an almost universal sentiment that serving on my jury ad been very worthwhile. The jurors all said they had learned a t. In my opinion, Rich put on an absolute clinic on how to try a ase. He knew every piece of evidence, how it could be misused by e government, and what it would take to put it in the proper con- ext. He was always respectful of even the most hostile witnesses— ut he didn't let them get away with their government-induced revisionism. His passion for the case was always just below the su face, occasionally emerging fully when a witness was particular intransigent or when he really wanted to make a point to Judg Carney.

Now What?

I am thankful for a lot of little things and some big things. For on messages from attorneys are no longer 90 percent of my incomir e-mail. I no longer have to make weekly calls or monthly visits my pretrial services officer. We no longer have to schedule our liv around court appearances and trial preparation. We no longer liv in fear of loss of liberty or being driven into financial ruin by the SE or some plaintiffs' attorneys.

I can finally write this book without fear that it will be used again. me in a courtroom. I can enjoy the advisory work I do with dynam young companies without the cloud of a potential conviction threa ening my future.

Julie and I can now devote our full attention to family, friends, an causes we believe in. In the end, the American system of justic worked the way it is supposed to work. We will be forever gratefu

POSTSCRIPT

ow Did We Do It?

e have often been asked this question-by ourselves as well as by
hers. How do you cope with something of this magnitude? A whole
nge of emotional reactions are possible. One could be embittered
id outraged and demand to know, "why is this happening to me?"
:rtainly an understandable reaction, but not very productive. One
uld become seriously depressed and retreat into a shell. Again
iderstandable but not very productive. Another possibility is to
:come obsessed with planning a defense and spend every waking
oment trying to craft a defense. Even this is not, in my opinion, the
ost productive approach.

lie and I were fortunate to be able to find the right balance, with
e key word being balance. Our first requirement was to make
re we had the very best possible defense team. Our Skadden team
as more than up to that challenge. We worked closely with them
roughout the case, but left the detailed and excruciating research
the six million documents in their capable hands. This allowed us
not have to be obsessed with uncovering every little nuance of
e case. We were always there as a resource to suggest directions
the Skadden team and to vet their conclusions, but they had far
eater capability than we did to pore through all the documents.

om the outset we were determined that we were not going to
t the prosecutors take away our lives. Our relationship actually
arted some time after I was forced out of Broadcom and before
e indictments were handed down. We took great strength in each
her. Neither Julie nor I could be considered devoutly religious in
rms of participating in an organized religion. However we do both
ive deep faith in God and take comfort in prayers-both our own
id those others have offered for us.

I believe a very important element to remaining in control of your emotions is to have a sense of humor. It may sound strange with all the very heavy duty pressures surrounding us, but we were able laugh a lot, often at silly little things. I remember the day we we checking into a hotel for a pre-trial conference and we walked pa an open room door with rap music blasting from inside. I immec ately started making up rap verses to describe some of the expect trial testimony.

We traveled, going frequently to Northern California to visit my far ily and our friends. We went to the East Coast so I could show Jul all the places I lived when I was growing up and going to school. V traveled to Texas to visit the places Julie lived and went to scho when she immigrated from Iran at age 18. We went to Hong Kor as part of the Pepperdine MBA program Julie had enrolled in. Sh started working on her MBA before the indictment in 2007 ar completed her degree a few months before trial.

We built an incredibly strong bond between us, getting engage in early 2008 and married later the same year. Our wedding was beautiful amalgam of Persian and American culture with parts the service in Farsi and parts in English. Both of our families we there. It was evident that many of them feared that we would nev be able to enjoy our married life as they feared I would be convicte

I wish I could say that we knew from the outset that I would nev be convicted, but that would not be true. What I did know for su was that I was innocent of the charges and I hoped and prayed th we would be able to establish that in a court of law. Ultimately v did.

By nature, I have always been calm-no Type A personality her That calm served us very well in the case. The senior members my defense team have told me on many occasions that my calmne was inspiring to them and it allowed them to focus all their energi on my defense instead of having to figuratively hold my hand or pu me down off the ceiling.

few words here about the support I felt from my family, specifically from each of my three grown children. Janine left her two teenage daughters with a friend so she could fly down from Santa Clara to spend some days with us in the courtroom. She even joined Julie and me in the hotel gym at 6:00 a.m. on the days she was there. Beth left her daughter in her husband's care while she flew out from Boston to be in the courtroom. Glenn left his three kids with his wife in Marin County so he could come down.

An experience like ours can be described, but to really internalize it you have to be there. Each of my kids was there for part of the case. They were grateful for the firsthand exposure, and I was extremely grateful for their support. They all believed in their dad!

Still, as Julie and I look back on the experience we do ask ourselves how we were able to remain so calm and collected. In the end, we did what we had to do. We had a superb defense team; we had a courageous and open-minded judge and we had the unconditional support of friends and family. To our friends and family who may be reading this, we send our most heartfelt thanks.

215

ACKNOWLEDGEMENTS

s a first time author I never could have completed this book without the total dedication and support of my wife, Julie. Not only was he always with me throughout the trial, she was my constant editor, critic and muse through the writing of the book.

he fact that I am able to write this book as a free man is largely thanks to the supreme efforts of my defense team at the law firm kadden, Arps, Slate, Meagher and Flom. In the book I talked in detail bout the lead partner on my case, Rich Marmaro and a little about is partner Jack DiCanio. Less mentioned, but equally important re all the members of the Skadden team who worked so tirelessly n the case. My thanks to Matt Sloan, Matt Umhofer, Kristin Tahler, teve Lybrand, Nicole Diaz, Patrick Hammon, Ryan Weinstein, Emily viad, Anil Antony, Sheryl Wu, Lisa Johnston, Aaron Shorr, Wayne ampbell, Kim Miller, Jason Breeding, Andrew Galvin, Kim Cooley, tephen Haydon-Kahn and the many document reviewers, paralegals and others who worked so well together as a team. Thanks to ur jury consultants, Dave Weinberg and Carrie Mason.

very special thanks to Judge Cormac J. Carney, whose reverence or the law and courage to stand up for his principles were and emain an inspiration to us.

want to acknowledge my family – my children, Janine, Beth and lenn and their spouses and children; my step-daughters, Sara and elara. They all had unconditional faith in my innocence. We had lany friends who stood by us. A few were particularly notable, ncluding Terry and Russ who came down from Northern California o be with us at trial, and Stephen and David who traveled all the ay from Australia several times to be with us.

I also want to thank the editorial and design staffs at CreateSpace an Amazon company, for their help in turning my ramblings into reasonably coherent book.

Appendix A

Thompson Memorandum

U.S. Department of Justice

Office of the Deputy Attorney General

The Deputy Attorney General · *Washington, D.C. 20530*

January 20, 2003

MEMORANDUM

TO: Heads of Department Components
        United States Attorneys

FROM: Larry D. Thompson
        Deputy Attorney General

SUBJECT: Principles of Federal Prosecution of Business Organizations

As the Corporate Fraud Task Force has advanced in its mission, we have confronted certain issues in the principles for the federal prosecution of business organizations that require revision in order to enhance our efforts against corporate fraud. While it will be a minority of cases in which a corporation or partnership is itself subjected to criminal charges, prosecutors and investigators in every matter involving business crimes must assess the merits of seeking the conviction of the business entity itself.

Attached to this memorandum are a revised set of principles to guide Department prosecutors as they make the decision whether to seek charges against a business organization. These revisions draw heavily on the combined efforts of the Corporate Fraud Task Force and the Attorney General's Advisory Committee to put the results of more than three years of experience with the principles into practice.

The main focus of the revisions is increased emphasis on and scrutiny of the authenticity of a corporation's cooperation. Too often business organizations, while purporting to cooperate with a Department investigation, in fact take steps to impede the quick and effective exposure of the complete scope of wrongdoing under investigation. The revisions make clear that such conduct should weigh in favor of a corporate prosecution. The revisions also address the efficacy of the corporate governance mechanisms in place within a corporation, to ensure that these measures are truly effective rather than mere paper programs.

Further experience with these principles may lead to additional adjustments. I look forward to hearing comments about their operation in practice. Please forward any comments to Christopher Wray, the Principal Associate Deputy Attorney General, or to Andrew Hruska, my Senior Counsel.

I. Charging a Corporation: General

A. General Principle: Corporations should not be treated leniently because of their artificial nature nor should they be subject to harsher treatment. Vigorous enforcement of the criminal laws against corporate wrongdoers, where appropriate results in great benefits for law enforcement and the public, particularly in the area of white collar crime. Indicting corporations for wrongdoing enables the government to address and be a force for positive change of corporate culture, alter corporate behavior, and prevent, discover, and punish white collar crime.

B. Comment: In all cases involving corporate wrongdoing, prosecutors should consider the factors discussed herein. First and foremost, prosecutors should be aware of the important public benefits that may flow from indicting a corporation in appropriate cases. For instance, corporations are likely to take immediate remedial steps when one is indicted for criminal conduct that is pervasive throughout a particular industry, and thus an indictment often provides a unique opportunity for deterrence on a massive scale. In addition, a corporate indictment may result in specific deterrence by changing the culture of the indicted corporation and the behavior of its employees. Finally, certain crimes that carry with them a substantial risk of great public harm, e.g., environmental crimes or financial frauds, are by their nature most likely to be committed by businesses, and there may, therefore, be a substantial federal interest in indicting the corporation.

Charging a corporation, however, does not mean that individual directors, officers, employees, or shareholders should not also be charged. Prosecution of a corporation is not a substitute for the prosecution of criminally culpable individuals within or without the corporation. Because a corporation can act only through individuals, imposition of individual criminal liability may provide the strongest deterrent against future corporate wrongdoing. Only rarely should provable individual culpability not be pursued, even in the face of offers of corporate guilty pleas.

Corporations are "legal persons," capable of suing and being sued, and capable of committing crimes. Under the doctrine of *respondeat superior*, a corporation may be held criminally liable for the illegal acts of its directors, officers, employees, and agents. To hold a corporation liable for these actions, the government must establish that the corporate agent's actions (i) were within the scope of his duties and (ii) were intended, at least in part, to benefit the corporation. In all cases involving wrongdoing by corporate agents, prosecutors should consider the corporation, as well as the responsible individuals, as potential criminal targets.

---

[1] While these guidelines refer to corporations, they apply to the consideration of the prosecution of all types of business organizations, including partnerships, sole proprietorships, government entities, and unincorporated associations.

Agents, however, may act for mixed reasons -- both for self-aggrandizement (both direct and indirect) and for the benefit of the corporation, and a corporation may be held liable as long as one motivation of its agent is to benefit the corporation. In *United States v. Automated Medical Laboratories*, 770 F.2d 399 (4th Cir. 1985), the court affirmed the corporation's conviction for the actions of a subsidiary's employee despite its claim that the employee was acting for his own benefit, namely his "ambitious nature and his desire to ascend the corporate ladder." The court stated, "*Partucci* was clearly acting in part to benefit AML since his advancement within the corporation depended on AML's well-being and its lack of difficulties with the FDA." Similarly, in *United States v. Cincotta*, 689 F.2d 238, 241-42 (1st Cir. 1982), the court held, "criminal liability may be imposed on the corporation only where the agent is acting within the scope of his employment. That, in turn, requires that the agent be performing acts of the kind which he is authorized to perform, and those acts must be motivated -- at least in part -- by an intent to benefit the corporation." Applying this test, the court upheld the corporation's conviction, notwithstanding the substantial personal benefit reaped by its miscreant agents, because the fraudulent scheme required money to pass through the corporation's treasury and the fraudulently obtained goods were resold to the corporation's customers in the corporation's name. As the court concluded, "Mystic--not the individual defendants--was making money by selling oil that it had not paid for."

Moreover, the corporation need not even necessarily profit from its agent's actions for it to be held liable. In *Automated Medical Laboratories*, the Fourth Circuit stated:

[B]enefit is not a "touchstone of criminal corporate liability; benefit at best is an evidential, not an operative, fact." Thus, whether the agent's actions ultimately redounded to the benefit of the corporation is less significant than whether the agent acted with the intent to benefit the corporation. The basic purpose of requiring that an agent have acted with the intent to benefit the corporation, however, is to insulate the corporation from criminal liability for actions of its agents which be inimical to the interests of the corporation or which may have been undertaken solely to advance the interests of that agent or of a party other than the corporation.

770 F.2d at 407 (emphasis added; quoting *Old Monastery Co. v. United States*, 147 F.2d 905, 908 (4th Cir.), cert. denied, 326 U.S. 734 (1945)).

2

II. Charging a Corporation: Factors to Be Considered

A. General Principle: Generally, prosecutors should apply the same factors in determining whether to charge a corporation as they do with respect to individuals. *See* USAM § 9-27.220, *et seq.* Thus, the prosecutor should weigh all of the factors normally considered in the sound exercise of prosecutorial judgment: the sufficiency of the evidence; the likelihood of success at trial,; the probable deterrent, rehabilitative, and other consequences of conviction; and the adequacy of noncriminal approaches. *See* id. However, due to the nature of the corporate "person," some additional factors are present. In conducting an investigation, determining whether to bring charges, and negotiating plea agreements, prosecutors should consider the following factors in reaching a decision as to the proper treatment of a corporate target:

1. the nature and seriousness of the offense, including the risk of harm to the public, and applicable policies and priorities, if any, governing the prosecution of corporations for particular categories of crime (*see* section III, *infra*);

2. the pervasiveness of wrongdoing within the corporation, including the complicity in, or condonation of, the wrongdoing by corporate management (*see* section IV, *infra*);

3. the corporation's history of similar conduct, including prior criminal, civil, and regulatory enforcement actions against it (*see* section V, *infra*);

4. the corporation's timely and voluntary disclosure of wrongdoing and its willingness to cooperate in the investigation of its agents, including, if necessary, the waiver of corporate attorney-client and work product protection (*see* section VI, *infra*);

5. the existence and adequacy of the corporation's compliance program (*see* section VII, *infra*);

6. the corporation's remedial actions, including any efforts to implement an effective corporate compliance program or to improve an existing one, to replace responsible management, to discipline or terminate wrongdoers, to pay restitution, and to cooperate with the relevant government agencies (*see* section VIII, *infra*);

7. collateral consequences, including disproportionate harm to shareholders, pension holders and employees not proven personally culpable and impact on the public arising from the prosecution (*see* section IX, *infra*); and

8. the adequacy of the prosecution of individuals responsible for the corporation's malfeasance;

9. the adequacy of remedies such as civil or regulatory enforcement actions (*see*

3

section X, infra).

B. Comment: As with the factors relevant to charging natural persons, the foregoing factors are intended to provide guidance rather than to mandate a particular result. The factors listed in this section are intended to be illustrative of those that should be considered and not a complete or exhaustive list. Some or all of these factors may or may not apply to specific cases, and in some cases one factor may override all others. The nature and seriousness of the offense may be such as to warrant prosecution regardless of the other factors. Further, national law enforcement policies in various enforcement areas may require that more or less weight be given to certain of these factors than to others.

In making a decision to charge a corporation, the prosecutor generally has wide latitude in determining when, whom, how, and even whether to prosecute for violations of Federal criminal law. In exercising that discretion, prosecutors should consider the following general statements of principles that summarize appropriate considerations to be weighed and desirable practices to be followed in discharging their prosecutorial responsibilities. In doing so, prosecutors should ensure that the general purposes of the criminal law -- assurance of warranted punishment, deterrence of further criminal conduct, protection of the public from dangerous and fraudulent conduct, rehabilitation of offenders, and restitution for victims and affected communities -- are adequately met, taking into account the special nature of the corporate "person."

II. Charging a Corporation: Special Policy Concerns

A. General Principle: The nature and seriousness of the crime, including the risk of harm to the public from the criminal conduct, are obviously primary factors in determining whether to charge a corporation. In addition, corporate conduct, particularly that of national and multi-national corporations, necessarily intersects with federal economic, taxation, and criminal law enforcement policies. In applying these principles, prosecutors must consider the practices and policies of the appropriate Division of the Department, and must comply with those policies to the extent required.

B. Comment: In determining whether to charge a corporation, prosecutors should take into account federal law enforcement priorities as discussed above. *See* USAM § 9-27-230. In addition, however, prosecutors must be aware of the specific policy goals and incentive programs established by the respective Divisions and regulatory agencies. Thus, whereas natural persons may be given incremental degrees of credit (ranging from immunity to lesser charges to sentencing considerations) for turning themselves in, making statements against their penal interest, and cooperating in the government's investigation of their own and others' wrongdoing, the same approach may not be appropriate in all circumstances with respect to corporations. As an example, it is entirely proper in many investigations for a prosecutor to consider the corporation's pre-indictment conduct, *e.g.*,voluntary disclosure, cooperation, remediation or restitution, in determining whether to seek an indictment. However, this would not necessarily be appropriate in an antitrust investigation, in which antitrust violations, by definition, go to the

4

223

heart of the corporation's business and for which the Antitrust Division has therefore established a firm policy, understood in the business community, that credit should not be given at the charging stage for a compliance program and that amnesty is available only to the first corporation to make full disclosure to the government. As another example, the Tax Division has a strong preference for prosecuting responsible individuals, rather than entities, for corporate tax offenses. Thus, in determining whether or not to charge a corporation, prosecutors should consult with the Criminal, Antitrust, Tax, and Environmental and Natural Resources Divisions, if appropriate or required.

IV. Charging a Corporation: Pervasiveness of Wrongdoing Within the Corporation

A. General Principle: A corporation can only act through natural persons, and it is therefore held responsible for the acts of such persons fairly attributable to it. Charging a corporation for even minor misconduct may be appropriate where the wrongdoing was pervasive and was undertaken by a large number of employees or by all the employees in a particular role within the corporation, *e.g.*, salesmen or procurement officers, or was condoned by upper management. On the other hand, in certain limited circumstances, it may not be appropriate to impose liability upon a corporation, particularly one with a compliance program in place, under strict *respondeat superior* theory for the single isolated act of a rogue employee. There is, of course, a wide spectrum between these two extremes, and a prosecutor should exercise sound discretion in evaluating the pervasiveness of wrongdoing within a corporation.

B. Comment: Of these factors, the most important is the role of management. Although acts of even low-level employees may result in criminal liability, a corporation is directed by its management and management is responsible for a corporate culture in which criminal conduct is either discouraged or tacitly encouraged. As stated in commentary to the Sentencing Guidelines:

> Pervasiveness [is] case specific and [will] depend on the number, and degree of responsibility, of individuals [with] substantial authority ... who participated in, condoned, or were willfully ignorant of the offense. Fewer individuals need to be involved for a finding of pervasiveness if those individuals exercised a relatively high degree of authority. Pervasiveness can occur either within an organization as a whole or within a unit of an organization.

USSG §8C2.5, comment. (n. 4).

V. Charging a Corporation: The Corporation's Past History

A. General Principle: Prosecutors may consider a corporation's history of similar conduct, including prior criminal, civil, and regulatory enforcement actions against it, in determining whether to bring criminal charges.

5

B. Comment: A corporation, like a natural person, is expected to learn from its mistakes. A history of similar conduct may be probative of a corporate culture that encouraged, or at least condoned, such conduct, regardless of any compliance programs. Criminal prosecution of a corporation may be particularly appropriate where the corporation previously had been subject to non-criminal guidance, warnings, or sanctions, or previous criminal charges, and yet it either had not taken adequate action to prevent future unlawful conduct or had continued to engage in the conduct in spite of the warnings or enforcement actions taken against it. In making this determination, the corporate structure itself, *e.g.*, subsidiaries or operating divisions, should be ignored, and enforcement actions taken against the corporation or any of its divisions, subsidiaries, and affiliates should be considered. *See* USSG § 8C2.5(c) & comment. (n. 6).

1. Charging a Corporation: Cooperation and Voluntary Disclosure

A. General Principle: In determining whether to charge a corporation, that corporation's timely and voluntary disclosure of wrongdoing and its willingness to cooperate with the government's investigation may be relevant factors. In gauging the extent of the corporation's cooperation, the prosecutor may consider the corporation's willingness to identify the culprits within the corporation, including senior executives; to make witnesses available; to disclose the complete results of its internal investigation; and to waive attorney-client and work product protection.

B. Comment: In investigating wrongdoing by or within a corporation, a prosecutor is likely to encounter several obstacles resulting from the nature of the corporation itself. It will often be difficult to determine which individual took which action on behalf of the corporation. Lines of authority and responsibility may be shared among operating divisions or departments, and records and personnel may be spread throughout the United States or even among several countries. Where the criminal conduct continued over an extended period of time, the culpable or knowledgeable personnel may have been promoted, transferred, or fired, or they may have quit or retired. Accordingly, a corporation's cooperation may be critical in identifying the culprits and locating relevant evidence.

In some circumstances, therefore, granting a corporation immunity or amnesty or pretrial diversion may be considered in the course of the government's investigation. In such circumstances, prosecutors should refer to the principles governing non-prosecution agreements generally. *See* USAM § 9-27.600-650. These principles permit a non prosecution agreement in exchange for cooperation when a corporation's "timely cooperation appears to be necessary to the public interest and other means of obtaining the desired cooperation are unavailable or would not be effective." Prosecutors should note that in the case of national or multi-national corporations, multi-district or global agreements may be necessary. Such agreements may only be entered into with the approval of each affected district or the appropriate Department official. *See* USAM §9-7.641.

6

In addition, the Department, in conjunction with regulatory agencies and other executive branch departments, encourages corporations, as part of their compliance programs, to conduct internal investigations and to disclose their findings to the appropriate authorities. Some agencies, such as the SEC and the EPA, as well as the Department's Environmental and Natural Resources Division, have formal voluntary disclosure programs in which self-reporting, coupled with remediation and additional criteria, may qualify the corporation for amnesty or reduced sanctions.[2] Even in the absence of a formal program, prosecutors may consider a corporation's timely and voluntary disclosure in evaluating the adequacy of the corporation's compliance program and its management's commitment to the compliance program. However, prosecution and economic policies specific to the industry or statute may require prosecution notwithstanding a corporation's willingness to cooperate. For example, the Antitrust Division offers amnesty only to the first corporation to agree to cooperate. This creates a strong incentive for corporations participating in anti-competitive conduct to be the first to cooperate. In addition, amnesty, immunity, or reduced sanctions may not be appropriate where the corporation's business is permeated with fraud or other crimes.

One factor the prosecutor may weigh in assessing the adequacy of a corporation's cooperation is the completeness of its disclosure including, if necessary, a waiver of the attorney-client and work product protections, both with respect to its internal investigation and with respect to communications between specific officers, directors and employees and counsel. Such waivers permit the government to obtain statements of possible witnesses, subjects, and targets, without having to negotiate individual cooperation or immunity agreements. In addition, they are often critical in enabling the government to evaluate the completeness of a corporation's voluntary disclosure and cooperation. Prosecutors may, therefore, request a waiver in appropriate circumstances.[3] The Department does not, however, consider waiver of a corporation's attorney-client and work product protection an absolute requirement, and prosecutors should consider the willingness of a corporation to waive such protection when necessary to provide timely and complete information as one factor in evaluating the corporation's cooperation.

Another factor to be weighed by the prosecutor is whether the corporation appears to be protecting its culpable employees and agents. Thus, while cases will differ depending on the circumstances, a corporation's promise of support to culpable employees and agents, either

---

[2] In addition, the Sentencing Guidelines reward voluntary disclosure and cooperation with a reduction in the corporation's offense level. *See* USSG §8C2.5)g).

[3] This waiver should ordinarily be limited to the factual internal investigation and any contemporaneous advice given to the corporation concerning the conduct at issue. Except in unusual circumstances, prosecutors should not seek a waiver with respect to communications and work product related to advice concerning the government's criminal investigation.

7

through the advancing of attorneys fees,[4] through retaining the employees without sanction for their misconduct, or through providing information to the employees about the government's investigation pursuant to a joint defense agreement, may be considered by the prosecutor in weighing the extent and value of a corporation's cooperation. By the same token, the prosecutor should be wary of attempts to shield corporate officers and employees from liability by a willingness of the corporation to plead guilty.

Another factor to be weighed by the prosecutor is whether the corporation, while purporting to cooperate, has engaged in conduct that impedes the investigation (whether or not rising to the level of criminal obstruction). Examples of such conduct include: overly broad assertions of corporate representation of employees or former employees; inappropriate directions to employees or their counsel, such as directions not to cooperate openly and fully with the investigation including, for example, the direction to decline to be interviewed; making presentations or submissions that contain misleading assertions or omissions; incomplete or delayed production of records; and failure to promptly disclose illegal conduct known to the corporation.

Finally, a corporation's offer of cooperation does not automatically entitle it to immunity from prosecution. A corporation should not be able to escape liability merely by offering up its directors, officers, employees, or agents as in lieu of its own prosecution. Thus, a corporation's willingness to cooperate is merely one relevant factor, that needs to be considered in conjunction with the other factors, particularly those relating to the corporation's past history and the role of management in the wrongdoing.

VII. Charging a Corporation: Corporate Compliance Programs

A. General Principle: Compliance programs are established by corporate management to prevent and to detect misconduct and to ensure that corporate activities are conducted in accordance with all applicable criminal and civil laws, regulations, and rules. The Department encourages such corporate self-policing, including voluntary disclosures to the government of any problems that a corporation discovers on its own. However, the existence of a compliance program is not sufficient, in and of itself, to justify not charging a corporation for criminal conduct undertaken by its officers, directors, employees, or agents. Indeed, the commission of such crimes in the face of a compliance program may suggest that the corporate management is not adequately enforcing its program. In addition, the nature of some crimes, *e.g.*, antitrust violations, may be such that national law enforcement policies mandate prosecutions of corporations notwithstanding the existence of a compliance program.

---

[4] Some states require corporations to pay the legal fees of officers under investigation prior to a formal determination of their guilt. Obviously, a corporation's compliance with governing law should not be considered a failure to cooperate.

8

B. Comment: A corporate compliance program, even one specifically prohibiting the very conduct in question, does not absolve the corporation from criminal liability under the doctrine of *respondeat superior. See United States v. Basic Construction Co.,* 711 F.2d 570 (4th Cir. 1983) ("a corporation may be held criminally responsible for antitrust violations committed by its employees if they were acting within the scope of their authority, or apparent authority, and for the benefit of the corporation, even if... such acts were against corporate policy or express instructions."). In *United States v. Hilton Hotels Corp.,* 467 F.2d 1000 (9th Cir. 1972), *cert. denied,* 409 U.S. 1125 (1973), the Ninth Circuit affirmed antitrust liability based upon a purchasing agent for a single hotel threatening a single supplier with a boycott unless it paid dues to a local marketing association, even though the agent's actions were contrary to corporate policy and directly against express instructions from his superiors. The court reasoned that Congress, in enacting the Sherman Antitrust Act, "intended to impose liability upon business entities for the acts of those to whom they choose to delegate the conduct of their affairs, thus stimulating a maximum effort by owners and managers to assure adherence by such agents to the requirements of the Act."[5] It concluded that "general policy statements" and even direct instructions from the agent's superiors were not sufficient; "Appellant could not gain exculpation by issuing general instructions without undertaking to enforce those instructions by means commensurate with the obvious risks." *See also United States v. Beusch,* 596 F.2d 871, 878 (9th Cir. 1979) ("[A] corporation may be liable for the acts of its employees done contrary to express instructions and policies, but ... the existence of such instructions and policies may be considered in determining whether the employee in fact acted to benefit the corporation."); *United States v. American Radiator & Standard Sanitary Corp.,* 433 F.2d 174 (3rd Cir. 1970) (affirming conviction of corporation based upon its officer's participation in price-fixing scheme, despite corporation's defense that officer's conduct violated its "rigid anti-fraternization policy" against any socialization (and exchange of price information) with its competitors; "When the act of the agent is within the scope of his employment or his apparent authority, the corporation is held legally responsible for it, although what he did may be contrary to his actual instructions and may be unlawful.").

While the Department recognizes that no compliance program can ever prevent all criminal activity by a corporation's employees, the critical factors in evaluating any program are whether the program is adequately designed for maximum effectiveness in preventing and detecting wrongdoing by employees and whether corporate management is enforcing the program

---

[5]   Although this case and *Basic Construction* are both antitrust cases, their reasoning applies to other criminal violations. In the Hilton case, for instance, the Ninth Circuit noted that Sherman Act violations are commercial offenses "usually motivated by a desire to enhance profits," thus, bringing the case within the normal rule that a "purpose to benefit the corporation is necessary to bring the agent's acts within the scope of his employment." 467 F.2d at 1006 & n4. In addition, in *United States v. Automated Medical Laboratories,* 770 F.2d 399, 406 n.5 (4th Cir. 1985), the Fourth Circuit stated "that Basic Construction states a generally applicable rule of corporate criminal liability despite the fact that it addresses violations of the antitrust laws."

9

r is tacitly encouraging or pressuring employees to engage in misconduct to achieve business bjectives. The Department has no formal guidelines for corporate compliance programs. The indamental questions any prosecutor should ask are: "Is the corporation's compliance program ell designed?" and "Does the corporation's compliance program work?" In answering these uestions, the prosecutor should consider the comprehensiveness of the compliance program; the xtent and pervasiveness of the criminal conduct; the number and level of the corporate mployees involved; the seriousness, duration, and frequency of the misconduct; and any emedial actions taken by the corporation, including restitution, disciplinary action, and revisions corporate compliance programs.[6] Prosecutors should also consider the promptness of any isclosure of wrongdoing to the government and the corporation's cooperation in the overnment's investigation. In evaluating compliance programs, prosecutors may consider vhether the corporation has established corporate governance mechanisms that can effectively etect and prevent misconduct. For example, do the corporation's directors exercise independent view over proposed corporate actions rather than unquestioningly ratifying officers' ecommendations; are the directors provided with information sufficient to enable the exercise of idependent judgment, are internal audit functions conducted at a level sufficient to ensure their idependence and accuracy and have the directors established an information and reporting ystem in the organization reasonable designed to provide management and the board of directors ith timely and accurate information sufficient to allow them to reach an informed decision garding the organization's compliance with the law. *In re: Caremark*, 698 A.2d 959 (Del. Ct. han. 1996).

Prosecutors should therefore attempt to determine whether a corporation's compliance rogram is merely a "paper program" or whether it was designed and implemented in an effective anner. In addition, prosecutors should determine whether the corporation has provided for a :aff sufficient to audit, document, analyze, and utilize the results of the corporation's compliance fforts. In addition, prosecutors should determine whether the corporation's employees are dequately informed about the compliance program and are convinced of the corporation's ommitment to it. This will enable the prosecutor to make an informed decision as to whether the orporation has adopted and implemented a truly effective compliance program that, when onsistent with other federal law enforcement policies, may result in a decision to charge only the orporation's employees and agents.

Compliance programs should be designed to detect the particular types of misconduct iost likely to occur in a particular corporation's line of business. Many corporations operate in omplex regulatory environments outside the normal experience of criminal prosecutors. ccordingly, prosecutors should consult with relevant federal and state agencies with the xpertise to evaluate the adequacy of a program's design and implementation. For instance, state nd federal banking, insurance, and medical boards, the Department of Defense, the Department

---

For a detailed review of these and other factors concerning corporate compliance rograms, see United States Sentencing Commission, GUIDELINES MANUAL, §8A1.2, mment. (n.3(k)) (Nov. 1997). *See also* USSG §8C2.5(f)

10

of Health and Human Services, the Environmental Protection Agency, and the Securities and Exchange Commission have considerable experience with compliance programs and can be very helpful to a prosecutor in evaluating such programs. In addition, the Fraud Section of the Criminal Division, the Commercial Litigation Branch of the Civil Division, and the Environmental Crimes Section of the Environment and Natural Resources Division can assist U.S. Attorneys' Offices in finding the appropriate agency office and in providing copies of compliance programs that were developed in previous cases.

VIII. Charging a Corporation: Restitution and Remediation

A. General Principle: Although neither a corporation nor an individual target may avoid prosecution merely by paying a sum of money, a prosecutor may consider the corporation's willingness to make restitution and steps already taken to do so. A prosecutor may also consider other remedial actions, such as implementing an effective corporate compliance program, improving an existing compliance program, and disciplining wrongdoers, in determining whether to charge the corporation.

B. Comment: In determining whether or not a corporation should be prosecuted, a prosecutor may consider whether meaningful remedial measures have been taken, including employee discipline and full restitution.[7] A corporation's response to misconduct says much about its willingness to ensure that such misconduct does not recur. Thus, corporations that fully recognize the seriousness of their misconduct and accept responsibility for it should be taking steps to implement the personnel, operational, and organizational changes necessary to establish an awareness among employees that criminal conduct will not be tolerated. Among the factors prosecutors should consider and weigh are whether the corporation appropriately disciplined the wrongdoers and disclosed information concerning their illegal conduct to the government.

Employee discipline is a difficult task for many corporations because of the human element involved and sometimes because of the seniority of the employees concerned. While corporations need to be fair to their employees, they must also be unequivocally committed, at all levels of the corporation, to the highest standards of legal and ethical behavior. Effective internal discipline can be a powerful deterrent against improper behavior by a corporation's employees. In evaluating a corporation's response to wrongdoing, prosecutors may evaluate the willingness of the corporation to discipline culpable employees of all ranks and the adequacy of the discipline imposed. The prosecutor should be satisfied that the corporation's focus is on the integrity and credibility of its remedial and disciplinary measures rather than on the protection of the wrongdoers.

---

[7]   For example, the Antitrust Division's amnesty policy requires that "[w]here possible, the corporation [make] restitution to injured parties...."

11

In addition to employee discipline, two other factors used in evaluating a corporation's remedial efforts are restitution and reform. As with natural persons, the decision whether or not to prosecute should not depend upon the target's ability to pay restitution. A corporation's efforts to pay restitution even in advance of any court order is, however, evidence of its "acceptance of responsibility" and, consistent with the practices and policies of the appropriate Division of the Department entrusted with enforcing specific criminal laws, may be considered in determining whether to bring criminal charges. Similarly, although the inadequacy of a corporate compliance program is a factor to consider when deciding whether to charge a corporation, that corporation's quick recognition of the flaws in the program and its efforts to improve the program are also factors to consider.

IX. Charging a Corporation: Collateral Consequences

A. General Principle: Prosecutors may consider the collateral consequences of a corporate criminal conviction in determining whether to charge the corporation with a criminal offense.

B. Comment: One of the factors in determining whether to charge a natural person or a corporation is whether the likely punishment is appropriate given the nature and seriousness of the crime. In the corporate context, prosecutors may take into account the possibly substantial consequences to a corporation's officers, directors, employees, and shareholders, many of whom may, depending on the size and nature (e.g., publicly vs. closely held) of the corporation and their role in its operations, have played no role in the criminal conduct, have been completely unaware of it, or have been wholly unable to prevent it. Prosecutors should also be aware of non-penal sanctions that may accompany a criminal charge, such as potential suspension or debarment from eligibility for government contracts or federal funded programs such as health care. Whether or not such non-penal sanctions are appropriate or required in a particular case is the responsibility of the relevant agency, a decision that will be made based on the applicable statutes, regulations, and policies.

Virtually every conviction of a corporation, like virtually every conviction of an individual, will have an impact on innocent third parties, and the mere existence of such an effect is not sufficient to preclude prosecution of the corporation. Therefore, in evaluating the severity of collateral consequences, various factors already discussed, such as the pervasiveness of the criminal conduct and the adequacy of the corporation's compliance programs, should be considered in determining the weight to be given to this factor. For instance, the balance may tip in favor of prosecuting corporations in situations where the scope of the misconduct in a case is widespread and sustained within a corporate division (or spread throughout pockets of the corporate organization). In such cases, the possible unfairness of visiting punishment for the corporation's crimes upon shareholders may be of much less concern where those shareholders have substantially profited, even unknowingly, from widespread or pervasive criminal activity. Similarly, where the top layers of the corporation's management or the shareholders of a closely-held corporation were engaged in or aware of the wrongdoing and the conduct at issue

12

was accepted as a way of doing business for an extended period, debarment may be deemed not collateral, but a direct and entirely appropriate consequence of the corporation's wrongdoing.

The appropriateness of considering such collateral consequences and the weight to be given them may depend on the special policy concerns discussed in section III, *supra*.

X. Charging a Corporation: Non-Criminal Alternatives

A. General Principle: Although non-criminal alternatives to prosecution often exist, prosecutors may consider whether such sanctions would adequately deter, punish, and rehabilitate a corporation that has engaged in wrongful conduct. In evaluating the adequacy of non-criminal alternatives to prosecution, *e.g.*, civil or regulatory enforcement actions, the prosecutor may consider all relevant factors, including:

1. the sanctions available under the alternative means of disposition;

2. the likelihood that an effective sanction will be imposed; and

3. the effect of non-criminal disposition on Federal law enforcement interests.

B. Comment: The primary goals of criminal law are deterrence, punishment, and rehabilitation. Non-criminal sanctions may not be an appropriate response to an egregious violation, a pattern of wrongdoing, or a history of non-criminal sanctions without proper remediation. In other cases, however, these goals may be satisfied without the necessity of instituting criminal proceedings. In determining whether federal criminal charges are appropriate, the prosecutor should consider the same factors (modified appropriately for the regulatory context) considered when determining whether to leave prosecution of a natural person to another jurisdiction or to seek non-criminal alternatives to prosecution. These factors include: the strength of the regulatory authority's interest; the regulatory authority's ability and willingness to take effective enforcement action; the probable sanction if the regulatory authority's enforcement action is upheld; and the effect of a non-criminal disposition on Federal law enforcement interests. *See* USAM §§ 9-27.240, 9-27.250.

XI. Charging a Corporation: Selecting Charges

A. General Principle: Once a prosecutor has decided to charge a corporation, the prosecutor should charge, or should recommend that the grand jury charge, the most serious offense that is consistent with the nature of the defendant's conduct and that is likely to result in a sustainable conviction.

13

B. Comment: Once the decision to charge is made, the same rules as govern charging natural persons apply. These rules require "a faithful and honest application of the Sentencing Guidelines" and an "individualized assessment of the extent to which particular charges fit the specific circumstances of the case, are consistent with the purposes of the Federal criminal code, and maximize the impact of Federal resources on crime." *See* USAM § 9-27.300. In making this determination, "it is appropriate that the attorney for the government consider, *inter alia*, such factors as the sentencing guideline range yielded by the charge, whether the penalty yielded by such sentencing range ... is proportional to the seriousness of the defendant's conduct, and whether the charge achieves such purposes of the criminal law as punishment, protection of the public, specific and general deterrence, and rehabilitation." *See* Attorney General's Memorandum, dated October 12, 1993.

XII. Plea Agreements with Corporations

A. General Principle: In negotiating plea agreements with corporations, prosecutors should seek a plea to the most serious, readily provable offense charged. In addition, the terms of the plea agreement should contain appropriate provisions to ensure punishment, deterrence, rehabilitation, and compliance with the plea agreement in the corporate context. Although special circumstances may mandate a different conclusion, prosecutors generally should not agree to accept a corporate guilty plea in exchange for non-prosecution or dismissal of charges against individual officers and employees.

B. Comment: Prosecutors may enter into plea agreements with corporations for the same reasons and under the same constraints as apply to plea agreements with natural persons. *See* USAM §§ 9-27.400-500. This means, *inter alia*, that the corporation should be required to plead guilty to the most serious, readily provable offense charged. As is the case with individuals, the attorney making this determination should do so "on the basis of an individualized assessment of the extent to which particular charges fit the specific circumstances of the case, are consistent with the purposes of the federal criminal code, and maximize the impact of federal resources on crime. In making this determination, the attorney for the government considers, inter alia, such factors as the sentencing guideline range yielded by the charge, whether the penalty yielded by such sentencing range ... is proportional to the seriousness of the defendant's conduct, and whether the charge achieves such purposes of the criminal law as punishment, protection of the public, specific and general deterrence, and rehabilitation." *See* Attorney General's Memorandum, dated October 12, 1993. In addition, any negotiated departures from the Sentencing Guidelines must be justifiable under the Guidelines and must be disclosed to the sentencing court. A corporation should be made to realize that pleading guilty to criminal charges constitutes an admission of guilt and not merely a resolution of an inconvenient distraction from its business. As with natural persons, pleas should be structured so that the corporation may not later "proclaim lack of culpability or even complete innocence." *See* USAM §§ 9-27.420(b)(4), 9-27.440, 9-27.500. Thus, for instance, there should be placed upon the record a sufficient factual basis for the plea to prevent later corporate assertions of innocence.

14

A corporate plea agreement should also contain provisions that recognize the nature of the corporate "person" and ensure that the principles of punishment, deterrence, and rehabilitation are met. In the corporate context, punishment and deterrence are generally accomplished by substantial fines, mandatory restitution, and institution of appropriate compliance measures, including, if necessary, continued judicial oversight or the use of special masters. *See* USSG §§ 8B1.1, 8C2.1, *et seq.* In addition, where the corporation is a government contractor, permanent or temporary debarment may be appropriate. Where the corporation was engaged in government contracting fraud, a prosecutor may not negotiate away an agency's right to debar or to list the corporate defendant.

In negotiating a plea agreement, prosecutors should also consider the deterrent value of prosecutions of individuals within the corporation. Therefore, one factor that a prosecutor may consider in determining whether to enter into a plea agreement is whether the corporation is seeking immunity for its employees and officers or whether the corporation is willing to cooperate in the investigation of culpable individuals. Prosecutors should rarely negotiate away individual criminal liability in a corporate plea.

Rehabilitation, of course, requires that the corporation undertake to be law-abiding in the future. It is, therefore, appropriate to require the corporation, as a condition of probation, to implement a compliance program or to reform an existing one. As discussed above, prosecutors may consult with the appropriate state and federal agencies and components of the Justice Department to ensure that a proposed compliance program is adequate and meets industry standards and best practices. *See* section VII, *supra*.

In plea agreements in which the corporation agrees to cooperate, the prosecutor should ensure that the cooperation is complete and truthful. To do so, the prosecutor may request that the corporation waive attorney-client and work product protection, make employees and agents available for debriefing, disclose the results of its internal investigation, file appropriate certified financial statements, agree to governmental or third-party audits, and take whatever other steps are necessary to ensure that the full scope of the corporate wrongdoing is disclosed and that the responsible culprits are identified and, if appropriate, prosecuted. *See* generally section VIII, *supra*.

15

Appendix B

Wall Street Journal Article

This article appeared on the front page, above the fold, of the *Wall Street Journal* on February 16, 2007, in what appeared to me to be part of a carefully orchestrated plan by the prosecutors to call attention to the case they were about to bring.

You will note that the lead topic in the article is an email that I wrote on January 4, 2002 regarding an option granting decision that had been made the previous December 24. This same e-mail was hammered at by Mr. Stolper in his opening statement at trial, when he said:

> Let's take a look at what was going on inside Broadcom, to see if the option committee actually met and granted on Christmas Eve, 2001.
>
> E-mail from the defendant to the option committee, to Henry Nicholas and to Henry Samueli.
>
> What does he say?
>
> "I" – all caps – "VERY strongly recommend these options be priced as of December 24. Given the recent market performance" – as you can see, the price is going up – "I think we should grab the December 24 price. If we wait beyond Friday, we will have missed the deadline and will be subject to market risk."
>
> Outside, he granted options on December 24; inside, 10 days later, "I think we should grab the December 24 price."
>
> If the option committee were meeting and granting in real time, if they weren't backdating stock options, this e-mail cannot exist.

Inflammatory comments, to say the least. Because of the prominence given to this email I want to provide context to show how the attempt to make it sound nefarious was misguided.

The grant date of December 24, 2001 was not just chosen at random nor was it chosen opportunistically, as the prosecutors would have you believe. The prosecutors tried to put further spin on the date by constantly referring to it as "Christmas Eve", with the implication being it would be highly unlikely for any serious corporate work to be done on Christmas Eve.

The history of that grant is that it was an important part of the company's attempt to maintain equity incentives for our employees in the face of the meltdown of the NASDAQ market that began in 2000. As described earlier, the company conducted a so-called *tender offer* that allowed employees to cancel their old high-priced options for ones that would be repriced on the new grant date.

The tender offer process was closely regulated by the SEC. An important provision was that the repricing could take place no sooner than six months and one day after the old options were surrendered. This meant that participating employees had no option incentives at all for the intervening period. The first possible date the options could be granted was December 24, 2001. The option committee, with the full support of the senior executive staff and board members, had decided back in June when the tender offer was launched that the regrant would be done on the first possible day. That day was December 24.

This point was brought out during the prosecutors' case as Rich cross-examined Werner Wolfen, a board member:

> Rich Marmaro: Did you understand from meetings at the board level that it was always the intent of management to grant those new options at the first available time that they could because the employees for that six-month-and-a-day period were without options?

> Werner Wolfen: That's correct.

Q: And the first day available to grant those options was December 24, 2001, was it not?

A: I don't know that, but I believe that's right.

Q: So it was no secret at Broadcom that the grant date of this grant, the grant taking care of the employees who had tendered their shares, was going to be December 24th, 2001?

A: You want me to comment on that? I think that's right.

During the defense case, Rich revisited the issue with David Dull:

Rich Marmaro: And was there an understanding among many people at the company that Broadcom would do its best to grant replacement options at the earliest day it was legally permitted to do so?

David Dull: Yes.

Q: And was that a common understanding among the management of the company?

A: Yes. I think it was a common understanding with the management and the board. And we had some flexibility. We actually provided, in the tender offer, documents that we had, as it turned out, I believe until the end of January 2002 to make the grants. But the expectation had always been that these grants would be made at the earliest possible date because we had – the principal reason being that the employees were sitting there bare in the meantime.

Later, Rich probed David on why there was continual discussion of the grant date if the decision had already been made. David responded:

Well, I didn't – I guess the reason I'm having trouble with your question is that, from my perspective, December 24 was the default date. It was the date the grants were going to occur. So it wasn't an issue, in that particular case, of getting Dr. Nicholas to release, if you will, make a decision, because the decision had already been made.

Rich went on to ask David if he knew why I had written the January 4 e-mail if the decision had already been made. David replied:

I viewed this, as I just indicated a moment ago, as a response from Bill to what he perceived to be an attempt by Nick to re-litigate the decision to price as of December 24. And I know the phraseology of the e-mail doesn't jump out and doesn't use words like "re-litigate", but I understood this is the way we wrote e-mails to Nick when we basically wanted him to give up trying to re-litigate a decision.

Later in the trial, Rich posed a similar line of questioning to Henry Samueli:

Rich Marmaro: Did you have a pre-arrangement or pre-agreement with Dr. Nicholas?

Henry Samueli: My recollection is yes, before we all left on our Christmas vacations, that we had discussed many times the fact that we had intended to grant these shares on the first available date, which was December 24. So that is my understanding that we had that agreement.

So with that background, here is the WSJ article:

(For reference, a copy of this article was included as Exhibit 6 to Prosecutorial Misconduct motion filed by the defense as Document 135-4 on 10/20/2008.)

THE WALL STREET JOURNAL

FRIDAY, FEBRUARY 16, 2007 ~ VOL. CCXLIX NO. 39

BEARING DOWN

Probes of Backdating Move to Faster Track

Stock-Option Emails At Broadcom Are Focus; Monster Worldwide Plea

By JAMES BANDLER
and CHARLES FORELLE

On Jan. 4, 2002, the chief financial officer of Broadcom Corp. tapped out an email about stock options to his chief executive and others.

"I VERY strongly recommend that these options be priced as of December 24," he wrote.

They were, and that was fortunate for recipients. Broadcom's share price rose 23% between the two dates. The pretense that the options had been granted on the earlier date made them extra valuable.

It also violated the rationale of stock options. They give recipients a right to buy stock in the future at the price when the options are granted, so that recipients can profit only if the price of their company's stock goes up. Setting a lower "exercise price" for the options gives recipients a head start on profiting.

The Broadcom correspondence, and in an internal investigation at the maker of communication chips, is just one of a number internal documents that have drawn the attention federal prosecutors and Federal Bureau of Investigation agents in Orange County, Calif. Prosecutors are strongly considering filing criminal charges against the former Broadcom chief financial officer who wrote the email, William J. Ruehle, and at least one other former executive, according to people familiar with the situation.

Mr. Ruehle's lawyer said his client didn't break the law.

The Broadcom probe is a sign of how long-running investigations of stock-options back-

William J. Ruehle

dating are heating up. Yesterday, a former general counsel of Monster Worldwide Inc. pleaded guilty to securities fraud in federal court in Manhat-

tan. The day before, the founder of Take-Two Interactive Software Inc. pleaded guilty to a New York State charge in a backdating scheme.

Prosecutors in a half-dozen jurisdictions are zeroing in on other cases. The filing of criminal charges in some of these in coming months would mark a watershed in the scandal, as prosecutors and regulators winnow the roster of some 140 companies with options problems to a tighter list of promising cases.

The government is nearing charges against a former official of computer-security company McAfee Inc., say people familiar with the situation, and is strongly considering bringing cases against ex-executives of Apple Inc. and semiconductor-equipment maker KLA-Tencor Corp. In St. Louis, at least one former executive of Engineered Support Systems Inc., a defense contractor now owned by DRS Technologies Inc. of Parsippany, N.J., has been told of a likely charge, says a person close to the matter.

The former Monster Worldwide general counsel who pleaded guilty yesterday is Myron Olesnyckyj, 45. He admitted that he and others conspired to systematically backdate stock options, inflate the company's earnings and mislead auditors. Separately, the Securities and Exchange Commission filed a civil complaint against him. Mr. Olesnyckyj agreed to forfeit $381,000 in personal gains. He faces sentencing in August.

Mr. Olesnyckyj, fired last year, is expected to cooperate with prosecutors investigating Monster founder Andrew McKelvey. Mr. McKelvey, who hasn't been charged, quit late

last year rather than be interviewed in an internal company probe of options. A lawyer for him declined to comment.

In a 1999 email cited by the government, Mr. Olesnyckyj wrote to a human-resources official: "No written document should ever state lowest price over next 30 days! The auditor will view that as backdating options and we'll have a charge to earning in the amount of the difference between price on day 30 and any lower price which is used."

That's the type of evidence investigators are looking for—"plus factors" that can give a case more promise of success. Such factors might include written indications of deliberate backdating; falsified documents; efforts to hide manipulation from auditors or investigators; or indications that top executives gave themselves backdated options. With so many companies admitting to an improper options practice, investigators have an abundance of possible cases.

Broadcom illustrates some of the elements investigators are focusing on as they set their priorities. The Irvine, Calif., company is one of the biggest companies in the options spotlight. It makes chips that help power all sorts of communications devices and has a stock-

market value of more than $19 billion. The SEC in addition to the Justice Department is looking at Broadcom.

Also being investigated are Henry Nicholas—the former chief executive to whom the CFO's email was addressed—and Henry Samueli, Broadcom's chairman. Messrs. Nicholas and Samueli co-founded Broadcom. The two made up the committee that handed out options Broadcom has admitted were backdated.

Mr. Nicholas said in a statement his focus was on running Broadcom, and "the minutiae of employee paperwork and documentation were not at the top of my list." Mr. Samueli's attorney declined to comment except to say that some of the Journal's information was "misleading."

Mr. Nicholas founded the company in 1991 with help from Mr. Samueli, his former engineering professor. After they took it public in 1998, its stock soared 20-fold in two years. Together the men sold more than $1 billion in Broadcom shares near the end of the tech boom. Each still holds about $1 billion of Broadcom stock.

A domineering figure, Mr. Nicholas routinely scheduled late-night staff meetings and boasted of working for days without sleep. At a yearly sales conference, he quizzed subordinates about chip designs, forcing those who erred to gulp down shots of hard liquor. He stepped down from his CEO post in 2003. Along the way, he settled into a 15,000-square-foot mansion, which he outfitted with a billionaire's toys: waterfalls, secret tunnels into the hills, a sports bar.

Deepening Probe

Federal prosecutors are investigating whether Broadcom executives pretended stock-option grants were awarded when the company's shares were particularly low, giving the recipients a chance at extra profit. Two of the grants being examined:

● Date of grant

Grant to nonofficer employees

Grant to executives

Jan 4: Finance chief William Ruehle sends email to CEO Henry Nicholas, "I VERY strongly recommend that these options be priced as of December 24."

Sources: FactSet Research Systems; WSJ research

Mr. Samueli cuts a less flamboyant figure. A leading philanthropist in Orange County, he also owns the Mighty Ducks hockey franchise. Two University of California engineering schools bear his name.

Last year Broadcom admitted rampant backdating. It restated several years of results, taking $2.24 billion in charges against earnings—the biggest restatement so far in the scandal.

Mr. Ruehle stepped down as Broadcom's chief financial officer a few days before he was to be interviewed by outside lawyers doing the internal investigation. Broadcom said in a securities filing that Mr. Ruehle was "at the center" of backdating. Mr. Ruehle's lawyer, Richard Marmaro, said that if his client is charged, he "will not plead guilty because he did not commit any crime."

Broadcom in its filing also blamed a former human-resources chief, Nancy Tullos. It said she "encouraged, assisted in and enabled" the backdating. A lawyer for Ms. Tullos, who left in 2003, declined to comment for this article. The lawyer has said previously that Ms. Tullos followed the directives of superiors, didn't select any grant dates and always acted in the company's best interests.

Broadcom's backdating, which it has said occurred from 1998 to 2003, took place amid a heated technology industry in which valued employees were often poached by others with big options packages. Broadcom emails, described by people who have seen them, suggest that executives sometimes deliberately gave grants earlier dates and sometimes cautioned others not to mention the dating process in writing.

Broadcom's auditor, Ernst & Young, raised concerns in 2000 about an aspect of the options process and reminded executives about the rules, say people familiar with the matter. At that time, options granted at the current stock price didn't affect companies' earnings. But a grant at below-market prices was considered compensation, so that companies had to count it as an expense.

In 2000 Broadcom made a giant options grant to a large number of employees, purportedly on a day in May when the stock had its lowest close for the quarter. Ernst discovered that the company hadn't finished divvying up the grant among employees until months later. Accounting rules say an option isn't recorded as granted until recipients are determined.

Ernst warned company officials, including Mr. Ruehle, "not to make such "subsequent allocations" again, according to people familiar with the matter. Ernst reminded executives of how options should be accounted for, taking them through the rules.

Like many stocks, Broadcom's sank after the Sept. 11,

2001, terrorist attacks. It hit its lowest price in three years on Oct. 1, before recovering and then more than doubling by year-end. Broadcom claimed to have granted a slew of options to non-officers on Oct. 1. Investigators are looking at whether the company may actually have made this grant later and backdated it, say people familiar with the situation.

Broadcom said in its federal filing that co-founder Mr. Nicholas was "at times" involved in the backdating, and bore a large responsibility for the problems because of "the tone and style of doing business he set." A person familiar with the grant dated Oct. 1 said it engendered jealousy among those who didn't get options then, and that Mr. Nicholas and others appear to have retroactively added more people to the list.

In an email on Jan. 2, 2002, Mr. Nicholas sent a list of employees included in the Oct. 1 grant to at least two people, including Ms. Tullos, say people familiar with the email's contents. "I found my old share grant spreadsheet from before October," he wrote.

But the electronic time stamp on the computer file indicated the spreadsheet had been created toward the end of 2001, long after Oct. 1, say people familiar with the matter. The discrepancy has led investigators to examine whether the email and spreadsheet might be an attempt to provide written cover for manipulated grants.

Broadcom said in its federal filing that co-founder Mr. Samueli was "involved with" the "flawed option granting process." The company cleared him, saying he "reasonably relied on management and other professionals" regarding proper treatment of the options. According to people familiar with the matter, Mr. Samueli, as a member of the Equity Award Committee, received a number of emails that discussed retroactive date selection.

Mr. Samueli cooperated with the internal probe but so far has declined a request to speak to government investigators—unusual for a sitting chairman. When weighing how much responsibility corporations themselves bear for fraudulent conduct, prosecutors are supposed to consider how cooperative top officials have been, according to Justice Department guidelines.

An outside lawyer for Broadcom said it wouldn't comment on the investigation except to say that it was cooperating fully. "Dr. Samueli did cooperate fully and voluntarily with the company's independent internal investigation," said the lawyer, David Siegel.

In any effort to link backdating to Messrs. Nicholas and Sam-

ueli, prosecutors would fac[ ] potential hurdle: The [ ] founders didn't regularly [ ]ceive option grants themsel[ ] The two received just one gra[ ] for a million options each, [ ] 2002. Broadcom has said [ ] grants to the founders or to[ ] rectors were among those n[ ] dated.

Ms. Tullos and Mr. Rue[ ] by contrast, received num[ ] ous options, including gra[ ] the company has said w[ ] manipulated. Mr. Ruehle h[ ] $32 million of unexercised [ ] tions when he left last ye[ ] The company canceled the[ ] Last year the company c[ ]celed $4 million of opti[ ] Ms. Tullos held.

Several emails written [ ] Ms. Tullos suggest she m[ ] have been aware the dat[ ] practices were troubleso[ ] In a period when Broadco[ ] stock was falling, a busine[ ] unit head repeatedly ask[ ] get options. Eventually, [ ] told him "I cannot tell y[ ] what we are doing" in a "p[ ] Enron" world, according [ ] people familiar with the m[ ]ter. In a message to anot[ ] employee asking about op[ ] tions, she wrote, "I cannot [ ]swer in writing."

Prosecutors would n[ ] more than suggestive email[ ] make a successful crim[ ] case. A document that see[ ] like a smoking gun can g[ ] cold when the context is [ ]plained to a jury by an exp[ ]enced defense lawyer.

Another obstacle to [ ] government in prosecut[ ] backdating is at some com[ ]nies the practice was discus[ ] openly, making it harder to [ ]gue that executives knew t[ ] were engaged in wrongful c[ ]duct.

Defense lawyers will dou[ ]less pass blame around. Th[ ] representing CEOs are likel[ ] argue that their clients—b[ ] business leaders, not acco[ ]tants—relied on others to [ ]ure out how options should b[ ] sued and accounted for. Th[ ] representing subordinates [ ] likely to argue that the b[ ] made them do it.

Helping boost momentu[ ] ward the filing of charges is[ ] statute of limitations. It's [ ] years for securities fraud [ ] wire fraud. But there's s[ ] flexibility, based on the not[ ] that misdated options might [ ]fect earnings in later years.

—Paul Da[ ]
contributed to this art[ ]

Appendix C

Judge Carney's Ruling of December 15, 2009

UNITED STATES DISTRICT COURT

CENTRAL DISTRICT OF CALIFORNIA

SOUTHERN DIVISION

THE HON. CORMAC J. CARNEY, JUDGE PRESIDING

UNITED STATES OF AMERICA,	)	
	)	
PLAINTIFF,	)	
	)	
VS.	)	NO. SACR 08-00139-CJC
WILLIAM J. RUEHLE,	)	
DEFENDANT.	)	

REPORTER'S TRANSCRIPT OF PROCEEDINGS

SANTA ANA, CALIFORNIA

TUESDAY,DECEMBER 15, 2009

9:00

MARIA BEESLEY-DELLANEVE, CSR 9132
OFFICIAL FEDERAL REPORTER
RONALD REAGAN FEDERAL BUILDING
411 W. 4TH STREET, ROOM 1-053
SANTA ANA, CA 92701
(714) 564-9259

Page 5193

```
 1   APPEARANCES:

 2   FOR THE PLAINTIFF:      GEORGE S. CARDONA
                             UNITED STATES ATTORNEY
 3                           BY:   ANDREW STOLPER
                             AND ROBB ADKINS,
 4                               GREG STAPLES,
                             ASSISTANT UNITED STATES ATTORNEY
 5                           411 W. 4TH STREET, 8TH FLOOR
                             SANTA ANA, CALIFORNIA 92701
 6

 7

 8

 9

10   FOR THE DEFENDANT RUEHLE:    SKADDEN ARPS SLATE MEAGHER
                             BY:   RICHARD MARMARO, ESQ.
11                           AND   JACK DICANIO, ESQ.
                                   MATTHEW UMHOFER, ESQ.
12                           300 SOUTH GRAND AVENUE
                             LOS ANGELES, CALIFORNIA 90071
13                           (213)687-5535

14   FOR HENRY SAMUELI:      MCDERMOTT WILL & EMERY
                             BY:   GORDON GREENBERG, ESQ.
15                           2049 CENTURY PARK EAST, SUITE 3800
                             LOS ANGELES, CALIFORNIA 90067-3218
16                           (310) 551-9398

17
     FOR HENRY NICHOLAS:     WILLIAMS & CONNOLLY LLP
18                           BY:   BRENDAN SULLIVAN, ESQ.
                             725 TWELFTH STREET N.W.
19                           WASHINGTON D.C. 20005
                             (202) 434-5460
20

21   FOR DAVID DULL:         QUINN EMANUEL URQUHART OLVER & HEDGES
                             BY:   JAMES ASPERGER, ESQ.
22                           AND SETH ARONSON, ESQ.
                             865 S. FIGUEROA ST 10TH FL
23                           LOS ANGELES, CALIFORNIA 90017

24

25
```

```
 1        SANTA ANA, CALIFORNIA; TUESDAY, DECEMBER 15, 2009

 2                          -oOo-

 3        THE CLERK:  ITEM NUMBER ONE, SACR 08-139-CJC. UNITED

 4   STATES VERSUS WILLIAM J. RUEHLE.

 5        COUNSEL, PLEASE STATE YOUR APPEARANCES FOR THE RECORD.

 6        MR. ADKINS:  GOOD MORNING, YOUR HONOR.  ROBB ADKINS,

 7   GEORGE CARDONA, ANDREW STOLPER, AND GREG STAPLES ON BEHALF OF THE

 8   UNITED STATES.

 9        THE COURT:  GOOD MORNING, GENTLEMEN.

10        MR. MARMARO:  GOOD MORNING, YOUR HONOR.  RICHARD MARMARO

11   AND JACK DICANIO FOR MR. RUEHLE, WHO IS PRESENT.

12        THE COURT:  GOOD MORNING.

13        AND I THINK WE HAVE SOME OTHER LAWYERS; RIGHT?  AND

14   PARTIES?

15        MR. SULLIVAN, I SEE YOU THERE, SIR.

16        MR. SULLIVAN:  BRENDAN SULLIVAN OF WILLIAMS AND CONNOLLY

17   FOR DR. HENRY NICHOLAS.

18        MR. ASPERGER:  GOOD MORNING, YOUR HONOR.  JIM ASPERGER

19   AND SETH ARONSON FOR MR. DULL.

20        MR. GREENBERG:  GORDON GREENBERG ON BEHALF OF DR. HENRY

21   SAMUELI, WHO IS PRESENT BEFORE THE COURT.

22        THE COURT:  GOOD MORNING TO ALL OF YOU.

23        WHAT I THOUGHT I WOULD DO IS READ INTO THE RECORD MY

24   DECISION, AND THEN I'LL GIVE EVERYONE A NOTICE AND OPPORTUNITY TO

25   SAY WHATEVER THEY WANT TO SAY ON THE RECORD.
```

243

1   I HEARD ALL THE EVIDENCE PRESENT AT MR. RUEHLE'S TRIAL

2   AND AT THE EVIDENTIARY HEARINGS. I NOW KNOW THE ENTIRE STORY OF

3   WHAT HAPPENED. THIS DECISION SUPERSEDES ANY PRIOR FINDINGS,

4   RULINGS OR CREDIBILITY DETERMINATION THAT I HAD MADE ON A PARTIAL

5   RECORD WITHOUT THE BENEFIT OF ALL THE FACTS.

6   BASED ON THE COMPLETE RECORD NOW BEFORE ME, I FIND THAT

7   THE GOVERNMENT HAS INTIMIDATED AND IMPROPERLY INFLUENCED THE THREE

8   WITNESSES CRITICAL TO MR. RUEHLE'S DEFENSE. THE CUMULATIVE EFFECT

9   OF THAT MISCONDUCT HAS DISTORTED THE TRUTH-FINDING PROCESS AND

10   COMPROMISED THE INTEGRITY OF THE TRIAL.

11   TO SUBMIT THIS CASE TO THE JURY WOULD MAKE A MOCKERY OF

12   MR. RUEHLE'S CONSTITUTIONAL RIGHT TO COMPULSORY PROCESS AND A FAIR

13   TRIAL. THE SIXTH AMENDMENT TO THE UNITED STATES CONSTITUTION

14   GUARANTEES THE ACCUSED THE RIGHT TO COMPULSORY PROCESS FOR

15   WITNESSES IN ITS DEFENSE. FOR THIS CONSTITUTIONAL RIGHT TO HAVE

16   TRUE MEANING, THE GOVERNMENT MUST NOT DO ANYTHING TO INTIMIDATE OR

17   IMPROPERLY INFLUENCE WITNESSES. SADLY, GOVERNMENT DID SO IN THIS

18   CASE.

19   MR. RUEHLE'S PRIMARY DEFENSE HERE HAS BEEN THAT HE HAD

20   NO CRIMINAL INTENT TO VIOLATE THE SECURITIES LAWS. TO SUCCEED, IT

21   WAS IMPERATIVE FOR MR. RUEHLE TO CALL THE THREE AVAILABLE

22   WITNESSES WHO HAD KNOWLEDGE OF BROADCOM'S STOCK-OPTION GRANTING

23   PRACTICES. THOSE THREE WITNESSES WERE NANCY TULLOS, THE VICE

24   PRESIDENT OF HUMAN RESOURCES; DAVID DULL, THE GENERAL COUNSEL; AND

25   DR. HENRY SAMUELI, COFOUNDER AND CHIEF TECHNICAL OFFICER. FOR

1 WHATEVER REASON, THE GOVERNMENT INTIMIDATED AND IMPROPERLY

2 INFLUENCED EACH OF THEM.

3   LET ME FIRST FOCUS ON MS. TULLOS. AFTER MS. TULLOS

4 DECLINED TO COOPERATE WITH THE GOVERNMENT, THE LEAD PROSECUTOR

5 CALLED THE GENERAL COUNSEL OF MS. TULLOS' NEW EMPLOYER AND MADE

6 INAPPROPRIATE STATEMENTS TO HIM THAT CAUSED MS. TULLOS TO LOSE HER

7 JOB.

8   AFTER THOSE EVENTS AND A REVERSE PROFFER SESSION THAT

9 LEFT HER UNDERSTANDABLY SCARED, MS. TULLOS ENTERED INTO AN UNUSUAL

10 COOPERATION PLEA AGREEMENT CONTAINING A QUESTIONABLE FACTUAL

11 BASIS, THAT SEVEN YEARS BEFORE ANY GOVERNMENT INVESTIGATION

12 COMMENCED INTO BROADCOM, MS. TULLOS OBSTRUCTED JUSTICE BY ASKING

13 AN EMPLOYEE TO DELETE AN E-MAIL THAT MS. TULLOS HERSELF NEVER

14 DELETED AND, IN FACT, COPIED TO ANOTHER PERSON.

15   THE GOVERNMENT ALSO TOLD MS. TULLOS THAT SHE WOULD HAVE

16 TO PLEAD TO A FELONY BECAUSE IT LOOKED MORE CONVINCING TO A JURY.

17 AND, MOST TROUBLING, THE GOVERNMENT MET WITH MS. TULLOS ON 26

18 SEPARATE OCCASIONS AND SUBJECTED HER TO GRUELING INTERROGATION

19 DURING WHICH THE GOVERNMENT INTERJECTED ITS VIEWS OF THE EVIDENCE

20 AND, AT LEAST ON ONE OCCASION, TOLD HER THAT SHE WOULD NOT RECEIVE

21 THE BENEFITS OF COOPERATION UNLESS SHE TESTIFIED DIFFERENTLY THAN

22 SHE HAD INITIALLY IN AN EARLIER SESSION.

23   NOT SURPRISINGLY, MS. TULLOS' TESTIMONY AT TRIAL CAME

24 OFF SCRIPTED AND NOT CONSISTENT WITH THE EXTENSIVE E-MAIL TRAIL

25 BROUGHT OUT DURING CROSS-EXAMINATION.

1   I HAVE ABSOLUTELY NO CONFIDENCE THAT ANY PORTION OF MS.

2   TULLOS'S TESTIMONY WAS BASED ON HER OWN INDEPENDENT RECOLLECTION

3   OF EVENTS AS OPPOSED TO WHAT THE GOVERNMENT THOUGHT HER

4   RECOLLECTION SHOULD BE ON THOSE EVENTS.

5   LET ME NEXT FOCUS ON MR. DULL. THE GOVERNMENT BELIEVED

6   THAT MR. DULL WAS A COCONSPIRATOR YET IT DECIDED NOT TO SEEK

7   CHARGES AGAINST HIM FOR SECURITIES FRAUD. IN EFFECT, THE

8   GOVERNMENT LEFT MR. DULL HANGING IN THE WIND AND UNCERTAIN OF HIS

9   FATE FOR ALMOST TWO YEARS. DURING TRIAL, I GRANTED MR. DULL

10   IMMUNITY SO HE COULD TESTIFY FOR THE DEFENSE.

11   AFTER I HAD DONE SO, THE LEAD PROSECUTOR CONTACTED

12   COUNSEL FOR MR. DULL AND THREATENED TO PROSECUTE MR. DULL IF HE

13   TESTIFIED CONSISTENTLY WITH HIS PRIOR TESTIMONY BEFORE THE SEC.

14   COMPOUNDING HIS MISCONDUCT, THE LEAD PROSECUTOR ATTEMPTED TO

15   NEGOTIATE THE TESTIMONY OF MR. DULL BY, AMONG OTHER THINGS,

16   PROMISING A SOFT CROSS IF MR. DULL INCRIMINATED OR DISPARAGED MR.

17   RUEHLE. THE LEAD PROSECUTOR SOMEHOW FORGOT THAT TRUTH IS NEVER

18   NEGOTIABLE.

19   FINALLY, LET ME FOCUS ON DR. SAMUELI. THE

20   UNCONTROVERTED EVIDENCE AT TRIAL ESTABLISHED THAT DR. SAMUELI WAS

21   A BRILLIANT ENGINEER AND A MAN OF INCREDIBLE INTEGRITY. THERE WAS

22   NO EVIDENCE AT TRIAL TO SUGGEST THAT DR. SAMUELI DID ANYTHING

23   WRONG, LET ALONE CRIMINAL. YET, THE GOVERNMENT EMBARKED ON A

24   CAMPAIGN OF INTIMIDATION AND OTHER MISCONDUCT TO EMBARRASS HIM AND

25   BRING HIM DOWN.

1   AMONG OTHER WRONGFUL ACTS THE GOVERNMENT, ONE,

2 UNREASONABLY DEMANDED THAT DR. SAMUELI SUBMIT TO AS MANY AS 30

3 GRUELING INTERROGATIONS BY THE LEAD PROSECUTOR.

4   TWO, FALSELY STATED AND IMPROPERLY LEAKED TO THE MEDIA

5 THAT DR. SAMUELI WAS NOT COOPERATING IN THE GOVERNMENT'S

6 INVESTIGATION.

7   THREE, IMPROPERLY PRESSURED BROADCOM TO TERMINATE DR.

8 SAMUELI'S EMPLOYMENT AND REMOVE HIM FROM THE BOARD.

9   FOUR, MISLED DR. SAMUELI INTO BELIEVING THAT THE LEAD

10 PROSECUTOR WOULD BE REPLACED BECAUSE OF MISCONDUCT.

11   FIVE, OBTAINED AN INFLAMMATORY INDICTMENT THAT REFERRED

12 TO DR. SAMUELI 72 TIMES AND ACCUSED HIM OF BEING AN UNINDICTED

13 COCONSPIRATOR WHEN THE GOVERNMENT NEW, OR SHOULD HAVE KNOWN, THAT

14 HE DID NOTHING WRONG.

15   AND SEVEN, CRAFTED AN UNCONSCIONABLE PLEA AGREEMENT

16 PURSUANT TO WHICH DR. SAMUELI WOULD PLEAD GUILTY TO A CRIME HE DID

17 NOT COMMIT AND PAY A RIDICULOUS SUM OF $12 MILLION TO THE UNITED

18 STATES TREASURY.

19   ONE MUST CONCLUDE THAT THE GOVERNMENT ENGAGED IN THIS

20 MISCONDUCT TO PRESSURE DR. SAMUELI TO FALSELY ADMIT GUILT AND

21 INCRIMINATE MR. RUEHLE OR, IF HE WAS UNWILLING TO MAKE SUCH A

22 FALSE ADMISSION AND INCRIMINATION, TO DESTROY DR. SAMUELI'S

23 CREDIBILITY AS A WITNESS FOR MR. RUEHLE.

24   NEEDLESS TO SAY, THE GOVERNMENT'S TREATMENT OF DR.

25 SAMUELI WAS SHAMEFUL AND CONTRARY TO AMERICAN VALUES OF DECENCY

1 AND JUSTICE.

2   IN LIGHT OF MY FINDING OF GOVERNMENT MISCONDUCT AND

3 DENIAL OF MR. RUEHLE'S CONSTITUTIONAL RIGHT TO COMPULSORY PROCESS,

4 I MUST NOW EXERCISE MY SUPERVISORY AUTHORITY AND ISSUE THE

5 **FOLLOWING ORDER:**

6   NUMBER ONE, I'M GOING TO DISMISS, WITH PREJUDICE, THE

7 STOCK-OPTION BACKDATING INDICTMENT AGAINST MR. RUEHLE AND ENTER A

8 JUDGMENT OF ACQUITTAL. THIS DISMISSAL AND JUDGMENT ARE BASED ON

9 TWO SEPARATE, BUT RELATED GROUNDS.

10   FIRST, AS I PREVIOUSLY STATED, THE GOVERNMENT MISCONDUCT

11 HAS DEPRIVED MR. RUEHLE OF THE RIGHT TO COMPULSORY PROCESS AND A

12 FAIR TRIAL. AND SECOND, THERE IS INSUFFICIENT EVIDENCE TO SUSTAIN

13 A CONVICTION AGAINST MR. RUEHLE. BECAUSE THE GOVERNMENT

14 IMPROPERLY INFLUENCED MS. TULLOS, HER TRIAL TESTIMONY IS

15 UNRELIABLE AND MUST BE STRICKEN.

16   WITHOUT MS. TULLOS' TAINTED TESTIMONY THERE IS

17 INSUFFICIENT EVIDENCE THAT MR. RUEHLE HAD THE CRIMINAL INTENT

18 NECESSARY TO VIOLATE ANY OF THE LAWS ALLEGED IN THE INDICTMENT.

19   I SHOULD NOTE THAT THIS LATTER GROUND PROHIBITS THE

20 GOVERNMENT FROM PROSECUTING MR. RUEHLE AGAIN FOR ANY CRIME RELATED

21 TO THE STOCK OPTION PRACTICES AT BROADCOM. TO DO SO WOULD VIOLATE

22 THE DOUBLE JEOPARDY CLAUSE OF THE FIFTH AMENDMENT.

23   NUMBER TWO, I'M GOING TO DISMISS, WITH PREJUDICE, THE

24 STOCK-OPTION BACKDATING INDICTMENT AGAINST DR. NICHOLAS. THE

25 THREE WITNESSES THAT MR. RUEHLE NEEDED TO PROVE HIS INNOCENCE ARE

Page 5200

1 THE SAME THREE WITNESSES THAT DR. NICHOLAS NEEDS TO PROVE HIS

2 INNOCENCE. CONSEQUENTLY, DR. NICHOLAS IS DENIED HIS RIGHT TO

3 COMPULSORY PROCESS AND HE CANNOT RECEIVE A FAIR TRIAL.

4   NUMBER THREE, I'M GOING TO ORDER GOVERNMENT TO SHOW

5 CAUSE, ON FEBRUARY 2, 2010, AT 9:00 A.M. WHY THE DRUG DIRECTION

6 INDICTMENT AGAINST DR. NICHOLAS SHOULD NOT BE DISMISSED. THE

7 THREE MATERIAL WITNESSES IN THE STOCK-OPTION BACKDATING CASE WILL

8 UNDOUBTEDLY BE WITNESSES IN THE DRUG DISTRIBUTION CASE, BUT I'M

9 NOT SURE WHETHER THE DIFFERENT NATURE OF THE DRUG CHARGES REDUCES

10 THE PREJUDICE TO DR. NICHOLAS SO HE CAN STILL EXERCISE HIS RIGHT

11 TO COMPULSORY PROCESS AND RECEIVE A FAIR TRIAL.

12   I DO ASK THAT THE GOVERNMENT KEEP IN MIND TWO ISSUES IN

13 ITS DECISION WHETHER TO GO FORWARD WITH THE DRUG DISTRIBUTION CASE

14 AGAINST DR. NICHOLAS. FIRST, THERE WILL BE OTHER EVIDENCE OF

15 GOVERNMENT MISCONDUCT INTRODUCED AT THAT TRIAL, SUCH AS THE

16 GOVERNMENT'S THREAT TO ISSUE A GRAND JURY SUBPOENA TO DR.

17 NICHOLAS' 13-YEAR-OLD-SON AND FORCE THE BOY TO TESTIFY AGAINST HIS

18 FATHER.

19   AND SECOND, DR. NICHOLAS'S E-MAIL TO HIS FORMER WIFE

20 ENTITLED "BRETT'S HOME RUN" WILL NOT BE ADMITTED AT TRIAL UNDER

21 ANY CIRCUMSTANCE. THE E-MAIL IS VERY PRIVATE AND PERSONAL AND

22 WILL NOT BE PUBLICLY AIRED IN THIS COURT AGAIN.

23   FOUR, I'M GOING TO LIFT THE STAY IMPOSED IN THE SEC

24 CIVIL STOCK-OPTION BACKDATING CASE AND DISMISS THAT COMPLAINT

25 WITHOUT PREJUDICE. THE SEC HAS 30 DAYS TO FILE AN AMENDED

Page 5201

1 COMPLAINT. I DO, HOWEVER, DISCOURAGE THE SEC FROM PROCEEDING

2 FURTHER WITH THE CASE.

3   THE GOVERNMENT'S MISCONDUCT HAS COMPROMISED THE

4 INTEGRITY AND LEGITIMACY OF THE CASE AND THE EVIDENCE AT MR.

5 RUEHLE'S TRIAL ESTABLISHED THE SEC WILL HAVE GREAT DIFFICULTY

6 PROVING THAT THE DEFENDANTS ACTED WITH THE REQUISITE SCIENTER.

7   THE ACCOUNTING STANDARDS AND GUIDELINES WERE NOT CLEAR,

8 AND THERE WAS CONSIDERABLE DEBATE IN THE HIGH-TECH INDUSTRY AS TO

9 THE PROPER ACCOUNTING TREATMENT FOR STOCK OPTION GRANTS. INDEED,

10 APPLE AND MICROSOFT WERE ENGAGING IN THE EXACT SAME PRACTICES AS

11 THOSE OF BROADCOM.

12   NOW, I'M SURE THERE ARE GOING TO BE MANY PEOPLE WHO ARE

13 GOING TO BE CRITICAL OF MY DECISION IN THIS CASE AND ARGUE THAT

14 I'M BEING TOO HARD ON THE GOVERNMENT. I STRONGLY DISAGREE. I

15 HAVE A SOLEMN OBLIGATION TO HOLD THE GOVERNMENT TO THE

16 CONSTITUTION. I'M DOING NOTHING MORE AND NOTHING LESS. AND I ASK

17 MY CRITICS TO PUT THEMSELVES IN THE SHOES OF THE ACCUSED.

18   YOU ARE CHARGED WITH SERIOUS CRIMES AND, IF CONVICTED ON

19 THEM, YOU WILL SPEND THE REST OF YOUR LIFE IN PRISON. YOU ONLY

20 HAVE THREE WITNESSES TO PROVE YOUR INNOCENCE AND GOVERNMENT HAS

21 INTIMIDATED AND IMPROPERLY INFLUENCED EACH ONE OF THEM. IS THAT

22 FAIR? IS THAT JUSTICE? I SAY ABSOLUTELY NOT.

23   I'D LIKE TO CONCLUDE WITH THE POWERFUL AND INSIGHTFUL

24 PASSAGE FROM THE U.S. SUPREME COURT IN THE CASE OF BERGER V.

25 UNITED STATES.

Page 5202

```
 1              "THE UNITED STATES ATTORNEY IS THE REPRESENTATIVE, NOT

 2    OF AN ORDINARY PARTY TO A CONTROVERSY, BUT OF A SOVEREIGNTY WHOSE

 3    OBLIGATION TO GOVERN IMPARTIALLY IS AS COMPELLING AS ITS

 4    OBLIGATION TO GOVERN AT ALL, AND WHOSE INTEREST, THEREFORE, IN A

 5    CRIMINAL PROSECUTION IS NOT THAT IT SHALL WIN A CASE, BUT THAT

 6    JUSTICE SHALL BE DONE.  AS SUCH, HE IS IN A PECULIAR AND A VERY

 7    DEFINITE SENSE THE SERVANT OF THE LAW, THE TWOFOLD AIM OF WHICH IS

 8    THAT GUILT SHALL NOT ESCAPE OR INNOCENT SUFFER.

 9              HE MAY PROSECUTE WITH EARNESTNESS AND VIGOR.  INDEED, HE

10    SHOULD DO SO.  BUT WHILE HE MAY STRIKE HARD BLOWS, HE IS NOT AT

11    LIBERTY TO STRIKE FOUL ONES.  IT IS MUCH HIS DUTY TO REFRAIN FROM

12    IMPROPER METHODS CALCULATED TO PRODUCE A WRONGFUL CONVICTION AS IT

13    IS TO USE EVERY LEGITIMATE MEANS TO BRING ABOUT A JUST ONE."

14              I SINCERELY REGRET THAT THE GOVERNMENT DID NOT HEED THE

15    RIGHTEOUS WORDS OF THE SUPREME COURT.

16              MR. MARMARO, I'LL HEAR FROM YOU FIRST, SIR, IF THERE IS

17    ANYTHING YOU OR MR. RUEHLE WOULD LIKE TO STATE ON THE RECORD.

18              MR. MARMARO:  YOUR HONOR, IT'S VERY DIFFICULTY

19    OBVIOUSLY, HAVING HEARD THE COURT'S COMMENTS, TO GIVE A COMPOSED

20    RESPONSE OR A STATEMENT, BUT I JUST WANT TO SAY ONE THING, YOUR

21    HONOR.  YOU HAVE SAID ALL ALONG THAT YOU WANTED TO HEAR THE WHOLE

22    STORY.  BUT IF IT WEREN'T FOR WHAT YOU DID, WE WOULD NOT HAVE

23    HEARD THE WHOLE STORY.  IF IT WEREN'T FOR YOUR DECISION TO GRANT

24    DEFENSE WITNESSES IMMUNITY, WE WOULD NOT HAVE HEARD FROM DR.

25    SAMUELI AND MR. DULL.  AND YOU WOULD HAVE BEEN STUCK WITH ONLY
```

Page 5203

```
1    PART OF THE STORY.

2         SO IN A VERY LARGE SENSE, YOUR HONOR, WHAT HAPPENED,

3    WHAT YOU ANNOUNCED TODAY IS THE DIRECT RESULT OF WHAT YOU DID.

4         AND I HAVE TO TELL YOU, YOUR HONOR, 34 YEARS AGO TODAY,

5    TO THE DAY, DECEMBER 15, 1975, I PASSED THE BAR.  WHAT HAPPENED IN

6    THIS COURT WAS VERY DIFFICULT TO WATCH, BUT WHAT HAPPENED TODAY

7    RESTORES MY FAITH AND I CAN HONESTLY SAY I HAVE NEVER BEEN MORE

8    PROUD TO BE A LAWYER.

9         THE COURT:  MR. SULLIVAN, I KNOW I'M PROBABLY CATCHING

10   YOU A LITTLE OFF GUARD, BUT GIVEN THE MANY ORDERS THAT I HAVE

11   ISSUED, I DON'T KNOW IF THERE IS ANYTHING YOU WOULD LIKE TO SAY ON

12   THE RECORD, SIR.

13        MR. SULLIVAN:  OF COURSE, MR. MARMARO IS A YOUNG LAWYER.

14   I HAVE BEEN DOING THIS 42 YEARS, BUT I ADOPT HIS MOVING WORDS.

15        I GUESS THAT WHEN I WAS A YOUNG LAWYER, I WAS NAIVE AND

16   I THOUGHT THAT FAIRNESS WAS ASSURED IN OUR COURTROOMS BECAUSE OUR

17   FOUNDING FATHERS HAD DEVISED THIS MAGICAL CONSTITUTION AND THIS

18   MAGICAL BILL OF RIGHTS, AND SOMEHOW IF THE GOVERNMENT LIVED BY

19   THAT, THAT WE WOULD ALWAYS BE JUST FINE.  BUT I WAS NAIVE.  I

20   LEARNED IN SHORT ORDER THAT THE ONLY THING THAT ASSURES FAIRNESS

21   IN THE COURTROOM ARE JUDGES WITH COURAGE TO KEEP THEIR EYES OPEN,

22   WATCH WHAT IS HAPPENING, KEEP AN OPEN MIND AND MAKE FAIR

23   DECISIONS, FAIR TO BOTH SIDES.

24        AND, YOUR HONOR, I STAND IN AWE OF WHAT YOU HAVE DONE

25   HERE TODAY BASED UPON THE MANY DAYS OF TEDIOUS TRIAL THAT WE HAVE
```

1 SEEN.

2   I'LL ADD ONLY ONE THING TO YOUR SUPREME COURT ARGUMENT.

3 AND WE ALL KNOW, WITHOUT SAYING, THAT THERE ARE MANY, MANY FINE

4 MEN AND WOMEN IN GOVERNMENT SERVICE, IN PROSECUTOR'S OFFICES AND

5 ALSO IN THE FBI. AND WE APPLAUD THEM. AND SOMETIMES WE DO SEE

6 THE KIND OF MISCONDUCT ON THE PART OF AN INDIVIDUAL OR SEVERAL

7 INDIVIDUALS.

8   BUT I'M REMINDED WHEN I HEARD YOUR SUPREME COURT QUOTE,

9 HOW SIMILAR IT WAS TO THE QUOTE I HEARD EIGHT MONTHS AGO, APRIL 8,

10 2008, FROM THE ATTORNEY GENERAL HIMSELF, A MESSAGE THAT WAS

11 DELIVERED TO ALL STATE DEPARTMENT U.S. ATTORNEYS. AND I QUOTE

12 HIM.

13   "YOUR JOB AS U.S. ATTORNEYS IS NOT TO CONVICT PEOPLE,

14 YOUR JOB IS NOT TO WIN CASES. YOUR JOB IS TO DO JUSTICE. YOUR

15 JOB IS IN EVERY CASE, EVERY DECISION THAT YOU MAKE, TO DO THE

16 RIGHT THING. ANYBODY WHO ASKS YOU TO DO SOMETHING OTHER THAN THAT

17 IS TO BE IGNORED. ANY POLICY THAT IS AT TENSION WITH THAT IS TO

18 BE QUESTIONED AND BROUGHT TO MY ATTENTION."

19   THE MESSAGE DELIVERED BY THIS COURT TODAY HAD BEEN HEARD

20 THROUGHOUT THE COUNTRY BY ALL WHO ENFORCE THE LAW, AND WE ARE ALL

21 BETTER OFF AND THE SYSTEM OF JUSTICE WILL BE BETTER OFF FOR THE

22 COURAGE DEMONSTRATED IN THIS COURT ON THIS DATE. THANK YOU.

23   **THE COURT:** MR. GREENBERG, IS THERE ANYTHING YOU WOULD

24 LIKE TO SAY ON BEHALF OF DR. SAMUELI?

25   **MR. GREENBERG:** THANK YOU, YOUR HONOR.

1   I'M IN A DANGEROUS POSITION, A LAWYER WHO IS BREATHLESS.

2   I REALLY -- MY BREATH IS TAKEN AWAY BECAUSE, ECHOING THE

3   SENTIMENTS OF MY COLLEAGUES HERE, THIS TRULY IS A TURNING POINT, I

4   BELIEVE, THAT WILL BE HEARD THROUGHOUT THE COUNTRY.

5   I SAT AT THAT TABLE AS A PROSECUTOR AND ENJOYED IT. IT

6   WAS THE GREATEST JOB I HAD IN MY LIFE. THE MOST ENJOYABLE BECAUSE

7   THE PRESUMPTION OF CREDIBILITY, YOU ARE CLOAKED WITH IT FROM THE

8   MOMENT THAT YOU WALK INTO THE COURTROOM. USUALLY, FROM THE

9   JUDGE'S PERSPECTIVE, FRANKLY FROM THE CLERK'S PERSPECTIVE, IT'S

10   YOUR CREDIBILITY TO LOSE.

11   AND IT'S A TREMENDOUS BURDEN DOING IT ON THE OTHER SIDE

12   OF THE EQUATION, YOUR HONOR, TO PIERCE THAT. AND TODAY THE

13   COURT'S ACKNOWLEDGMENT, ESPECIALLY IN LIGHT OF WHERE WE STARTED IN

14   THIS CASE, YOUR HONOR, WHICH I CAN ONLY SAY TO YOUR HONOR, THAT

15   IT'S REMARKABLE BECAUSE IN A PUBLIC SETTING, YOUR HONOR HAS SET

16   THE RECORD STRAIGHT AND INDICATED INITIALLY THAT IT WANTED TO HEAR

17   THE FACTS OF THIS AND REJECTED OUR PLEA, AND I COULD ONLY BE

18   THANKFUL FOR THAT.

19   I SAY THAT TO YOU SINCERELY BECAUSE IT TAKES NOT ONLY A

20   TREMENDOUS JUDGE, BUT A TREMENDOUS HUMAN BEING TO RECOGNIZE THAT

21   THAT WAS, FRANKLY, THE WRONG DECISION, IF I MAY SAY SO, YOUR

22   HONOR, AT THE TIME IN TERMS OF HOW IT WAS POSTURED AT THAT TIME.

23   AND I THANK YOUR HONOR FOR LISTENING CAREFULLY AND

24   KEEPING AN OPEN MIND, AND TRULY LOOKING AT THE EVIDENCE, AND

25   UNDERSTANDING AND GETTING TO THE POINT OF EXACTLY WHAT HAPPENED

```
                                                      Page 5206
 1   HERE.

 2            AND I THINK THAT OUR JUSTICE SYSTEM WILL EMBRACE THIS.

 3   THERE HAVE BEEN MANY CIRCUMSTANCES AROUND THE COUNTRY MOST

 4   RECENTLY WHERE A NUMBER OF CASES HAVE BEEN TOSSED BECAUSE OF

 5   PROSECUTORS PLACING THEIR THUMB ON THE SCALES OF JUSTICE.  AND

 6   SADLY, THE OFFICE THAT I LOVED SO MUCH, HERE, WHICH IS A

 7   TREMENDOUS OFFICE, THE U.S. ATTORNEY'S OFFICE, DID SO IN THIS

 8   CASE.

 9            AND I THANK YOUR HONOR FOR THE COURAGE TO GO FORWARD AND

10   SET THE RECORD STRAIGHT.  I HAVE REPRESENTED A HUMAN BEING HERE

11   THAT I HAVE NEVER HAD MORE RESPECT FOR, OF ANYONE I HAVE

12   REPRESENTED.  AND NO DISRESPECT TO ANYONE ELSE.  HE TRULY IS A

13   WONDERFUL HUMAN BEING.  AND I HAVE WATCHED THE FAMILY GO THROUGH

14   THIS PROCESS FOR THREE AND A HALF YEARS.  AND IT'S BEEN UGLY.  AND

15   IT JUST GOT UGLIER AND UGLIER UNTIL TODAY IN WHICH WE CAN ALL GO

16   HOME AND CELEBRATE.

17            THANK YOU, YOUR HONOR.

18            **THE COURT:**  MR. ASPERGER?

19            **MR. SLOAN:**  THANK YOU, YOUR HONOR.

20            AS THE COURT KNOWS, MR. ARONSON AND I AND MR. DULL HAVE,

21   IN MANY WAYS, BEEN BYSTANDERS TO THESE CRIMINAL PROCEEDINGS, BUT

22   THIS HAS NONETHELESS BEEN EXTREMELY CHALLENGING AS I'M SURE THE

23   COURT IS WELL AWARE, FOR MR. DULL AND HIS FAMILY.  AND WE APPLAUD

24   THE COURT.  WE ECHO WHAT OUR COLLEAGUES HAVE SAID AND APPLAUD THE

25   COURT FOR THE GREAT COURAGE THAT THE COURT HAS SHOWN IN ITS RULING
```

1 TODAY.

2   ONE OF THE THINGS THAT STRUCK ME IN THE LAST TWO WEEKS

3 WAS WHEN THE COURT SAID THAT YOU'RE HERE TO DO JUSTICE, TO DO THE

4 RIGHT THING, AND THAT'S WHY YOU TOOK THE BENCH. THAT'S WHY I WAS

5 A FEDERAL PROSECUTOR FOR 10 YEARS, YOUR HONOR, AND WAS PROUD TO BE

6 ABLE TO SAY I REPRESENT THE UNITED STATES OF AMERICA. IT'S WHY,

7 IN REPRESENTING MR. DULL AND TRYING TO SUPPORT HIM AND HIS FAMILY,

8 WE'RE VERY PROUD TO BE REPRESENTING A MAN OF SUCH INTEGRITY WHO

9 WAS ALWAYS THERE TO DO THE RIGHT THING.

10   AND THIS WILL BE A GREAT RELIEF OF THE BURDENS AND

11 TRYING CIRCUMSTANCES THAT HE HAS HAD TO GO THROUGH.

12   AND I WILL ECHO WHAT, AGAIN, MR. MARMARO AND

13 MR. SULLIVAN AND MR. GREENBERG HAD SAID. IT'S JUDGES LIKE YOU WHO

14 HAVE SHOWN THE COURAGE TO MAKE THE RULING THAT YOU HAVE MADE; TO

15 DO THE RIGHT THING; TO LOOK AT THE FACTS WITH AN OPEN MIND; AND TO

16 BE OPEN TO CHANGING YOUR VIEW OF THE FACTS AND COMING UP WITH

17 DOING THE RIGHT THING AND DOING FAIRNESS THAT RESTORES OUR FAITH

18 IN THE SYSTEM OF JUSTICE.

19   AGAIN, IT STRUCK ME THAT THE BIGGEST DISAPPOINTMENT FOR

20 MR. DULL, WHEN THE EVENTS THAT HAPPENED OCCURRED IN THIS CASE, WAS

21 HIS PROFOUND DISAPPOINTMENT IN OUR JUSTICE SYSTEM. I'M SURE I

22 SPEAK FOR HIM AS FOR ALL OF US THAT YOUR RULING TODAY DOES RESTORE

23 THAT FAITH, AND WE'RE VERY GRATEFUL FOR IT, YOUR HONOR.

24   AS THE COURT IS WELL AWARE, WE HAVE A PROPOSED ORDER

25 THAT WHENEVER YOU FEEL IT APPROPRIATE TO TAKE UP, WE CAN, BUT I

1   REALIZE TODAY IS NOT THE TIME.

2   THANK YOU, YOUR HONOR.

3   **THE COURT:** VERY WELL.

4   I SINCERELY APPRECIATE ALL THE COMPLIMENTS THAT COUNSEL

5   HAVE GIVEN, ESPECIALLY THEY'RE FROM THE TITANS IN THE LEGAL

6   PROFESSION. SO THEY MEAN A LOT TO ME. BUT IT'S REALLY IMPORTANT

7   I THINK, TO ME, THAT YOU AND MR. RUEHLE, DR. NICHOLAS, MR. DULL,

8   AND DR. SAMUELI REALIZE, I DON'T NEED TO BE COMPLIMENTED. THE

9   WISDOM, THE BRILLIANCE WAS IN THE FRAMERS OF OUR CONSTITUTION.

10 I'M JUST DOING MY JOB.

11   MR. ADKINS, IS THERE ANYTHING THE GOVERNMENT WOULD LIKE

12 TO SAY? MR. CARDONA?

13   **MR. CARDONA:** YOUR HONOR, VERY BRIEFLY. FIRST, AS YOU

14 KNOW, THIS IS THE FIRST TIME I HAVE BEEN DOWN HERE IN THIS CASE.

15 I APOLOGIZE FOR NOT HAVING BEEN OVER HERE THE LAST TWO WEEKS WHEN

16 THESE EVENTS WERE GOING DOWN. I WOULD HAVE HOPED I COULD HAVE

17 SAID SOMETHING THAT MIGHT HAVE CONVINCED THE COURT TO RULE

18 DIFFERENTLY THAN IT DID TODAY.

19   I DON'T KNOW IF YOU WERE TOLD, BUT I WAS OUT OF, FIRST

20 THE STATE AND OUT OF THE COUNTRY SO COULD NOT BE HERE.

21   **THE COURT:** I WAS.

22   **MR. ADKINS:** WITH THAT, YOUR HONOR, OBVIOUSLY WE HAVE

23 HEARD YOUR DECISION. RESPECTFULLY, WE DISAGREE WITH IT. I DON'T

24 THINK THAT WILL COME AS A SURPRISE TO YOU. WE HAVE SUBMITTED OUR

25 PAPERS. WE BELIEVE WE HAVE SET FORTH OUR POSITION IN OUR PAPERS

```
 1   AND THE OTHER PLEADINGS.  AND I DON'T BELIEVE THERE IS ANY POINT

 2   IN SAYING ANYTHING FURTHER HERE.  YOU UNDERSTAND OUR POSITIONS.  I

 3   UNDERSTAND YOU DISAGREE WITH THEM.  I HOPE YOU UNDERSTAND WE

 4   DISAGREE WITH YOUR RULING AND WE WILL NEED TO DECIDE WHAT WE DO

 5   NEXT.  THANK YOU.

 6           THE COURT:  AND I APPRECIATE THAT, SIR.

 7           ALL RIGHT.  I DON'T THINK ANYTHING NEEDS TO BE SAID

 8   FURTHER OTHER THAN, MR. RUEHLE, YOU ARE A FREE MAN.

 9           THE DEFENDANT:  THANK YOU, YOUR HONOR.

10               (WHEREUPON THE PROCEEDINGS WERE ADJOURNED AT 9:33.)

11

12

13

14

15

16

17

18

19

20

21

22

23

24

25
```

```
                                                          Page 5210
 1

 2                                -OOO-

 3

 4                              CERTIFICATE

 5

 6             I HEREBY CERTIFY THAT PURSUANT TO SECTION 753, TITLE 28,

 7   UNITED STATES CODE, THE FOREGOING IS A TRUE AND CORRECT TRANSCRIPT

 8   OF THE STENOGRAPHICALLY REPORTED PROCEEDINGS HELD IN THE

 9   ABOVE-ENTITLED MATTER.

10

11   DATE:   DECEMBER 15, 2009

12

13

14   MARIA DELLANEVE, U.S. COURT
     CSR NO. 9132

15

16

17

18

19

20

21

22

23

24

25
```

Made in the USA
San Bernardino, CA
10 January 2013